ENERGY, LAND, AND PUBLIC POLICY

Energy Policy Studies

John Byrne and Daniel Rich, editors

ENERGY, LAND, AND PUBLIC POLICY

Energy Policy Studies
Volume 5

Edited by
J. Barry Cullingworth

Transaction Publishers
New Brunswick (U.S.A.) and London (U.K.)

ISBN: 0-88738-770-5
ISSN: 0882-3537
Printed in the United States of America

Contents

ACKNOWLEDGEMENT

I wish to thank Professor John Byrne for his editorial assistance in the preparation of this book. Sincere thanks are due to Patricia Grimes for preparing the manuscript with skill, patience and good humor. Finally, I would like to recognize the considerable work of Cecilia Martinez and Kyunghee Ham in preparing the Select Bibliography.

Tables

Figures

Acronyms

BRC	Below Regulatory Concern
CBA	Cost benefit analysis
CBDC	Cardiff Bay Development Corporation
CHP/DH	Combined heat and power, and district heating systems
CHP	Combined heating and power systems
CMA	Census Metropolitan Area (Canada)
DH	District heating
DHC	District heating and cooling
DOE	Department of Energy
EEG	Environmental Evaluation Group (New Mexico)
EPA	Environmental Protection Agency
ERDA	Energy Research and Development Administration
GLC	Greater London Council
GTCC	Greater-than-class-C wastes
HLW	High level wastes
IPP	Intermountain Power Project
KHEs	Kilowatt hour equivalents
LLRWPA	Low Level Radioactive Wastes Policy Amendment Act
LLW	Low level wastes
MAB	Man in Biosphere Program (UNESCO)
MKDC	Milton Keynes Development Corporation
MRS	Monitored retrievable storage
MTHM	Metric tons of heavy metal
NIMBY	"Not in my back yard"
NRC	Nuclear Regulatory Commission
NTIS	National Technical Information Service
OECD	Organization for Economic Cooperation and Development
OPEC	Organization of Petroleum Exporting Countries
PV	Photovoltaics
SMSA	Standard Metropolitan Statistical Area (U.S.)

SRP	Savannah Waste Plant
TMI	Three Mile Island
TRU	Transuranic wastes
WIPP	Waste Isolation Pilot Plant

Introduction

J. Barry Cullingworth

The relationships between energy and urban form are paradoxically both simple and complex, obvious and elusive, dramatic and subtle. It is obvious that energy supply systems shape land use forms while, at the same time, spatial structures influence levels of energy consumption. The land use patterns which emerge in an economy dependent upon a coal based energy system are quite different from those emerging in economies with an energy system based upon cheap oil. Similarly, a low density development "obviously" demands much more gasoline than a tight high density development. Much has been written on this (e.g. Beaumont and Keys, 1982; Burchell and Listokin, 1982; Owens, 1986). Yet the relationships between energy and land use remain problematic. Scholars have typically chosen their words carefully. Thus, in our first paper, "The Future of Urbanization", Lester R. Brown and Jodi Jacobson neatly (and enigmatically) comment that "Technological change and the availability of vast energy supplies dovetailed (sic) in the nineteenth century to foster the development of large, modern cities."

There is, of course, no doubt that energy supply systems have had (and continue to have) a major impact on urbanization, suburbanization, and counterurbanization. However, as Brown and Jacobson argue, other factors have conspired to stimulate urban spatial forms - to the point that they "have outgrown the capacity of natural and social systems to support them." By implication, they have also surpassed the

1

management   capability of governments. The result is uncontrollable "excessive urbanization" in the Third World (and
equally uncontrollable counterurbanization in the U.S. - a point
which is not developed in the current volume).

The paper by Brown and Jacobson is a wide ranging survey of some major ecological and economic factors in land use
and urbanization. The comparisons which are made between
European and U.S. cities are particularly telling. Drawing upon
the work of Australian researchers (Newman and Kenworthy,
1987), they point up the fact that average per capita gasoline
consumption in U.S. cities is over four times that of European
cities, and over ten times that of the Asian cities of Tokyo,
Singapore, and Hong Kong. Cheap gasoline has not only made
urban deconcentration possible: it has also greatly increased
demand for the fuel. The resultant urban forms are not easy to
change, even if it were politically possible (or desirable) to do
so.

In the Third World, a major force for urbanization is rural
poverty and the relatively greater opportunities which are to be
found in the cities. The impact on energy demands has been
dramatic, with an ever widening search for firewood (leading to
massive deforestation) and a shift to fossil fuels (kerosene).
However, in widely different areas (in both the Third World and
the developed nations) there are indications of a shift to renewable energy resources. If this shift were to gain momentum, "it
would slow the urbanization process, perhaps reversing it in
some cases." The cautious tone of the comment is justified. As
in so many aspects of the energy/land use conundrum, there is
no certainty.

Energy and land use problems have acute political dimensions, as instanced by the violence which erupted at U.S. gas
stations during the 1974 oil crisis, or by the "food related" riots
instanced by Brown and Jacobson. The former is clear and
direct; the latter less so. But, as frequently noted in this
volume, energy and land use matters are interrelated with many
others. Thus, the food related riots were a result of food price
policies which provided unrealistically cheap food for city dwellers, and discouraged private investment in food production and

therefore in rural employment. The result was increased pressures for urbanization and its related energy demands. Another relationship explored in the Brown/Jacobson paper is nutrient recycling (particularly night soil). The collection of nutrient wastes for use as fertilizer has a long history; but it has become salient in recent times as land, water, and energy resources have become more scarce and as waste management strategies have been modernized.

Human organic waste is the oldest of the waste outputs. The modern world has added many more. "New Yorkers alone annually produce enough garbage to cover all 340 hectares of Central Park to a depth of four meters" (Spirn, 1984). Dealing with this colossus is not only energy intensive: it also has major land use dimensions which increase with city size. The problems are fiscal as well as physical: in the words of Brown and Jacobson: "Of all the investments needed to sustain cities, the shortfall is perhaps greatest in the treatment and disposal of human and industrial wastes." Urban transportation vies for priority in investment policies. Automobiles are the creators of both pollution and congestion. "Industrial and developing countries alike need a new ethic of urban development - one that embraces the concept of the city as an ecosystem in which population size and urban form are matched to available resources."

The problem is more easily stated than resolved. Brown and Jacobson conclude their wide ranging paper by touching upon some of the issues in a discussion of "Seeking a Rural-Urban Balance."

A major question arising from this paper has to do with the practicability of incorporating energy issues in land use planning. Susan Owens addresses this in "Land Use Planning for Energy Efficiency." She starts with the contention that "the case for including an energy dimension in the land use planning process is both simple and compelling." Energy supply, distribution and use are related in significant ways to the spatial organization of society and, since planners are concerned with influencing the evolution of this spatial structure, they must necessarily deal with energy supply, demand, and conservation.

Nevertheless, interest was minimal until the energy crisis of the 1970s: at that time, a potential shortfall in energy supply was the issue; conditions have now changed, but some momentum is maintained by the need to use energy efficiently in order to minimize environmental externalities.

Unfortunately, "the relationship between the energy system and spatial structure is complex, dynamic and inadequately understood." Although there is a growing body of literature concerned with energy/spatial structure interactions, many uncertainties remain. It is difficult to predict either the energy implications of current urban trends or the spatial impact of energy system changes. Nor is it possible to identify uniquely energy efficient forms, because relative efficiency is influenced by factors specific to particular locations (such as climate and topography), and by non-spatial variables (such as lifestyle preferences) which are inherently difficult to predict. It is possible, however, to identify some of the characteristics of spatial structure at different scales which contribute to energy efficiency, or robustness, and to develop some guidelines for energy conscious urban design.

The simplest scale is the local one: there is "a fairly good understanding of the energy implications of built form and of the ways in which siting, orientation, layout and landscaping can make the optimum use of microclimatic conditions to minimize the need for space heating from conventional sources". For example, a detached house can require three times as much energy input as an intermediate apartment (though the lifestyles of the occupants can affect this significantly). At the wider urban and regional scale, matters become more complex. After reviewing the various spatial forms, Owens concludes that there is no single ideal configuration, but "the form which emerges most consistently as robust involves a pattern of sub-centers providing access to a reasonable choice of jobs and services without the need for long journeys"; but again all models are dependent on assumptions about lifestyles and about the ways in which people value mobility and choice. Similarly with models which are aimed at reducing travel needs: whatever spatial form is chosen, its efficacy in reducing energy demands is dependent upon a wide range of variables.

The extent to which energy conscious planning actually takes place is extremely variable. In some countries, for example Sweden and Denmark, there is a strong national commitment to energy conservation, and this is reflected in urban planning; elsewhere, as in the U.S. and the U.K., energy conscious planning has been much more the result of local initiatives, and there are important institutional constraints to be overcome. Though there are encouraging indications that energy efficient land use planning is both feasible and effective in any given location, it is unlikely to be widely adopted until a crisis situation emerges.

Owens suggests that future research in this area should focus on gaining a better understanding of the interaction between energy trends and evolving urban and regional structures, with emphasis on the social and economic factors underlying this relationship. It is also important that results of theoretical work are made accessible, that experience of energy efficient planning is shared, and that its effectiveness is monitored.

In "The Energy Use Focus of Energy Impacts," Martin J. Pasqualetti complements Owens' analysis. He focuses on "the role of land use in the environmental impact of energy development." This, he submits, is the single central theme common to the wide diversity of energy impacts. These include air emissions, water pollution, aesthetics, noise, subsidence, and radioactivity. When the land use in an impact area changes, so too does the potential for impact. For example, air pollution from a power plant has different impacts, depending on whether it is in a city where the air is already polluted or in an area of pristine air quality. The relationships between energy impacts and land use are more difficult to avoid when the resource is more site specific, as is the case with wind and geothermal energy. This theme is tracked through various environments and energy resources, including oil, natural gas, coal, uranium, wind, solar and geothermal energy. Examples include coal development in areas of mine fires and subsidence in eastern Pennsylvania, geothermal energy and subsidence in the agricultural oasis of the Imperial Valley, California; land use requirements of solar energy and coal in Arizona; and power plant location in the Intermountain west. Such impacts have implications on the direction and intensity of development.

Pasqualetti concludes that virtually all energy/ environmental problems originate in conflicting land use, even though most environmental concerns tend to be defined in terms of resources (such as air or water), or of some other environmental quality (such as aesthetics or wilderness). Moreover, the advantage of a land use perspective on the environmental impact of energy development is that it produces a change of emphasis about the individual sources of energy as well as about the importance of the sites used for its exploitation.

One of the most dramatic and intractable energy/ environmental problems is that of nuclear waste disposal. In their paper, "Nuclear Waste Landscapes: How Permanent?", Diane M. Cameron and Barry D. Solomon explore the time dimensions of this. The time dimension is an important aspect of nuclear waste management. Different stakeholders have different concepts of the proper time frame in which to view nuclear waste issues. These time frames differ according to the set of values which each group holds, as well as the factual knowledge available to each group and judgments about this set of facts which each group makes. Each stakeholder group in turn develops a different policy statement about nuclear waste disposal which is in part due to their particular time perspective. In this paper, the time perspectives of scientists, federal agencies, Indian tribes, environmental groups, and the nuclear industry are described vis-a-vis the nuclear waste management and disposal problem. In addition, lessons and conclusions are drawn from experience to date with nuclear waste storage and disposal in the United States. These perspectives are, in turn, used to illuminate the current debate over storage versus disposal of nuclear wastes, considering in turn the categories of high level, transuranic, and low level waste, and the related issue of retrievability. Finally, conclusions are drawn which point to the need for a reclassification of certain nuclear wastes, so that they can be segregated by half life and stored or disposed according to the length of their hazardous lives.

It is shown that long term scientific concerns have played little part in nuclear waste policy. On the contrary, short term political considerations have been dominant. The objectives of policy have been to provide immediate protection from radiological hazards, to appease public opponents or public anxieties over waste related hazards, to eliminate the political liabilities that result from these public anxieties, and to remove waste from densely populated areas. Cameron and Solomon argue that nuclear wastes require long range planning because of the long range hazards they pose: "any nuclear waste policy must be based on the hazardous life of the waste if it is to be both responsible and realistic. To date, neither the nuclear industry, nor the federal agencies charged with regulating it, have developed comprehensive policies which take hazardous life of nuclear waste into account."

Most of the literature dealing with the connection between energy prices and land use planning has focused on demand or energy use implications. While these are important, they overlook the fact that in the United States and Canada there are many regional economies whose fortunes are directly tied to the production of petroleum. In these regions, the supply side implications of energy price changes dominate those arising from the demand side. The rapid economic growth in these regions during the 1970s and the sharp reversal of their economic fortunes in recent years amply demonstrate the power of changes in oil prices to significantly and swiftly alter the regional pattern of growth and prosperity.

In his paper on "Economic Development, Growth and Land Use Planning in Oil and Gas Producing Regions", Robert L. Mansell discusses this regional dimension of fluctuations in energy prices. In the first part of the paper, the role of the energy sector in shaping the character, structure and performance of the oil and gas surplus regional economy is outlined, along with the macro and sectoral impacts of shifts in oil and gas prices. Using Texas, Oklahoma and Alberta as representative cases, Mansell shows that the oil and gas sector tends to

produce regional economies with certain distinguishing characteristics. They are capital intensive and largely investment
driven; they have an industrial structure dominated by backward and forward linkages to the petroleum sector; a very
mobile population and labor force; regional governments that
rely heavily on petroleum as a source of revenue; an above average exposure to fluctuations in international commodity markets and in national policies; and regional markets with a high
degree of price and wage flexibility.

The unpredictability of future oil prices and the high
degree of variability of these economies pose serious problems
for land use planners. In particular, traditional techniques for
generating demographic and economic forecasts cannot be used.
Thus a key element in planning is missing. Planning therefore
has to operate under conditions of uncertainty. Mansell points
to various approaches which can be made to this, including the
employment of a range of scenarios, cost benefit analysis, game
theory, risk analysis, and more emphasis on incrementalism. It
is, however, as yet unclear how far such approaches can be
incorporated into the land use planning system.

In "Energy Flows in a Spatial Context: A Comparison
between Canada and the U.S.," Stephen Lonergan examines the
trends in energy consumption per unit of output in the
manufacturing sector in Canada and the United States, and
categorizes these trends by metropolitan areas in the two countries. The spatial energy intensities that result indicate wide
variations in the energy dependencies across regions, both
between and within countries. These variations fit well into
theories of energy use and efficiency that have been developed
for natural systems, and provide a base for speculation on the
ability of metropolitan areas to absorb rapid fluctuations in
energy prices and availability. The paper does not account for
variations in climate or prices (except nationally) that may have
as much of an influence on energy consumption as does industrial mix, but does present an additional factor to consider in
future U.S./Canada trade and for regional competitiveness in
general.

The final paper, "A Sustainable Tomorrow Means Transitioning Today," by Andrew Euston, is of a different character from the others. It is essentially a personal testament: a statement of conviction that action needs to be taken to make the future "sustainable." Such action would require transitions from our present situation of environmental degradation, ecological unconcern, and rampant waste.

The paper starts by surveying the contemporary conditions in the urbanized world and, in particular, the dependence on fossil fuel. He stresses the need for changes in public attitudes as a prerequisite for changes in energy use. Current patterns of consumption are regarded as unsustainable in terms of both supply and environmental deterioration. The latter includes not only the atmosphere (and global warming), but also the oceans' oxygen producing organisms and aquatic life generally, lakes and forests killed by acid rain, soil erosion, and increasingly inadequate water supplies. A complete list would be as lengthy as it would be horrifying. The tragedy, so Euston argues, is that ecological decline is not yet perceived as a crisis and (the most influential factor of all on behavior) energy remains inexpensive.

"Transitioning" involves the adoption of life sustaining options which meet today's needs without jeopardizing tomorrow's. Euston lightly touches upon a number of possibilities including a rejection of planned obsolescence; a shift to energy reducing materials; the adoption of district heating and cooling, and recycling; greater conservation of resources; and the employment of strategic energy planning and more sensitive urban environmental design. The argument in essence is that "an abundance of remedial technologies and remedial methodologies are attainable."

REFERENCES

Beaumont, J.R. and P. Keys, 1982, *Future Cities: Spatial Analysis of Energy Issues,* New York, NY: Research Studies Press/Wiley.

Burchell, R.W. and D. Listokin, 1982, *Energy and Land Use,* New Brunswick, NJ: Center for Urban Policy Research, Rutgers University.

Newman, P.W.G. and J.R. Kenworthy, 1987, "Gasoline Consumption and Cities: A Comparison of U.S. Cities with a Global Survey," *Journal of the American Planning Association* 55: 24-37.

Owens, S., 1986, *Energy, Planning and Urban Form,* London: Pion.

Spirn, A.W., 1984, *The Granite Garden: Urban Nature and Human Design,* New York: Basic Books.

Land Use and Urbanization: Ecological and Economic Factors

Lester R. Brown and Jodi L. Jacobson

Aside from the growth of world population itself, urbanization is the dominant demographic trend of the late twentieth century. The number of people living in cities increased from six hundred million in 1950 to over two billion in 1986. If this growth continues unabated, more than half of humanity will reside in urban areas shortly after the turn of the century (Renaud, 1981; Population Reference Bureau, 1986).

Historically, world population has been overwhelmingly rural. The number and size of urban settlements increased sporadically over the past several millennia. But the widespread urbanization now evident around the globe is largely a twentieth-century phenomenon: as recently as 1900, fewer than fourteen percent of the world's people lived in cities (Renaud, 1981).

Technological change and the availability of vast energy supplies dovetailed in the nineteenth century to foster the development of large, modern cities. In 1800, on the eve of the Industrial Revolution, for example, about a quarter of the British lived in cities; by 1900, two-thirds of the population was

Author's Note: This paper is based on the authors' *The Future of Urbanization: Facing the Ecological and Economic Constraints,* Worldwatch Paper 77, Worldwatch Institute, 1987.

urban. Coal, replacing firewood as the dominant energy source in Europe, fueled this urban growth. It was later supplanted by oil, which has supported the massive urbanization of the late twentieth century, providing fuel for transportation and the consolidation of industrial processes (Lees, 1985).

Petroleum has also enabled cities to lengthen their supply lines and draw basic resources, such as food and raw materials, from distant points. Cheap oil and economic policies encouraging rapid industrialization together led to a phenomenal surge in urban growth that is still rippling through developing countries.

The evolution of urban settlements placed in the context of human history, has long been considered a benchmark of social and economic success. But signs of urban stress now apparent around the world call into question the continuing expansion of cities. City dwellers (currently some forty-three percent of the world's population) command a disproportionate share of society's fiscal and natural resources and create a disproportionate share of its wastes. Land and water scarcity, inefficient energy use and waste disposal, and the resultant problems of pollution all contribute to the escalating ecological and economic costs of supporting modern cities (Salas, 1986).

Accelerated urbanization in the Third World has spurred the concentration of political powers within cities, leading to policies that favor urban over rural areas. Overvalued exchange rates that reduce the cost of imports, and preferential urban subsidies often make food and other basic goods cheaper in the city, discouraging agricultural investment and attracting people to urban areas. Now, mounting external debts are forcing Third World governments to scale back urban subsidies just as the demand for services multiplies.

The rapid economic growth and abundant resources that contributed to the rise of cities in an earlier era can no longer be taken for granted. Urban areas, larger and more numerous than ever, have outgrown the capacity of natural and social systems to support them. As a result, today's cities may be inhibiting, rather than aiding, efforts to raise living standards in an equitable fashion.

The Growth and Role of Cities

Cities are a relatively recent phenomenon, lagging by several millennia the emergence of agriculture some 12,000 years ago. Agricultural surpluses, expanding populations, and the sense of common interests among peoples of a region fostered the initial growth of urban areas. The first known cities evolved 5,000 years ago on the Nile, Tigris, and Euphrates rivers when traditionally nomadic peoples began to cultivate crops. Food surpluses resulting from successive agricultural advances, such as the harnessing of draft animals and the development of irrigation, enabled farmers to support nascent villages and towns.

Diversification of trade and the production of a wider array of goods encouraged the continued development of human settlements. Pre-industrial cities, such as second-century Rome and Chang'an (Xian), imperial capital of the Chinese T'ang dynasty, arose on nearly every continent. Advances in science and the arts seem to have depended on the dynamics of a "human implosion" as the population density of ancient cities speeded the exchange of ideas and innovations. Mumford (1961) has noted that the maturation of cities in Greece, for example, culminated in a "collective life more highly energized, more heightened in its capacity for aesthetic expression and rational evaluation" than ever before.

Despite the importance of cities in past social and economic development, their history only foreshadowed the dominant role that cities now play. Contemporary urban areas are integral centers of production and communications in a highly interdependent global network. But particularly in the Third World, where urban growth is most rapid, the economic gains normally attributed to cities are being offset by increasingly inefficient use of human and natural resources as a result of uncontrolled urban expansion.

Urbanization has three demographic components: migration, natural increase, and reclassification of rapidly developing rural areas to cities. Migration is most important in the early stages of urbanization, as in Africa today, while natural increase now dominates city growth in parts of Asia and throughout Latin America. At the current growth rate of 2.5 percent yearly (half again as fast as world population) the number of people living in cities throughout the world will double in the next twenty-eight years. Nearly nine-tenths of this expansion will occur in the Third World, where the annual urban growth rate is 3.5 percent: more than triple that of the industrial world (Salas, 1986).

Latin America, with 65 percent of its people in urban areas, is the site of some of the world's largest cities: Mexico City and Sao Paulo contain eighteen million and fourteen million people, respectively. By the turn of the century, over three-fourths of Latin America's 563 million people are expected to inhabit cities (Jordan, 1986).

Table 2.1

Urban Share of Total Population, 1950 and 1986
with Projections to 2000 (%)

Region	1950	1986	2000
North America	64	74	78
Europe	56	73	79
Soviet Union	39	71	74
East Asia	43	70	79
Latin America	41	65	77
Oceania	61	65	73
China	12	32	40
Africa	15	30	42
South Asia	15	24	35
World	29	43	48

Source: Population Reference Bureau, 1986.

In Africa, the least urbanized continent, urban population is growing five percent yearly as millions of Africans fleeing environmental degradation and rural poverty migrate to cities. Today, 175 million Africans live in cities: thirty percent of the continent's total. If current projections materialize, this number will reach 368 million in 2000, a tenfold increase since 1950 (Adepoju, 1986).

Most East Asian countries (Japan, Taiwan, North and South Korea) have predominantly urban advanced economies. China, now in the early stages of industrialization, is the exception to this pattern. Scarcely thirty-two percent of its population live in cities. This divergence is due in part to the strict regulations on internal migration that prevailed prior to 1978, and in part to growing rural prosperity as government policies stimulate agricultural development. Urbanization rates in China have stepped up recently, however, as the government encourages the development of towns and small cities to reduce rural population pressures (Laquian, 1986).

South Asia presents a mixed picture of urban development. Although city dwellers make up a relatively small share of total population in most countries of the region, urbanization seems to be accelerating. India is predominantly rural, with only twenty-four percent of its 765 million people in cities. Indian cities, however, grow by 600,000 people each month: large cities such as Bombay, Calcutta, Delhi, and Madras continue to expand, and rural migration to smaller metropolitan areas is rising. The urban share of population in countries such as Indonesia, the Philippines, Thailand, and Vietnam (ranging from eighteen to thirty-nine percent) is also increasingly rapidly.

Cities of more than five million can now be found on every continent. Urban projections for the year 2000 indicate that three out of the five cities with populations of fifteen million or more will be in the Third World: Mexico City, Sao Paulo, and Calcutta. Asia will contain fifteen of the world's thirty-five largest cities. In Africa, only Cairo is now in the five million category, but by the end of the century, the continent is projected to have at least eight such centers (Salas, 1986).

Most governments in the Third World have indirectly encouraged the rise of large cities through a combination of investment and fiscal policies that triggered rapid economic growth during the fifties and sixties. Accelerated industrialization based on capital intensive industries and imported technologies was promoted to forge links between domestic and international economies. Such policies had a major impact on population distribution, influencing people's employment and residence options. Over the past decade, however, fluctuating energy prices, soft commodity markets, and burdensome external debts have taken their toll on Third World economies. Few countries now have the capital to provide services for growing urban areas.

As a result of investment and migration patterns, one city, usually the capital, often dominates a country, controlling urban trade with both rural and international markets. The large population in principal Third World cities reinforces their concentrated wealth, power, and status. As the U.N. Fund for Population Activities notes, Manila and Bangkok have more in common with Tokyo and Washington than with their rural hinterlands (Salas, 1986).

Rapid urbanization is not surprising given that so much national wealth in otherwise poor Third World countries is tied up in one or a few cities. In 1983, an estimated forty-four percent of Mexico's gross domestic product, fifty-two percent of its industrial product, and fifty-four percent of its services were concentrated within metropolitan Mexico City - home of a fifth of the country's population. Similarly, more than sixty percent of Philippine manufacturing establishments in 1979 were located in Greater Manila (Hardoy and Satterthwaite, 1984).

The polarization of rural and urban economies in developing countries has two negative side effects. First, the demand for services within the largest cities is so great that few resources are available for investment in other regions. Large cities provide greater economies of scale for certain high technology and export industries. But industrial investments comprise only a small part of an integrated development strategy.   Moreover, once metropolitan areas reach a population of two or three million, they offer no unique advantages to small and medium sized enterprises: and the costs of rapidly growing urban areas can quickly outweigh the benefits. Second, because the success of the principal city becomes so critical to the national economy, the rest of the country is highly vulnerable to economic shocks or natural disasters that may affect it (Rondinelli, 1986).

Population growth in Third World cities is outpacing city and national budgets and straining urban institutions. The result is a profusion of sprawling, unplanned cities in which access to adequate housing, transportation, water supplies, and education is severely limited. This pattern of uncontrolled growth reduces urban productivity and efficiency, affecting not only urban areas but entire national economies.

The sharp income stratifications characteristic of Third World urban populations result in part from too many people chasing too few jobs. In metropolitan Manila, sixteen percent of the labor force is unemployed and forty-three percent is underemployed. The government's own program for economic development, including an industrial policy which emphasized capital-intensive rather than labor-intensive industries, has shut many out of the job market (DIESA, 1986a).

Low incomes, high land costs, and a dearth of affordable financing leave a growing number of families unable to buy or rent homes, even ones subsidized by the government. In Lima and La Paz, the tin and tarpaper shacks of the urban poor are found in the shadow of tall, modern office buildings. Mexico City has gained notoriety for the large number of people living in makeshift burrows in a hillside garbage dump. Scenes like these are repeated in shantytowns and illegal settlements ringing cities throughout the Third World.

Excessive urbanization is evident in the increasingly disparate standards of living within cities, and between urban and rural dwellers. In reviewing the impact of urban economic concentration on Brazil's development, Hamer (1982), found that in 1975 Sao Paulo had less than ten percent of the country's population but accounted for forty-four percent of the electricity consumption, thirty-nine percent of the telephones, and well over half the industrial output and employment. He concluded that "Sao Paulo has been the beneficiary of preferential public sector treatment for most of the last century [while] large segments of the population and even larger segments of the national territory were subject to benign neglect".

Few Third World governments have adopted national development policies that balance urban and rural priorities. Michael Lipton, an analyst of rural-urban relationships in developing countries, graphically describes the conflicts that arise: "The most important class conflict in the poor countries of the world today is not between labor and [those who control] capital, nor is it between foreign and national interests. It is between the rural classes and the urban classes. The rural sector contains most of the poverty and most of the low cost sources of potential advance. But the urban sector contains most of the articulateness and power." As a result, the urban classes "have been able to win most of the rounds of the struggle with the countryside; but in doing so they have made the development process needlessly slow and unfair." This strong urban bias in the provision of services, such as education, health, electricity, and water, increases social inequities: it deprives rural individuals of opportunities and societies of sorely needed talent (Lipton, 1975).

Urban Energy Needs

Urbanization over the last two centuries has been closely tied to the use of fossil fuels. Coal, used to run the steam engines that powered both factories and rail transport, gave rise to industrial society and the first industrial cities. It dominated the fossil fuel age until a few decades ago, but oil made massive urbanization possible. As world petroleum production turned sharply upwards after midcentury, the national and international transportation systems on which cities depend grew by leaps and bounds.

The amount of energy needed to support each urban dweller around the globe is increasing. Both the size and shape of cities are contributing to this trend. In some industrial countries, urbanization has slowed, but others, such as the United States, are still undergoing extensive suburbanization. In the Third World, where urbanization is proceeding rapidly, energy consumption is on the rise as well.

Whereas rural communities rely primarily on local supplies of food, water, and (to a lesser degree) fuel, cities must import these commodities, often over long distances. Likewise, rural areas can absorb their wastes locally at relatively small energy costs, but cities need far more energy to collect garbage and treat sewage.

Urban energy budgets increase as cities expand their boundaries, pushing back the countryside and lengthening supply lines. The amount of energy needed for households, industry, and transportation is closely related to the structure of urban and social and economic activity. The efficiency with which energy is used depends less on the size of the urban population than on choices regarding land use and transportation. Considerably higher levels of energy are required where settlement patterns are highly dispersed than where people live in close proximity to jobs and markets.

Taken together, the many intimately related yet often uncoordinated decisions made by urban residents and local and national governments shape urban forms. Is the city compact or sprawling? Are most of its needs met within a defined region or must resources be imported over long distances? How are wastes handled? The way these questions are answered influences how dependent a city is on external energy resources.

Poor planning leads to inefficient energy use. Suburbs invade the countryside and perpetuate the need for automobiles. Traffic congestion leads to reduced vehicle efficiency and health-strengthening pollution levels.

Cities built of concrete, stone, and asphalt absorb and retain solar energy, raising energy consumption in summer by creating the need for air conditioning. A study of twelve U.S. cities showed that while heating was required on eight percent fewer days in city centers than in outlying areas, air conditioning (a more energy intensive process) was needed on twelve percent more days, more than offsetting any gains from energy savings on heat (Spirn, 1984).

The amount of energy it takes to satisfy food needs also increases in urban settings. Not only are supply lines longer for cities, frequently extending across national borders, but food shipped long distances needs more processing and packaging. Fresh fruits, vegetables, and livestock products often require refrigerated transport. Of the total energy expended in the food system of the United States, roughly one-third is used in the production of food; one-third in transporting, processing, and distributing it; and one-third in preparing it (Pimentel, 1980).

As with food, water needs of large cities often exceed nearby supplies, forcing municipalities to pump and convey water over great distances. Local surface water supplies, frequently polluted by urban wastes, require physical and chemical purification, another energy consuming process.

Most cities can realize dramatic savings in transport energy use - one of the largest urban energy expenditures - by reducing their reliance on automobiles. Studies of the major petroleum consuming sectors in the U.S. for example, have shown that compared to residential and industrial users, savings in oil consumption in the transport sector have been negligible. Fuel switching and conservation have been important contributors to lowering oil consumption in all but the auto-dominated transport sector.

No single technology has had greater impact on urban form in the last several decades than the internal combustion engine. The first industrial cities, clustered around rail and trolley lines, were limited in size and form by these modes of transportation. But the proliferation of automobiles earlier in this century eclipsed mass transit. Automobiles encourage the growth of suburbs, and give city dwellers an insatiable appetite for fossil fuels. In addition, the urban sprawl characteristic of auto-based societies has forestalled efficiency gains in other areas such as district heating and some forms of renewable energy that require relatively high levels of population density to be economical.

Automobile dependent societies consume far more energy moving people and goods than those relying more heavily on other modes of transportation. When large and growing populations spread out in widening circles, road networks must expand. Commuting distances lengthen and more fuel is required for urban and suburban transportation.

More intensive land use shortens the average distances that urban dwellers travel and strengthens urban transit systems. Public transit becomes more viable when there are more people per stop; as the number of passengers per kilometer rises, the amount of energy used to move each passenger falls.

Newman and Kenworthy have shown that the amount of energy devoted to transport depends on "activity intensity" - a measure of city land use based on the concentration of residents and jobs per hectare in a metropolitan area. In a global sample of thirty-one cities, including ten in the United States, twelve in Europe, five in Australia, and three in Asia, Newman and Kenworthy (1987) found that average per capita gasoline consumption in the U.S. cities was nearly twice as high as in the Australian ones, over four times the European ones, and over ten times more than the Asian cities of Tokyo, Singapore, and Hong Kong (see Table 2.2).

In each case, intensive land use correlated with substantial savings in transport energy. The difference between U.S. cities and those in other regions lies in the distances covered and the degree of reliance on automobiles. For example, in Los Angeles, Denver, Detroit, and Houston, the share of population driving to work ranges from eighty-eight to ninety-four percent. In contrast, only forty percent of urban residents in Europe drive to work. Thirty-seven percent use public transit and the remainder walk or ride bicycles. Only fifteen percent of the population in industrialized Asian cities such as Tokyo commute to work by car (Newman and Kenworthy, 1987).

Table 2.2
Urban Gasoline Consumption Per Capita
United States and Other Countries

Urban Areas	Consumption Per Capita	Relationship of Consumption in U.S. Cities to Other Cities
	(gallons)	(ratio)
U.S. Cities	416	1.0
Toronto	248	1.7
Australian Cities	218	1.9
European Cities	97	4.3
Asian Cities	40	10.4

Source: Newman and Kenworthy, 1987.

The distances urban Europeans travel to work and on daily errands are fifty percent shorter on average than similar trips in North American and Australian cities, which have more extensively suburbanized since World War II. Newman and Kenworthy found in these international urban comparisons that land use patterns are more important for energy consumption than income levels, gasoline prices, or the size of cars.

Once a city becomes dependent on automobiles, inefficient land use patterns and automobile reliance tend to become self-reinforcing, making the transition to mass transportation more difficult. Unfortunately, Third World cities (where transportation needs are multiplying rapidly) are now repeating the urban development patterns of industrial countries.

Sao Paulo provides a dramatic example of urban sprawl in a developing country. In 1930, Sao Paulo's population of one million covered approximately 150 square kilometers. The city, with a population of four million, had spread to 750 square kilometers in 1962, a fivefold increase in area. By 1980, less than two decades later, Sao Paulo's dimensions had nearly doubled again, reaching 1,400 square kilometers and a population of twelve million (World Bank, 1986).

Poor land use controls and weak public transit systems have greatly increased auto use at the expense of energy efficiency. But, aside from fuel costs, cities reliant on automobiles face substantial hidden costs as well. As a rule of thumb, urban planners must set aside one-quarter to one-third of a city's land to accommodate autos: an extravagant use of an increasingly scarce resource. Road maintenance requires constant infusions of money, while traffic congestion reduces commercial and industrial productivity (Morris, 1982).

Land use patterns, population size, and level of development determine both the quantity and nature of urban fuel needs for other purposes, such as domestic and industrial activity. Typically, during the process of development reliance shifts from firewood to fossil fuels. As petroleum output expanded after midcentury, for example, kerosene began to replace wood as a cooking fuel in Third World cities. It was convenient and, for many urban dwellers, cheaper than firewood. The oil price surge of the seventies reversed this trend, catching many countries unprepared for the dramatic growth in urban firewood demand.

Rising fuel prices and a scarcity of foreign exchange to import oil for kerosene have forced residents of Third World cities to turn to the surrounding countryside for cooking fuel. As a result, forests are being devastated in ever widening circles around cities, particularly in the Indian subcontinent and Africa. No forests remain within seventy kilometers of Niamey, Niger, or of Ouagadougou, Burkina Faso (Postel, 1984).

One country now carefully measuring the loss of tree cover is India, where satellite images have been used to monitor deforestation. Bowonder et al (1985) report that the areas of closed forest within a 100 kilometer radius of nine of India's principal cities fell sharply between mid-seventies and early eighties. In well under a decade, the loss of forested area ranged from a comparatively modest fifteen percent decline around Coimbatore to a staggering sixty percent decline around Delhi.

Unfortunately for low income urban dwellers, this depletion of fuelwood supplies has boosted prices. Data for forty-one Indian cities, including the nine referred to above, show a rise of two-fifths in real fuelwood prices from 1977 to 1984. Even though food prices in India have remained remarkably stable, rising firewood prices directly affect the food consumption patterns of the urban poor, who are forced to spend more of their small incomes on cooking fuel (Bowonder et al, 1985). Even if India can produce enough food to feed its people by the end of the century, urban residents may lack the fuel to prepare it.

As forests recede from fuelwood dependent Third World cities, the cost of hauling wood rises. Eventually it becomes more profitable to convert the wood into charcoal, a more concentrated form of energy, before transporting it. This conserves transport fuel, but charcoal typically has less than half of the energy contained in the wood used in its manufacture. Not surprisingly, as urban fuel markets reach farther afield for wood supplies, village residents also suffer from depleted supplies and rising costs (Foley, 1986).

If firewood harvesting was properly managed and evenly distributed throughout a country's forests, this renewable resource could sustain far larger harvests. But, because the demand is often heavily concentrated around cities, nearby forests are decimated while more distant ones are left untouched. As urban firewood demand continues to climb, the inability to manage national forest resources for the maximum sustainable yield could prove to be economically costly and ecologically disastrous. The future availability of firewood hinges on better management of existing forests and a far greater tree-planting effort than is now in prospect.

Since the oil price hikes of the early seventies, some cities have increased the share of their energy budgets obtained from renewable sources, including wood and agricultural waste, hydroelectricity, garbage fueled electrical generation, solar collectors, wind turbines, and geothermal energy. If the transition from oil to renewable energy sources gains momentum in the years ahead, it could slow the urbanization process, perhaps even reversing it in some cases.

This effect can be seen in the contrasting prices of kerosene and firewood, the Third World's principal cooking fuels, in rural and urban areas. Kerosene prices are typically cheaper in the city and higher in the countryside because of higher distribution costs in rural areas. Firewood prices, by contrast, are typically lower in rural areas and much higher in the cities. As the shift to firewood and other renewable energy resources proceeds, the economic advantages of living in the countryside will become more obvious.

The cities now relying on renewable energy are as diverse as the sources they are drawing on: nearly forty percent of the homes in Perth, Australia rely on wood for heating, and about twenty-six percent of the city residents use solar energy to heat water. Reykjavik, Iceland, has long used geothermal energy for most of its space heating, while Philippine cities such as Manila derive a growing share of electricity from geothermically powered generating plants. San Francisco is obtaining a growing share of its electricity from nearby geothermal fields and wind farms. In Klamath Falls, Oregon, a city of 42,000 people, more than five hundred homes, a hospital, a nursing home, and a dairy creamery are heated geothermally. A new extension will serve fourteen government buildings and several blocks of residences at half the cost of oil heat (Spirn, 1984; Koenig, 1984).

Other cities have increased the efficiency of traditional sources of energy. District heating through cogeneration (an extremely efficient method widely used in the early part of this century) taps the waste heat produced in electric power generation. District heating permits major gains in energy efficiency where urban populations are sufficiently concentrated. Today, European cities lead in the use of waste heat. In an effort to conserve energy and reduce air pollution, Stuttgart, West Germany, pipes heated water from power plants through the city to homes and stores. Tapiola, Finland, has recaptured waste heat since 1953. Enough heat is generated in U.S. power plants to heat all the homes and commercial buildings in urban areas. But this potential resource remains largely untapped in the United States due to urban sprawl (Morris, 1982; Newman, 1982; Flavin and Pollock, 1985).

A few cities, such as Davis, California, have adopted integrated energy planning to reduce waste in all sectors of the urban economy. A survey done in the early seventies indicated that automobiles accounted for roughly half of all energy consumed within the city, while heating and cooling accounted for an additional twenty-five percent. Now, updated building codes combined with ordinances to encourage solar energy development have reduced the amount of energy needed for internal temperature control. And a low cost, convenient public transit system has markedly reduced automobile use (Spirn, 1984).

By far the largest share of the world's population lives in cities where energy consumption is rising, whether from sheer population growth or poor planning and urban sprawl. Urban planners, by assuming even greater automobile use, built cities that make it inevitable. In many countries, forms of energy favored by industry or government, including nuclear power and oil exploration, continue to receive subsidies that bias energy development away from renewable sources. However, as oil costs rise in the nineties, cities that have encouraged more intensive land use and developed vibrant urban centers and sub-centers linked by mass transit will be the most economically successful. Such cities will be able to rely to the greatest degree possible on local, renewable sources of energy to meet their needs.

Feeding Cities

When the shift from hunting and gathering to farming began, world population probably did not exceed fifteen million, no more than live in Greater London or Mexico City today. The first cities were fed with surpluses of wheat and barley produced in the immediately surrounding countryside, since the lack of efficient transportation prevented long distance movement of food. Residents of early Greek cities were aware of their dependence on agricultural bounty and sought to limit city size by design. Mumford (1961) describes the towns of Greece as "both small and relatively self contained, largely dependent on their local countryside for food and building materials."

During the Industrial Revolution this ancient pattern was altered when Britain began to export industrial products in exchange for food and raw materials. The practice spread, and soon much of Europe followed this trade pattern. On the eve of World War II, Asia, Africa, and Latin America, as well as North America, were all net grain exporters. Rural areas of these regions were producing grain to exchange for the manufactured products of European cities. Cities in the industrial countries were tapping not only the food surplus of their own countryside, but that of industrial lands as well.

These distant sources of food for cities grew in importance after World War II, as agricultural advances in North America created a huge exportable surplus of grain. Since midcentury, the growing food surplus of North America has underwritten much of the world's urban growth. Close to half North America's grain exports are consumed in Africa and Asian cities half a world away.

Recently, Western Europe (for over two centuries the dominant food importing region) has become a net exporter. This shift is attributable to agricultural support prices as well as above world market levels, advancing agricultural technology, and near stationary population sizes. Like cities in North America, those in Western Europe can now be supplied entirely with grain produced in the surrounding countryside. In good crop years, such as 1985, Latin America can also feed its cities.

Three major geographic regions (Asia, Africa, and Eastern Europe and the Soviet Union) still depend on grain from abroad. Major cities in these areas, such as Leningrad, Moscow, Cairo, Lagos, Dacca, Hong Kong, and Tokyo, depend heavily on grain produced in North America. And the Soviet Union is Argentina's main export market. In Africa, formerly a grain exporter, some of the world's fastest growing cities are being fed largely with imported grain.

Political instability has increased in regions where the food demands of growing urban populations outstrip domestic agricultural production. In Africa and elsewhere, food price and wage policies have been key factors in the process of urbanization. Many governments heavily subsidized food staples and other goods either to encourage urban development or to placate politically powerful urban residents. Now, these same governments are caught between the constraints of ballooning budget deficits, soaring foreign debts, and the demands of urban residents accustomed to low cost goods.

In Zambia, food policies were used in the fifties to encourage growth in the copper mining industry. Maize prices for European farmers were set at three times the level for those for native farmers, immediately changing income prospects for the two groups. Discouraged from farming by low prices, large numbers of native farmers sought work in the mining towns, where consumer food prices were heavily subsidized.

In the seventies, copper prices and government revenues fell dramatically; neither has recovered. Population growth is overwhelming a diminishing job market in urban areas and increasing the numbers of Zambians dependent on subsidized urban food supplies. A budget crisis forced cuts in the maize subsidy, sparking riots in December 1986. Although Zambian President Kaunda restored the subsidies, he noted that they would "divert money that Zambia should spend on development of public services" (New York Times, 1986a and 1986b).

Egypt, once a food exporter, now meets sixty percent of its daily food needs with imports bound primarily for urban markets. The government, which has barely recovered from the last spate of bread riots, is politically unable to reduce its $2 billion food subsidy but economically unable to sustain it. This precarious situation is increasingly common: between 1981 and 1986, more than a dozen food related riots and demonstrations have occurred in urban areas throughout the world (see Table 2.3).

Table 2.3
Food Related Riots
and Demonstrations, 1981-86

Country	Date	Triggering Event
Bolivia	July 1983	Drought induced food shortages
Brazil	Summer 1983	Food shortages in northeast
Dominican Republic	Spring 1984 January 1985	Food price increases Sharply increased prices for basic foodstuffs
Egypt	May 1984	Increased bread prices
Haiti	May, June 1984	Food shortages
Jamaica	January 1985	Food price increases
Morocco	January 1984	Cuts in government food subsidies
Philippines	January 1984	Fifty percent increase in food prices
Sierra Leone	Spring 1981	Scarcity of rice and increased retail food prices
Sudan	March 1985	Food price increases
Tunisia	December 1983	Sharply increased prices for wheat and wheat products
Zambia	December 1986	Cuts in government food subsidies

Source: U.S. Department of Agriculture, *Outlook and Situation Reports,* Washington, D.C.; various news articles.

Food price policies directly affect rural-urban relationships by providing unrealistically cheap food for city dwellers and discouraging private investments in food production and hence rural employment. Such policies hold down producer prices as well as rural incomes, thereby transferring net income to urban residents. Due to low domestic agricultural prices, the food surplus produced in the countryside may dwindle or disappear. The resulting distortion in the development process helps explain both the increasing reliance on imported food and the attraction cities hold for the rural unemployed.

Subsidies protect low income urban groups from fluctuating food prices, but for countries with growing populations, they carry prohibitive costs. Several factors limit the potential success of subsidies. To meet standards of equity and efficiency, subsidies must directly benefit a target group. In many countries, however, food subsidies are available to the population at large at high fiscal cost.

To forestall impending food shortages, governments spend scarce foreign exchange that would be better allocated to the purchase of fertilizer or irrigation pumps. Were such investments made, they would expand food output and the national product while creating employment. As the food riots in Zambia and other countries illustrate, the growing disparities between urban expectations and government revenues may lead to increasing social disorder.

Widespread food security has been achieved in those countries, such as China, where urban and rural priorities are in balance. The most effective urban food self sufficiency efforts are those where city governments orchestrate land use, nutrient recycling, and marketing, as in Shanghai. Increased local production of perishable vegetables facilitates the recycling of nutrients from waste and yields fresh produce at attractive prices, while shorter supply lines reduce dependency on energy intensive transportation.

As China worked towards national self sufficiency in cereals, some of its major cities have been seeking self sufficiency in the production of perishables, particularly fresh vegetables. To reach this goal, Shanghai, a city of eleven million, extended its boundaries into the surrounding countryside, increasing the city area to some 6,000 square kilometers. This shift of nearby land to city management greatly facilitates the recycling of nutrients in human wastes. As of 1986, Shanghai was self sufficient in vegetables and produced most of its grain and a good part of its pork and poultry. Vegetables consumed in Shanghai and many other Chinese cities typically travel less than ten kilometers from the fields in which they are produced, often reaching the market within hours of being harvested (Yeung, 1985).

Hong Kong, a city of five million occupying an area of just over 1,000 square kilometers, has a highly sophisticated urban agriculture which grows forty-five percent of its fresh vegetables. Fifteen percent of its pork needs are satisfied by pigs fed with indigenous food wastes, including some 130,000 tons per year from restaurants and food processing plants. Relying on imported feed, the city also produces sixty percent of its live poultry supply. A third of Hong Kong's agricultural land produces vegetables (Yeung, 1985).

In the industrial West, European cities have traditionally emphasized urban community gardens. Following the oil price increases of the seventies, many American cities also launched urban gardening projects, offering undeveloped land to inner-city residents. State governments, particularly in the Northeast, have organized farmers' markets in cities, producing a direct link between local farmers and consumers. Popular with urban dwellers, they are a valuable adjunct to the more traditional roadside stands in heavily populated areas (Spitler, 1986).

Nutrient Recycling

Each day thousands of tons of basic plant nutrients (nitrogen, phosphorus, and potassium) move from countryside to city in the flow of food that sustains urban populations. In turn, human organic wastes (society's most ubiquitous disposable materials) are created. Worldwide, over two-thirds of the nutrients present in human wastes are released to the environment as unreclaimed sewage, often polluting bays, rivers and lakes. As the energy costs of manufacturing fertilizer rise, the viability of agriculture (and, by extension, cities) may hinge on how successfully urban areas can recycle this immense volume of nutrients. Closing nutrient cycles is thus one of the building blocks of ecologically sustainable cities.

The collection of human wastes (known as night soil) for use as fertilizer is a long standing tradition in some countries, particularly in Asia. Door to door handcarts and special vacuum trucks are used to collect night soil in many of the older neighborhoods of Seoul, South Korea, for recycling to the city's green belt. The World Bank estimates that one-third of China's fertilizer requirements have been provided by night soil, maintaining soil fertility for centuries (Shuval, Gunnerson and Julius, 1981; DIESA, 1986c).

European cities equipped with waterborne sewage systems began fertilizing crops with human wastes in the late 1800s to minimize water pollution and to recycle nutrients. By 1875, nearly fifty sewage farms existed in Britain, some serving major cities such as London and Manchester. These early attempts at nutrient recycling failed for several reasons. The volume of wastes from growing cities soon overwhelmed the capacity of the sewage farms. As cities grew, sites to apply the sewage became even more distant from the nutrient sources. Untreated human wastes became recognized as a major source of health problems. Strong taboos developed and the practice was halted, resulting in an open ended nutrient flow (Shuval, Gunnerson and Julius, 1981).

Recently, attitudes toward nutrient recycling have come full circle. Higher fertilizer prices, a better understanding of natural resource and ecological constraints, and improved waste management technologies have renewed interest in nutrient recycling in industrial and developing countries alike. Such efforts protect scarce urban resources: municipalities that recycle organic wastes can simultaneously save money, land, and fresh water for other uses. Recycling treated sewage onto farms surrounding cities also enhances urban food self sufficiency, as indicated earlier. At least six Chinese cities produce within their boundaries more than eighty-five percent of their vegetable supplies, in part by reclaiming nutrients from human wastes and garbage (Yeung, 1985).

Efforts to devise a comprehensive recycling strategy depend on waste composition, collection and treatment, and on the disposable wastes that result. Different sewage treatment methods yield different end products, though they all mimic or enhance natural biological waste degradation. "Wet" or water-borne sewage systems yield raw or treated solids and waste-water effluents for recycling. "Dry" sanitation systems, predominant in developing regions, rely on night soil as the primary recyclable material.

Two waterborne sewage treatment methods are now used. In the first, air, sunlight, and microbial organisms break down wastes, settle solids, and kill pathogens in a series of wastewater ponds or lagoons. Because they are inexpensive and land-intensive, lagoons are used primarily in small urban areas and throughout developing countries. About a quarter of the municipalities in the United States use wastewater lagoons (EPA, 1984).

The second type of wastewater treatment uses energy and technology to replicate natural processes. Processing plants receive large volumes of sewage (domestic wastes often mixed with industrial wastes and stormwater), which undergo a variety of physical, biological, and chemical cleansing treatments. This method produces sludge (a substance of mud like consistency composed mainly of biodegradable organic material) and purified wastewater effluent.

Crop irrigation with wastewater treated in lagoons is practiced worldwide. The effluent is rich in nitrogen, phosphorus, and other nutrients, and represents a valuable water resource, particularly in arid regions. In the Mexican state of Hidalgo, effluents from Mexico City are recycled onto 50,000 hectares of cropland in the world's largest wastewater irrigation scheme. Falling water tables and rising energy costs for groundwater pumping are likely to make this practice even more attractive in the future (Shuval, Gunnerson and Julius, 1981).

Sewage fed aquaculture is another way to enhance food production using wastewater ponds. Here wastewater purification is complemented by cultivating fish on the nutrients and biomass in the lagoons. China, India, Thailand, and Vietnam are leaders in wastewater aquaculture. Fish ponds in Calcutta provide twenty tons of fish per day to city markets (Edwards, 1985).

More than 15,000 sewage treatment plants in the United States handled nearly ninety-eight billion liters of wastewater daily in 1985, generating an annual total of seven million tons of wastewater sludge (dry weight). The U.S. Environmental Protection Agency (EPA) estimated the nutrient content of this waste at some ten percent of that supplied to American farmers by chemical fertilizers, worth therefore over $1 billion per year (Bastian, 1986).

Sludge is not usually a complete fertilizer substitute because of variations in nutrient content. Nevertheless, it can provide significant quantities of nitrogen and phosphorus, while offering other agricultural benefits. Sludge is a soil builder; it adds organic bulk, improves soil aeration and water retention, combats erosion, and, as a result, boosts crop yields. Added to soil or used as incremental fertilizer, sludge can significantly reduce a farmer's commercial fertilizer bill.

Land application of treated sewage sludge has grown markedly over the past two decades. Approximately forty-two percent of sludge generated in the U.S. is applied to land; the rest goes to landfills or incinerators, or is composted (Bruce and Davis, 1984). Western Europe produces over 6.5 million dry tons of sludge each year, a figure that is expected to rise five percent annually as more stringent water pollution controls go into effect. Approximately forty percent of the sludge produced in Western Europe is now used in agriculture.

Collecting and treating waterborne sewage wastes is one of the largest items in municipal budgets. And sludge processing and disposal accounts for up to fifty percent or more of typical plant operating costs. Recycling can reduce these costs. Wyoming, Michigan, site of that state's largest land application program, discovered that while incinerating sludge cost thirteen cents per pound, land application cost only six cents per pound. Over 3,000 hectares of local farmland are now fertilized with sludge. In Muskegon, Michigan, where thirty-eight billion liters of wastewater fertilize cropland producing 450,000 bushels of corn each year, corn sales help defray the cost of the treatment facility (Licht and Johnson, 1986; Schauer, 1986).

Land application is not only cheaper than most other options, it reduces hidden costs that traditional waste disposal methods carry. A great deal of energy is needed to incinerate sludge, a low carbon material. An EPA survey estimated that 189 liters of fuel are consumed to burn one ton of dry sludge; at current annual rates of sludge incineration in the U.S. (about 1.7 million tons) the energy cost is roughly 322 million liters of fuel. In addition, about sixty-four million liters of oil is needed each year to manufacture for farm use the equivalent amount of nitrogen lost through incineration alone (Walker, 1979).

The chemical and biological makeup of sludge must be carefully monitored to protect the food chain from potentially harmful elements. For example, a high concentration of metals, particularly cadmium, is characteristic of sludges from heavily industrialized cities. In the United States, the EPA regulates wastewater treatment and various aspects of sludge application on land. Some sludges cannot be applied to cropland, but may be used on grazing land. Others may be used only in forests or in ecologically disturbed areas, such as stripmined land.

Composting sludge to produce a humus-like substance that is an excellent soil amendment is also increasingly popular. Although the nutrient value of composted sludge is reduced after processing, other benefits, such as the elimination of pathogens and reduced water content, makes this method of recycling more attractive in some situations. More significantly, compost enhances the ability of crops to draw on both natural and synthetic nutrients. Wheat yields in India increased from twenty-eight to forty-four percent with each five tons of compost added per hectare (Talashilkar and Vimal, 1984).

Appropriate technologies and practices for minimizing sewage-related health risks have been widely adopted in industrial countries, but they have not been fully exploited in developing countries. Installing Western style sanitation is a luxury   which few Third World cities can afford. Approximately forty percent of India's one hundred million urban households use dry buckets or latrines from which excreta is collected for disposal; only twenty percent are served by waterborne systems and the rest have virtually no sanitation (Strauss, 1986).

The lack of adequate organic waste collection and treatment in many Third World cities results in serious health and environmental problems. Raw night soil provides a microscopic blueprint of the enteric diseases prevalent in a community. Pathogens present in human wastes include hookworm, tapeworm, and the bacteria that cause typhoid and cholera. Unlike treated wastewater, sludge, or compost, the use of inadequately treated nightsoil in agriculture ensures the spread of these pathogens (Feacham et al, 1980; Shuval, Gunnerson and Julius, 1981).

U.S. Department of Agriculture scientists have devised a low cost composting method capable of killing all pathogens present in night soil (the Bettsville Aerated Rapid Composting System). The technique relies on the same principles as those employed in sludge composting but uses less energy, is labor-intensive, and results in a product with higher nutrient content. Adapting such low technology solutions to night soil management provides an affordable alternative to financially strapped municipalities (Shuval, Gunnerson and Julius, 1981).

Although human organic wastes are the single largest source of nutrients from cities, many organic materials (household food wastes and the by-products of food processing plants) can be recycled. Composting projects are now taking advantage of everything from brewery and yard wastes to apple pomace, animal manure, paper sludge, and wood chips.

Nutrient recycling is likely to increase in popularity as urban land, water, and energy resources become scarcer and as waste management strategies improve. Recycling sludge through land application and composting wherever waterborne sanitation exists is cheaper and more environmentally sound than any other disposal option. As part of a broad public health strategy, nutrient recycling can help Third World cities reach the goals of better health and sanitation, higher food self-sufficiency, and reduced environmental pollution.

Ecology and Economics of City Size

Cities require concentrations of food, water, and fuel on a scale not found in nature. Just as nature cannot concentrate the resources needed to support urban life, neither can it disperse the waste produced in cities. The waste output of even a small city can quickly overtax the absorptive capacity of local terrestrial and aquatic ecosystems.

The average urban resident in the United States uses approximately 568 liters of water, 1.5 kilograms of food, and 7.1 kilograms of fossil fuels per day, generating roughly 454 liters of sewage, 1.5 kilograms of refuse and 0.6 kilograms of air pollutants over the same period. New Yorkers alone annually produce enough garbage to cover all 340 hectares of Central Park to a depth of four meters (Spirn, 1984).

Not surprisingly, urban dwellers are far more energy dependent than their rural counterparts; suburbanites even more so. Moving large quantities of food, water, and fuel into large cities and moving garbage and sewage out are both logistically complex and energy-intensive. The larger and more sprawling the city, the more complex and costly its support systems become. Nutrient-rich human wastes that are an asset in a rural setting can become an economic liability in an urban environment. Indeed, the collection and treatment of sewage is a leading claimant on urban tax revenues, even when it is processed and sold as fertilizer.

Energy inefficient buildings and transport, and wasteful refuse disposal practices all combine to raise the fiscal and environmental costs of urban life. Cities are, in effect, larger than their municipal boundaries might imply: as urban material needs multiply through the effects of sprawl and mismanagement, they eventually exceed the capacity of the surrounding countryside, exerting pressure on more distant ecosystems to supply resources. Aquifers and wetlands, agricultural and open spaces are all as essential to a city's survival as transport networks, but are rarely ever the subject of urban planners' concerns.

Water, at once the most vital and the most abused urban resource, best illustrates the precarious relationship that now exists between cities and natural systems. The competition between cities and the other major water consumers - agriculture and industry - is rising just as the quantity and quality of available water is declining rapidly. Many cities are now searching farther and farther afield to augment supplies from overextended or contaminated aquifers. About three-quarters of all U.S. cities rely to some degree on groundwater. Yet only three of the thirty-five largest (San Antonio, Miami, and Memphis) can meet their needs solely from local supplies (Spirn, 1984).

Transporting water can involve enormous energy costs. Mexico City's elevated site means water must be lifted from progressively lower catchments. In 1982, Mexico City began pumping water from Cutzamala, a site one hundred kilometers away and 1,000 meters lower than the city. Douglas reports that "augmentation of the Mexico City supply in the 1990s will be from Tecolutla, which is some 200 kilometers away and 2000 meters lower." Pumping water this far will require some 125 trillion kilojoules of electrical energy annually, the output of six 1,000-megawatt power plants. Construction of these plants would cost at least $6 billion, an amount roughly equal to half the annual interest payments on Mexico's external debt. The city is thus faced with three rising cost curves in water procurement - increasing distance of water transport, increasing height of water lift, and, over the long term, rising energy prices. Escalating water costs, stringent rationing, or both are likely to prevent Mexico City from reaching the population of thirty million now projected by the United Nations (Douglas, 1983).

In many Third World cities, residents receive water that has undergone little or no purification. As Indian economist V. Nath points out, "The cost of providing adequate water... to the large cities is extremely high and that of providing safe water can be astronomical." Water containing dangerous levels of toxic wastes, and the viruses, protozoa, and bacteria that cause disease is routinely used for cooking, drinking and washing. In Jakarta, for example, less than 25 percent of the population's needs can be met by the current supply system. Sewage contamination and saltwater intrusion have rendered many wells useless. In Manila, a city of approximately nine million people, a scant eleven percent of the population is served by sewers. Road gutters, open ditches, and canals serve as conduits for the raw sewage that regularly contaminates water supplies (Nath, 1986; Lindh, 1983; DIESA, 1986a).

Cities are notorious for their waste and misuse of water. Aging water mains leak profusely. Until recently, few cities were replacing these antiquated pipes. Now, as the cost of obtaining new water supplies skyrockets, conservation is becoming attractive. London, for example, plans to spend $320 million to replace water mains originally installed during the reign of Queen Victoria some 125 years ago (Pearce, 1987).

Urban residents are accustomed to paying little for water, while fines levied against industries for dumping toxic wastes in public water supplies are traditionally light or go unenforced. In Peking, a ton of water costs less than a popsicle. Rationing went into effect in mid-1986, but shortages continue to plague the city (Browning, 1986).

Water supplies are not the only emerging constraint on urban growth. As noted earlier, for many Third World cities the rising price of oil, and hence of kerosene, since 1973 has put pressure on indigenous fuelwood resources. Research on fuelwood prices in India demonstrates a close relationship between city size and firewood costs (Bowonder et al, 1985).

In some smaller cities that are relatively close to forested areas, such as Darjeeling, fuelwood cost less than 350 rupees per ton in 1984. As city size increased, so did firewood prices. In the seven cities with populations between one million and five million, prices ranged from 500 to 700 rupees per ton. For the three cities with more than five million residents, fuelwood cost more than 700 rupees per ton, at least twice as much as in smaller cities. Some small cities also had expensive fuelwood, usually because they were in areas with little remaining forest cover. Thus small cities in India do not necessarily have low fuelwood prices, but all large cities have high prices.

Of all the investments needed to sustain cities, the shortfall is perhaps greatest in the treatment and disposal of human and industrial wastes. The number and concentration of urban pollutants toxic to humans and disruptive of other natural systems rise each year. Unchecked, these wastes pollute the air above cities, enter water and soil, and via many pathways, contribute to poor health. Urban pollutants inevitably transcend city limits; in time, they become the primary contributors to acid rain and the accumulation of carbon dioxide and other greenhouse gases that are changing the earth's chemistry.

Nitrogen and sulfur oxides, ozone, carbon compounds, and suspended particulates such as lead, arsenic, and cadmium foul city air. Reports on the adverse consequences of air pollution in Third World cities with few or no pollution controls are legion. Thomas (1985) found that automotive traffic is the largest single source of pollution in Sao Paulo, while industrial processes and power plants were the principal sources of particulates and sulfur dioxide. The more than 8,000 tons of pollutants poured into the air above Sao Paulo daily have been linked to increased mortality among infants and those over sixty-five years old. And an estimated sixty percent of Calcutta's residents are believed to suffer from respiratory diseases related to air pollution (Hardoy and Satterthwaite, 1984).

Automobiles (the predominant mode of transportation in many cities today) contribute most heavily to photochemical smog and carbon monoxide pollution (U.S. Bureau of the Census, 1986). Auto particulates represent only a small proportion of total urban pollution; but because they are emitted at street level and most easily inhaled, auto particulates are among the most insidious, contributing to respiratory ailments, and lead poisoning in children.

In the United States, federal air quality standards and emission control laws have decreased the level of pollutants in most urban areas. But persistent automobile dependence has kept the levels of some pollutants dangerously high. Despite standards set by the Clean Air Act, many cities are still exceeding standards allowed for several pollutants. Ozone levels in New York, Houston, and Chicago registered at least twice the maximum allowable level in mid-1986. In Los Angeles, the level was three times the maximum (Boorstin, 1986).

Urban pollution problems are multiplying rapidly in many Third World cities where automobile ownership symbolizes economic success. Chinese cities, with their traditional reliance on bicycles and buses for individual mobility, are perhaps the most efficient in their consumption of transport energy. Unfortunately, as Chinese living standards rise, autos are replacing these modes of transport, reducing energy efficiency and raising pollution levels.

While dwindling water and fuel supplies combine with mounting pollution levels to raise the ecological costs of urban life, fiscal costs are rising as well. Laying the foundations of a comprehensive transportation system is essential to an efficient, sustainable city, where goods can compete in world markets. A well planned transport network raises urban productivity by facilitating the flow of people and goods throughout the city. Higher levels of equity and social development can be achieved when transportation provides all economic groups with access to jobs and services. Yet developing countries, following the urban settlement patterns of their industrialized counterparts, face severe transport problems.

The demand for transportation in Third World cities is often met with inappropriate remedies that tax city budgets and indirectly encourage more widespread reliance on automobiles. Motivated by the desire to modernize rapidly, most cities in the Third World have invested in politically attractive but extremely costly modes of transportation that serve only a small fraction of their populations.

Expensive underground rail transit systems and elevated roadways have taken precedence over improvements on existing roads and establishment of low-cost bus operations. Costs have risen dramatically as a result. The World Bank notes that municipal governments commonly spend between fifteen and twenty-five percent of their annual budgets on transport related investments - sometimes much more. Due to high capital and operation costs, high technology mass transit systems often require continued financial support from government revenues. Each kilometer of a rail subway may cost as much as $100 million, for example (World Bank, 1986).

A wide gap already exists between the fiscal and ecological costs of supporting urban development in its present context and the resources required to sustain it. Now, industrial and developing countries alike need a new ethic of urban development - one that embraces the concept of the city as an ecosystem in which population size and urban form are matched to available resources. The question which policymakers face is how large cities should be in a world that depends primarily on renewable resources. The subsidies that distort the relationship between cities and natural systems and promote waste should be replaced by a set of policies based on more intensive land use in urban centers with a heavy emphasis on mass transit, conservation of resources, and energy efficiency.

A broader analytical framework is needed to guide planners and policymakers in assessing urban investments: namely, a broad social cost benefit analysis, integrating principles of ecological and economic sustainability, and the principle of financial viability. The benefits of any urban project should outweigh the social costs. And municipal investments should be undertaken only with the understanding that they be financially self sustaining. Wherever possible, the private sector should be encouraged to provide services, a policy that will heighten efficiency. User taxes can be enforced to reduce waste by maximizing the cost of pollution to individuals and industries.

Establishing green belts within and around urban areas safeguards and increases local water supplies. Land use controls and the preservation of wetlands and open space can greatly enhance groundwater recharge and help with the management and recycling of wastewater. A green belt strategy aimed at permanent protection of open lands within and between cities can also mitigate pollution problems and increase urban self-sufficiency in agriculture. Trees and soil absorb many airborne wastes; large expanses of open lands enhance urban air flow.

Creating denser, more efficient cities depends on curbing automobile use. This trend is already under way in many cities, most notably in Europe. Some two thousand years after Julius Caesar banned human borne litters from downtown Rome to ease congestion, cars and trucks are now prohibited from entering the city center during rush hour. Stockholm, Rotterdam, Bologna, and Vienna have all banned traffic from various parts of the central city; indeed, virtually all European cities have some restrictions on auto use in force. And in Hong Kong and Singapore, as well as in Korean cities, taxes and financial disincentives discourage the use of private vehicles. The Dutch have built streets to discourage auto use and to encourage walking and biking.

Public transport can markedly reduce both pollutants and urban energy costs. Bus service in Third World cities, often the only means of transportation affordable to the urban poor, routinely falls short of demand. The importance of buses cannot be overestimated: the World Bank (1986) estimates that in 1980, 600 million trips per day were made on buses in the cities of the Third World, a figure that is expected to double by the year 2,000.

Mass transit need not be a costly undertaking. Encouraging competition among private companies to provide bus service frees up scarce municipal dollars and increases the choices available to commuters. While autos rarely carry more than two people, one bus may carry up to eighty passengers. Yet a bus takes up the space of only two private cars on the road. Simultaneously reducing the number of private vehicles and setting up special bus lanes allows other traffic to move faster, and increases urban efficiency (World Bank, 1986).

Seeking a Rural-Urban Balance

The formation and growth of cities is an integral part of the economic and social development of nations. The development of early cities was closely associated with the emergence of civilization itself. Over the last two centuries, urban growth has enabled countries to capitalize on the economies of scale inherent in industrial processes, such as manufacturing, leading to the improvements in living standards associated with modernization.

Official U.N. projections show urbanization continuing for decades into the future. But as world oil production declines, and the costs of supplying the needs of large cities mount, questions arise over what rate of urbanization best serves national needs. Some national governments are now beginning to reassess the policies that are critical to achieving a better distribution of resources between urban and rural areas.

The optimal balance between countryside and city varies, of course, from country to country and within a country over time. For example, the optimum size of cities will be reduced as the age of oil slowly fades and the age of renewable energy begins to unfold. Oil is a concentrated resource, easily transported in the huge quantities that large cities require. In contrast, renewable energy resources, whether firewood, solar collectors, or small scale hydro, are more geographically diffuse. Both the ecology and economics of these energy sources suggest that the future will favor smaller cities and those who live in rural areas.

As the energy transition proceeds, the ability of highly oil dependent cities, such as Houston and Los Angeles, to compete in the world market will be seriously disadvantaged by high living costs and hence, high wages. The cities that move vigorously to improve their efficiency of resource use (energy, water, land, and materials) will strengthen their competitive position. Those that ignore these issues will eventually pay with depressed economic activity and unemployment.

The growth in the world's urban population from six hundred million in 1950 to two billion in 1986 is without precedent. Because urban expansion in the more advanced industrial societies has come to a virtual halt over the last decade or so, urbanization is now concentrated in the Third World. Part of this urban growth is a response to the needs of industrialization, the pull of urban job opportunities. But much of the urban growth now occurring in the Third World is the result of failed economic and population policies, a process driven more by rural poverty that urban prosperity. Such policies have needlessly distorted the development process in many developing countries.

The official exchange rate that governs the terms of trade between a country and the outside world, and the food price policy that governs urban-rural terms of trade are the principal means of favoring cities. All too often, official exchange rates are set up to promote the imports and consumer goods bound for urban markets, sometimes bringing the price of imported food for urban consumers below that of food produced domestically. Policies that kept food prices low discourage investment in agriculture, eventually creating national food deficits. Moreover, the effects of these two policies on rural areas are compounded by the lack of investment in human capital; per capita investments in urban social services such as education and health care are often several times as great as those in rural areas.

One way of reaching a nation's optimum rural-urban balance would be to let the market play a more prominent role in economic development. A rate of urbanization determined largely by market forces would almost certainly be more sustainable than that influenced heavily by subsidies. Removing urban bias from economic policy - adjusting exchange rates to reduce the attractiveness of imported consumer goods and food, and adopting food price policies to encourage investment in the countryside - would be a healthy first step in this direction.

The urban bias evident in the economic policies of so many Third World countries wastes both human talent and natural resources.   The second major adjustment required to reduce urban bias is the transfer of investment in social services to the countryside.   A more equitable distribution of education and basic health care services throughout the society would help cultivate the most abundant resources that many developing societies have: their people.

Population policies, environmental conditions, and landownership patterns also directly affect urbanization rates. Countries with ineffective or nonexistent family planning programs are invariably faced with rural populations under greater pressures to migrate to cities. Where the rural environment is deteriorating as a result of deforestation, soil erosion, and desertification, cities are likely to be besieged by ecological refugees. And where landownership is concentrated in a few hands, as in Latin America, landlessness also drives rural people into the cities.

Apart from the optimal rural-urban balance, the question of how urban population is distributed among cities also looms large in countries where a primary city dominates economic and political life. Secondary cities can serve the goals of economic development by acting as conduits for more geographically dispersed investment.

Small urban centers not only provide an alternative outlet for migrants, but also offer local access to agricultural processing industries, farm inputs, and markets. These economic benefits are enhanced when accompanied by decentralized public services, such as field offices of national ministries or regional and provincial administrative offices that can increase rural access to needed services and information.

A few countries have adopted national development strategies aimed at balancing urban and rural needs against available resources. South Korea is one such country. A mix of land use and industrial location policies was put in place in the seventies to reduce the country's reliance on Seoul, the principal city. At the same time, the Korean government initiated the New Village Movement, a program geared to raise rural incomes and discourage migration from rural areas. More than 450 rural industries   have been established, a major factor in narrowing the income gap between rural and urban households (DIESA, 1986b). China offers another example of a country that has managed to regulate the growth of cities, by restricting migration and investing heavily in the countryside. As a result of the government's strong support for agriculture, incomes of many rural Chinese are higher than those of their urban counterparts. Few Third World governments emphasize agriculture as strongly as China's does, however.

Pressures from international lending institutions to eliminate urban biases in Third World economic policies are mounting, largely because these biases are partly responsible for the soaring external debt of many countries. All too much of the urbanization in the Third World over the past generation has been "artificial", supported either at the expense of rural populations or through foreign assistance. In either case it is becoming increasingly more difficult to sustain. Whether vast cities with tens of millions of people (Mexico City or Calcutta in the year 2000, for example) can, or indeed should, be sustained is questionable, particularly if doing so requires heavy subsidies from the countryside.

Out of the current reexamination of undervalued exchange rates and food price policies by the International Monetary Fund and World Bank may come much more enlightened national economic development strategies. The adoption of policies to arrest the growth in external debt and the transition to renewable sources of energy seem certain to slow urban growth. It is even conceivable that in some instances urbanization will be reversed.

REFERENCES

Adepoju, Aderanti, 1986, *Population and the Planning of Large Cities in Africa,* paper presented at the International Conference on Population and the Urban Future sponsored by UNFPA, Barcelona, Spain, May 19-22.

Bastian, Robert K., 1986, (Environmental Protection Agency) Private communication.

Boorstin, Robert O., 1986, "Clean Air Deadline Nears, and City Ponders its Choices," *New York Times,* October 26, 1986.

Bowonder, B. et al, 1985, *Deforestation and Fuelwood Use in Urban Centres,* Hyderabad, India: Centre for Energy, Environment and Technology, and National Remote Sensing Agency.

Browning, Michael, 1986, "For a Town That's Going Dry, Peking Treats Water Cheaply," *Miami Herald,* July 15.

Bruce, A.M. and R.D. Davis, 1984, "Britain Uses Half Its Fertilizer As Sludge," *BioCycle,* March.

Caufield, Catherine, "The California Approach to Plumbing", *New Scientist,* February 21, 1985.

DIESA, 1986a, (United Nations Department of International Economic and Social Affairs), *Population Growth in Mega-Cities: Metro Manila,* Population Policy Paper No. 5, (New York).

_____, 1986b, *Population Growth and Policies in Mega-Cities: Bombay,* Population Policy Paper No. 6 (New York).

_____, 1986c, *Population Growth and Policies in Mega-Cities: Seoul,* New York.

Douglas, Ian, 1983, *The Urban Environment,* Baltimore, MD: Edward Arnold.

Edwards, Peter, 1985, *Aquaculture: A Component of Low Cost Sanitation Technology,* Washington, DC: United Nations Development Program and World Bank.

EPA, 1984, *Primer for Wastewater Treatment* (Washington, DC).

Feacham, Richard G. et al, 1980, *Health Aspects of Excreta and Sullage Management - A State of the Art Review,* Washington, DC: World Bank.

Flavin, Christopher and Cynthia Pollock, 1985, "Harnessing Renewable Energy," in Lester R. Brown et al, *State of the World,* New York: W.W. Norton.

Foley, Gerald, 1986, *Charcoal Making in Developing Countries,* Washington, DC: Earthscan/International Institute for Environment and Development.

Frederick, Kenneth D., 1986, "Watering the Big Apple," Washington, DC: Resources for the Future.

Hamer, Andrew, 1982, *Brazilian Industrialization and Economic Concentration in Sao Paulo: A Survey,* Washington, DC: World Bank.

Hardoy, Jorge E. and David Satterthwaite, 1984, "Third World Cities and the Environment of Poverty," *Geoforum* Vol. 15, No. 3.

Jordan, Ricardo, 1986, *Population and the Planning of Large Cities in Latin America,* paper presented at the International Conference on Population and the Urban Future sponsored by UNFPA, Barcelona, Spain, May 19-22.

Knudson, Thomas J, 1987, "Dry Cities of West Buy Up Farm Water Rights," *New York Times,* February 10.

Koenig, Herman E., 1984, "The Scientific and Technological Context of Today's Urban Problems," from *Critical Urban Issues in the 1980s: Problems and Responses,* Urban Affairs Programs, Michigan State University, East Lansing, Michigan.

Laquian, Aprodicio A., 1986, *Population and the Planning of Large Cities in Asia,* paper presented at the International Conference on Population and the Urban Future sponsored by UNFPA, Barcelona, Spain, May 19-22.

Lees, Andrew, 1985, *Cities Perceived: Urban Society in European and American Thought 1820-1940,* New York, NY: Columbia University Press.

Licht, Judy and Johnson, Jeff, 1986, "Sludge is an Awful Thing to Waste," *Sierra,* March/April.

Lindh, Gunnar, 1983, *Water and the City,* Paris: UNESCO.

Lipton, Michael, 1975, "Urban Bias and Food Policy in Poor Countries," *Food Policy,* November.

Morris, David, 1982, *Self-Reliant Cities: Energy and the Transformation of Urban America,* Washington, DC: Institute for Local Self-Reliance.

Mumford, Lewis, 1961, *The City in History,* Orlando: Harcourt, Brace, Jovanovich.

Nath, V., 1986, "Urbanization in India: Review and Progress," *Economic and Political Weekly,* February 22.

New York Times, 1986a, "Food Riots in Zambia: Borders Are Closed," *New York Times,* December 10.

_____, 1986b, "Zambia Halts Food Increases After Rioting and 11 Deaths," *New York Times,* December 12.

Newman, Peter W.G., 1982, "Domestic Energy Use in Australian Cities," *Urban Ecology,* No. 7.

Newman, Peter and Kenworthy, Jeffrey, 1987, *Gasoline Consumption and Cities - A Comparison of U.S. Cities with a Global Survey and Some Implications,* Transport Research Paper 8, School of Environmental and Life Sciences, Murdoch University, Australia.

Pearce, Fred, 1987, "Ring of Water Will End London's Bursts," *New Scientist,* January 29.

Pimentel, David, 1980, *Handbook of Energy Utilization in Agriculture,* Boca Raton, FL: CRC Press.

Population Reference Bureau, 1986, *1986 World Population Data Sheet,* Washington, DC (and personal communication).

Postel, Sandra, 1984, "Protecting Forests" in Lester R. Brown et al, *State of the World 1984,* New York: W.W. Norton.

Purnick, Joyce, 1986, "Water Meters Due in All City Houses," *New York Times,* November 13.

Renaud, Bertrand, 1981, *National Urbanization Policies in Developing Countries,* Washington, DC: World Bank.

Rondinelli, Dennis A., 1986, "Metropolitan Growth and Secondary Cities Development Policy," *Habitat International,* Vol. 10, No. 1/2.

Salas, Rafael M., 1986, *The State of World Population 1986,* New York: United Nations Fund for Population Activities.

Schauer, Dawn, 1986, "Saving Money While Land Applying," *BioCycle,* November/December.

Shuval, Hillel, Charles G. Gunnerson, and DeAnne S. Julius, 1981, *Night Soil Composting,* Washington, DC: World Bank.

Shuval, Hillel, et al, 1981, *Wastewater Irrigation in Developing Countries: Health Effects and Technical Solutions,* Washington, DC: United Nations Development Program and World Bank.

Spirn, Anne Whiston, 1984, *The Granite Garden: Urban Nature and Human Design,* New York: Basic Books.

Spitler, John, 1986, "Many Hard-Pressed U.S. Farmers Sell Produce Directly to Public," *Christian Science Monitor,* November 12.

Strauss, Martin, 1986, *About Wastewater and Excreta Use in India* (draft), World Health Organization International Reference Center for Waste Disposal, Duebendorf, Switzerland, June.

Talashilkar, S.C. and O.P. Vimal, 1984, "From Nutrient-Poor Compost to High Grade Fertilizer," *BioCycle,* March.

Thomas, Vinod, 1985, "Evaluating Pollution Control: The Case of Sao Paulo, Brazil," *Journal of Development Economics,* Vol. 19.

Todara, Michael P. and Stilkind, Jerry, 1981, *City Bias and Rural Neglect: The Dilemma of Urban Development,* New York: Population Council.

U.S. Bureau of the Census, 1986, *Statistical Abstract of the United States 1986,* U.S. Government Printing Office,

Walker, John M., 1979, "Using Municipal Sewage on Land Makes Sense," *Compost Science/Land Utilization,* September/October.

World Health Organization, *The Risk to Health of Microbes in Sewage Sludge Applied to Land,* Copenhagen, Denmark: W.H.O.

World Bank, 1986, *Urban Transport: A World Bank Policy Study,* Washington, DC.

Yeung, Yue-Man, 1985, *Urban Agriculture in Asia,* The Food Energy Nexus Programme of the United Nations University, Tokyo, September.

Land Use Planning for Energy Efficiency

Susan E. Owens

In broad outline, the case for including an energy dimension in the land use planning process is both simple and compelling. Energy is undeniably a crucial resource; the system of energy supply, distribution and use is related in significant ways to the spatial organization of society; and if land use planning is intended to influence the evolution of spatial structure, it must be legitimate for planners to be concerned with energy supply, demand and conservation.

The relationship between the energy system and the spatial organization of society is complex, dynamic and not yet fully analysed or understood, but in outline its main features are clear. The nature and availability of energy resources has always influenced the built environment and the distribution of human activities, and during the twentieth century cheap energy has permitted the outward spread of urban areas at decreasing densities (though *causal* factors are obviously much more complex). Physical infrastructure, once in place, has an important influence on energy demand, both directly through the need for space heating or cooling and for travel, and indirectly through its compatibility with particular energy supply or conservation technologies. In the U.K., transport and space heating account for well over half of delivered energy needs, and one Swedish study suggests that 60-75 percent of total energy use is related in some way to spatial structure (Lamm, 1986).

53

The case for including energy considerations in the planning process is strongly reinforced by the fact that physical structures are relatively permanent, but the energy future is at best uncertain. Planners should therefore be aware of the energy implications of alternative development policies, should include energy efficiency among their objectives, and may be able to make a more positive contribution to energy planning through urban design which is compatible with particular supply and conservation options. Neglect of energy considerations in the planning process risks the development of energy intensive land use patterns by default.

The validity of these arguments depends on acceptance of the need for state intervention, both in the development of land and in the energy system. It is sometimes suggested that market forces, with minimal guidance, will best take care of energy supply and conservation, as well as producing the most appropriate spatial structure in relation to energy availability and constraints. But market imperfections make it highly unlikely that the optimal outcome would be achieved, even in narrow economic efficiency terms, and the unplanned outcome is almost certain to be problematic on social and environmental grounds. Indeed, as world fossil fuel prices have fallen sharply in the 1980s and the energy situation has moved from scarcity to glut, it is the environmental externalities associated with energy supply and use that have come to dominate the rationale for energy efficiency. As the direct economic incentive to conserve energy has diminished, it has been replaced by growing anxiety about nuclear accidents, acid rain, the greenhouse effect and other alarming manifestations of environmental degradation. On a more local scale, NIMBY resistance to new energy supply facilities has grown rapidly, making their location in some areas almost a political impossibility. The environmental arguments alone should be enough to convince planners of the importance of energy efficiency, but anyone involved in the development of the built environment should also be conscious of longer term energy supply uncertainties: development planned in the 1980s will almost certainly outlast any temporary energy glut.

Some notes of caution must be sounded. First, energy can and should be only one of many considerations in land use planning, and energy efficiency may have to take lower priority than other objectives, though it is often much more compatible with social and environmental goals than has sometimes been implied. Perhaps more importantly, the limitations of planning itself must be recognized: it will always be a highly imperfect process with or without energy considerations. Many influences on the spatial organization of society fall outside the control of land use planning, and planners can sometimes have relatively little impact on development patterns which are shaped by underlying social and economic forces. This observation becomes more valid the larger the scale of intervention. As Cherry (1982) suggests:

> ... in the market economy countries of the West, public sector land policies have remarkably little effect at macro scale on the shaping of metropolitan form and regional distribution patterns.

In spite of these limitations and other constraints (considered in more detail later), the energy crises of the 1970s stimulated considerable interest in the energy/spatial structure relationship and in the potential contribution of land use planning to energy conservation. Research developed quite rapidly: Lamm (1986) comments that a search of the English and Swedish language literature uncovered one hundred relevant items in 1980, but five hundred by 1984. Unfortunately, research in this field has been uncoordinated, relying on many different methodologies and approaches, and has varied enormously in quality, sophistication and policy relevance. Nevertheless, some broad principles (and in some cases, detailed guidelines) for energy conscious land use planning have emerged, especially at the local scale. Occasionally these are put into practice, but energy integrated planning is still the exception rather than the rule.

The object of this paper is to provide an overview of the theory and practice related to energy, land use and planning, to examine possibilities and constraints, and to consider how research in this field might most fruitfully be developed in future. The following section explores the interactive relationship between energy and spatial structure, considering both the energy implications of current urban trends and the possible spatial implications of energy constraints: both areas are characterized by great uncertainty. This is followed by a discussion of theoretical work which has sought to identify energy efficient spatial structures at the local, urban and regional scales. A subsequent section looks at energy conscious planning in practice, selecting a variety of examples, and identifies factors which both encourage and inhibit the inclusion of an energy dimension in the land use planning process. The final section evaluates progress to date and considers prospects and research needs for the future.

Energy and Spatial Structure

Energy and Current Spatial Trends

Important changes, the root causes of which are not fully understood, are affecting settlement structure in many advanced countries, including the U.S. and the U.K., and these changes could have a significant long term impact on energy demand. The most striking recent trend, aptly named "counterurbanization" (Berry, 1976), has involved a substantial net flow of people and jobs out of the major conurbations into small and medium sized towns in non-metropolitan areas. Champion (1988) argues that the scale of change is such that:

> ... in both geographical and intellectual terms these recent developments are as important as the major changes in population distribution which took place during the nineteenth and early twentieth centuries.

The U.K., for example, has seen a consistent trend towards deconcentration during the past two decades, with a clear negative relationship emerging between the rate of growth of a place and its size (Champion, 1988). During the 1970s, a few very large cities lost eight percent or more of their population, while many small and medium sized places gained by more than fifteen percent. In other words:

> The British population is... becoming more evenly distributed over space, and not just as a result of suburbanization or local decentralization from the major metropolitan centers (Champion, 1988).

Although recent evidence suggests that the rate of population loss from the major cities (especially London) has slowed during the 1980s, Champion argues that deconcentration remains the major force.

Manufacturing employment has also decentralized: in Britain in the period 1960-1981, Keeble (1986) shows that manufacturing employment change "was almost invariably faster the further away from... a conurbation an area was located", and he demonstrates that "high tech" industry has become strongly associated spatially with rural, small town and less urban local environments.

The energy implications of macro level changes of this kind are intriguing, possibly very significant, and highly uncertain. Since there is no clear agreement about the causes of counterurbanization, or about its likely persistence, it is not possible to define the type of settlement pattern which might be its ultimate outcome. And even if it were clear that, in the early twenty-first century, we might see a much higher proportion of the population of Europe and North America living in small to medium sized freestanding towns, well away from the influence of the conurbations, the *energy* implications are still far from clear. Theoretical work (discussed later) tells us that such a settlement pattern is potentially energy efficient: a shift from a city/suburb structure to one involving smaller, quasi-autonomous urban units could result in lower travel requirements, but only if people choose to live, work, shop and take their leisure in the same small town and refrain from energy intensive cross commuting. Long commuter trips might be replaced in the new settlement pattern by shorter journeys, but would these now be by car instead of by energy efficient rail? Or would walking and cycling be encouraged by the proximity of facilities and a more pleasant environment? Another important question is whether time and energy saved by not commuting to the city would be used for other forms of travel, such as leisure driving in the countryside. Since it is difficult to answer any of these questions in the absence of relevant data, it can be argued just as convincingly that counterurbanization is an energy intensive trend as that it might be an energy efficient one: as will be shown later, much depends on personal mobility and propensity to travel, factors which are themselves related to energy costs.

Other trends, including the growth of out-of-town car-orientated facilities, long distance commuting and second home ownership, also have interesting energy implications. The last of these, for example, may involve short daily trips within the city combined with long car-based journeys at weekends, or even novel and completely non-routine trip patterns between home(s) and work, making maximum use of telecommunications technology. Again, the energy consequences are not immediately clear.

What we know is that significant social and structural change is taking place on a regional scale, as well as change due to growth and redevelopment within specific planning areas. But the outcome, both in terms of evolving settlement structure and its implications for travel and energy demand, is still very uncertain. Whether emerging patterns are more or less energy intensive than existing ones may itself depend upon energy availability and constraints: the system is interactive. We need therefore to be concerned not only with the possible effects of evolving spatial structure on energy demand, but with ways in which changes in the energy system might influence current urban trends.

Spatial Implications of Energy System Change

Since the influence of the energy system on spatial structure is complex and involves a large number of variables, it is difficult to envisage, let alone to predict with any confidence, how energy system changes might influence the way in which settlement structures evolve. A number of attempts have been made to do just this but, as Talarcheck (1984) points out:

> ... a review of the scholarly literature fails to provide a definitive answer to the question: will changing energy supplies and energy cost transform urban spatial structure?

Most attention has focused on the impact of possible future energy constraints (typically in the form of price increases) on urban structure, an issue which seemed very pertinent in the aftermath of the energy crises of the 1970s and stimulated much interest in the energy/urban form relationship. Some authors have broadened the analysis to consider the implications of alternative energy scenarios, ranging from "crisis" to "glut" (see, for example, Williams, Kruvant and Newman, 1979), and a few have explored more remote possibilities such as a return to the use of renewable energy resources on a relatively small scale as in the "soft energy path" advocated by Lovins (1977; for more detail, see Owens 1986a).

It is tempting to assume that if energy, especially fuel for transport, were to become scarce and expensive, the energy intensive centripetal urban trends which have characterized much of the twentieth century would be halted and reversed; it was in this spirit that some observers in the early 1970s looked forward to "squeezing spread city" (Downs, 1974) and to the "imploding metropolis" (Franklin, 1974). But the metropolis has not imploded, and it was highly unlikely to do so even if oil market disruptions had been sustained long enough to have a lasting effect on urban form. The energy system may permit or constrain urban change, but it is crudely deterministic to interpret it as a direct causal factor. Social and economic forces drive spatial evolution and, for this and other reasons energy constraints, while having some influence on urban trends, are unlikely to lead to any simple reversal of decentralization and dispersal of urban activity (Owens 1986a). A really effective analysis of possible spatial consequences of energy constraints would build upon an understanding of both the causal factors behind current spatial change and the social response to changes in energy availability. The lack of consensus in the first of these areas has already been noted, and is compounded by a dearth of reliable empirical evidence on the second (Dix and Goodwin 1982, 1981).

Faced with considerable complexity of both energy and urban and regional systems, much research in this field has involved the use of urban models, including adaptations of the Lowry model with energy costs represented in the deterrent effect of distance/cost parameter (Beaumont and Keys, 1982; Coelho and Williams, 1978) and equilibrium models based on utility analysis of the residential location decision, with energy costs included in the transport budget (Dendrinos, 1979; Romanos, 1978; Thrall 1982). Recently developed methods in dynamical systems analysis have also been applied, though as yet only to very simple representations of the problem (Beaumont, Clarke and Wilson, 1981). One of the major difficulties with this predictive approach is the implicit assumption in many of the models (of whatever kind) that aspects of individual behavior which might ultimately be reflected in spatial structure are *elastic* with respect to energy costs. But in practice there are many ways in which people can respond to increasing energy prices which do not have obvious spatial implications, so the nature of the individual response is fundamental to the spatial outcome. Unfortunately, evidence on responses to energy constraints is limited, and in the case of medium to long term reaction to sustained energy price increases, is non-existent for obvious reasons.

In the case of transport, such evidence as exists suggests that gas price increases are unlikely to have any marked effect in the short term (Dix and Goodwin, 1981). Marginal adjustments of trip patterns, especially less essential social and leisure trips, are associated with small changes in gas consumption, producing short run elasticities of around -0.25 (U.K. Department of Energy, 1977). Evidence that people adopt "coping" strategies in the short term is supported by "backtrack" interview surveys after cost changes (Carpenter and Dix, 1980; Corsi and Harvey, 1977), and by an interesting analysis of behavior after the collapse of the main bridge linking city to suburbs in Hobart, Australia (Wood and Lee, 1980).

Lagged time series analyses suggest higher long term than short term gas demand elasticities, but Dix and Goodwin (1981) suggest that a distinction must be made between "traffic" and "gas" elasticities. In the medium term these diverge, the former diminishing as people try to revert to their original trip patterns and the latter increasing as more efficient vehicles are acquired to save gas without loss of mobility. For longer term spatial readjustments to occur, *traffic* elasticities would have to increase as decisions on location and lifestyle were influenced by energy constraints. Dix and Goodwin (1981) argue that this is a possibility if (as they believe is likely) people respond rationally to energy costs in the long term and adjust their travel habits (by relocation) at the time of "life shocks", defined as important transitions between life cycle stages. There is some limited support for this hypothesis (Marche 1980), but the view that energy constraints will ultimately effect spatial adjustments must still fall into the realm of informed speculation.

If we do accept the fairly heroic assumption about elasticity of travel demand with respect to energy costs in the longer term, then the various models do indeed suggest some reversal of recent trends and a closer association once again between different activities in the urban system. Increasing the importance of transport costs in the "trip decision" in a Lowry model results in reduction of both the total amount of travel and the separation of different activities in the urban system (Beaumont and Keys, 1982). Higher energy costs in urban equilibrium models, some of which also include residential energy consumption, result in closer juxtaposition of residential areas and employment centers (Romanos, 1978), though such an outcome is not inevitable (Dendrinos, 1979; Thrall 1982). Dynamical systems theory applied to the location of shopping centers has produced similar results: increasing energy constraints leads to decentralization in terms of size and location (return to the corner shop from the supermarket) (for example, Beaumont, Clarke and Wilson, 1981). None of these findings is very

surprising given the input assumptions, and they serve to rein-
force Mogridge's (1984) point that what we really need to know
is whether the effects of changes in transport costs can satisfactorily be modeled in this way.

The interesting question of how energy constraints might
interact with current spatial trends like counterurbanization has
not really been addressed, though Romanos (1978) did try to
take account of suburbanization, with the result that energy
constraints caused his hypothetical urban areas to coalesce into
a pattern of "decentralized concentration". We might speculate
that coalescence could occur on a wider scale if higher energy
costs were superimposed on counterurbanization: the autonomy
of small and medium sized towns would be reinforced, and the
resulting pattern of self contained communities could, in a constrained energy situation, represent a more efficient spatial
structure than that of large cities with dependent and dispersed
suburban areas.

While transport forms the most obvious link, energy constraints might also influence urban form through the need for
space heating in buildings, but here the situation is more complex because there are much greater opportunities for fuel substitution. Nevertheless, we might expect energy constraints to
be reflected in the property sector and ultimately in spatial
structure, especially at the fine grain of urban development.
Again, any long term effect will depend on individual and institutional responses to increases in the price of fuel for space
heating. Faced with this situation, people may change fuels,
tolerate lower temperatures or make more effort to eliminate
waste, none of which will necessarily influence patterns of urban
development. But spatial structure might be affected if the
energy advantages of more efficient built forms, siting and layout are widely recognized. Increased demand for energy efficient
buildings could induce migration to areas where they predominate and influence the built form and density of new construction: the overall effect might be to encourage higher densities,
but any preference for the use of ambient energy sources as
these became more economic would provide a countervailing

factor and might even encourage development at the urban fringe.

There is little evidence as yet, at least in the U.K., that energy considerations have become an important factor in house purchase, though there are some indications that house buyers are no longer resistant to paying a modest premium for well designed, energy efficient homes (Heggie, 1988). Once again, however, there are so many ways in which energy consumption could be reduced that it is by no means clear how spatial structure might be influenced by energy constraints.

Comments on Energy and Spatial Structure

Neither the energy implications of current spatial trends nor the spatial implications of different energy futures can be determined with any confidence. Nor is further research likely to provide all the answers, since so much depends on lifestyle and behavior, which are notoriously difficult to predict. However, it is possible to speculate about this important relationship and to identify areas where more research would be helpful, for example, on the travel behavior of migrants from conurbations to small towns. But perhaps the most important implication of this work is that it emphasizes both the uncertainties and the potential significance of the energy/spatial structure relationship. While accurate prediction will never be possible (and never has been in any field of land use planning), it *should* be possible to make an intelligent assessment of current trends and to introduce a robustness into the planning system with respect to an uncertain energy future. We now turn, therefore, to research which has tried to identify those spatial structures which are energy efficient as well as those which are flexible with regard to energy supply and conservation technologies.

Energy Efficient Spatial Structure: The Theory

If the efficient use of energy resources is a legitimate goal of land use planning, we need to define what constitutes energy efficient spatial structure at different scales of development. Since the early 1970s, a considerable amount of research effort has been devoted to this issue, the main result of which has been a better appreciation of the complexities and magnitude of the task. Some degree of consensus about energy efficient form has emerged, but perhaps one of the most important conclusions to be drawn from a review of the literature is that it is impossible to define an ideal energy efficient form unambiguously: this issue is discussed in more detail below. The degree of certainty tends to diminish as the scale of spatial resolution increases. At the lower end of the scale (buildings and neighborhoods), where planners' responsibilities overlap with those of architects and developers, theory has advanced to the point where practical application is really a matter of overcoming inertia and conservative attitudes to urban design. At the urban and regional level, theoretical conclusions are more ambiguous and planning implications in the real world less clear, though there is still ample scope to incorporate energy considerations into land use planning policies.

In this section various theoretical approaches to defining energy efficient and flexible spatial structures are outlined, but two important points deserve emphasis at the outset. First, we are not working with a deterministic situation in which a given physical structure, be it a simple building or a whole city, leads to predictable levels of energy consumption. Energy demand is the outcome of many different factors, including both spatial and nonspatial variables, some of which are themselves difficult or impossible to predict (lifestyle preferences, for example). Complex interactions between these factors mean that we cannot conclude with confidence that a particular urban form will be more energy efficient than other forms under any set of future conditions, though some forms may be robust.

The second point, often overlooked, is that the object of energy conscious planning is not to minimize energy use *per se,* but to plan for a physical environment which permits people to carry out their daily activities using energy as efficiently as possible, subject to other reasonable constraints: the most energy conserving settlement would be one in which everybody stayed at home in the cold and dark! Rickaby (1987), stressing this point, has argued that comparison of energy use in different urban forms is of little value unless other factors, such as accessibility, are also taken into account. In fact, the costs of reducing energy consumption have not often been explicitly considered in analyses of alternative development patterns, perhaps contributing to the sense that such work is abstract and unrealistic.

Energy efficiency in the built environment can be achieved in two ways. One involves planning for an environment with relatively low *intrinsic* energy requirements, that is reducing the *need* to use energy for given purposes, such as transport or space heating. The other entails meeting unavoidable energy requirements in efficient ways - obtaining the greatest possible use out of a given primary energy input. This distinction provides a useful starting point for an analytical framework when considering the energy/spatial structure relationship. The framework is completed by spatial structural variables at different scales (Figure 3.1). Spatial variables can then be related to energy "needs" and energy efficiency at various scales of development, the most significant interactions occurring through travel and transport requirements and through energy use in buildings, mainly for space heating (sometimes known as "between place" and "within place" energy consumption respectively). Having established this basic framework, there is a number of different approaches to exploring the relationship between energy and spatial structure with a view to identifying energy efficient forms at different scales.

First, there are studies, like those described above, of the likely response of spatial structure to energy constraints. On the (possibly unreliable) assumption that higher fuel prices would stimulate a trend towards greater energy efficiency in spatial terms, the emerging land use patterns in these studies provide some insight into energy efficient characteristics. Second, there is empirical comparison of energy consumption in different geographical areas, involving an attempt to correlate patterns of energy use with structural variables and to draw conclusions about the energy implications of different spatial forms.

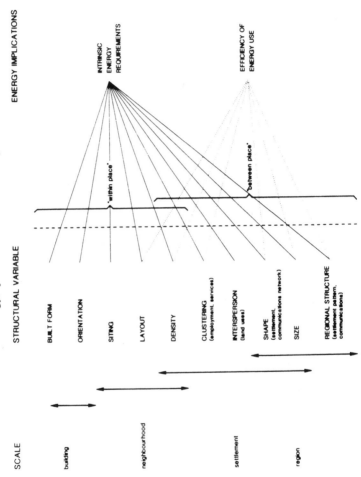

Figure 3.1
Framework for Analysis of
Energy/Spatial Structure Relationship

Empirical work tends to be problematic because of difficulties in controlling for the large number of variables involved, because spatial structure is typically treated as an *independent* variable and because regression studies tend to be cross-sectional rather than based on time series analysis (Talarcheck, 1984).

The third, and most commonly used, approach is to estimate the energy requirements associated with alternative hypothetical spatial structures and then to rank the alternatives in terms of energy efficiency. The use of models in this approach means that alternatives can be investigated in laboratory conditions, with variables other than those of direct interest being held constant though, as with the first approach, it is open to all the usual criticisms of these techniques, especially those concerned with over-simplification and unavoidable subjectivity (Owens, 1989). At the micro scale, most models have been designed specifically to explore the energy characteristics of buildings and groups of buildings, though even here the need to measure all variables empirically or to assume them subjectively presents unavoidable problems. At the urban scale simple linear programing and gravity models, Lowry-type models and integrated land use/transportation models have all been adapted, with varying degrees of sophistication, to explore the energy/spatial structure relationship in a broader context. A fourth approach is more normative, and involves identifying spatial *requirements* of energy supply and conservation measures, such as district heating or public transport networks, or the harnessing of renewable energy resources. This approach makes use of technical considerations, models and working experience.

All of these approaches, and sometimes combinations of them, have been used to explore the energy/spatial structure relationship. It is impossible here to review comprehensively what has become a large body of theoretical work but, in what follows, the most significant findings are outlined, focusing first on reducing intrinsic energy needs and then on compatibility with energy efficient technologies.

Intrinsic Energy Efficiency

Some spatial structures are efficient in the sense that they reduce the need for space heating or for travel, though not always without cost in other terms. This is true at all scales, but since we know most about the effect of structural variables at the fine grain of urban development, it is appropriate to begin with buildings, and work upwards.

At the local scale, there has been considerable progress in research aimed at reducing energy requirements, primarily for space heating. Many models have been developed to analyze thermal performance of buildings, to evaluate different conservation measures and to assist in the development of design guidelines. Even at this scale, the system is not deterministic: the behavior of occupants, for example, is an important but poorly understood variable (Bloomfield, 1986). But there is now a fairly good understanding of the energy implications of built form and of the ways in which siting, orientation, layout and landscaping can make the optimum use of microclimatic conditions to minimize the need for space heating from conventional sources.

At the most basic level, theoretical calculations show clearly that built form exerts a systematic influence on energy requirements for space heating: other things being equal, detached houses can require as much as three times the energy input of intermediate apartments (Barnes and Rankin, 1975; Building Research Establishment, 1975). The relationship is less easy to demonstrate empirically because of the large number of variables involved in determining heating requirements (Grot and Socolow, 1973; Loudon and Cornish, 1975), but there can be little doubt that any systematic trend towards built forms like row housing or low rise apartments could result in significant reductions in energy demand. Such a trend would imply generally higher net densities, so there is also a structural implication at the urban scale. However, although theoretical results on energy use and built form are fairly clear, this is arguably a case where energy efficiency can be achieved only at the cost of some loss of amenity, and at current energy prices other factors are likely to dominate the choice of different built

forms in the housing market. In contrast, energy conscious siting, layout, orientation and landscaping need involve no
sacrifice of amenity.

Again, these factors have been extensively explored, usually
with the help of computer models, and guidelines for architects
and builders working in different climatic and microclimatic
conditions are now readily available (Keplinger, 1978). Structural implications are primarily at the local scale, but microclimatic considerations could also influence the *location* of new
development (Lamm, 1986), and the need for solar access has
implications for development density. It is worth considering
the solar access question in more detail, since it has a number
of interesting spatial consequences.

The harnessing of solar energy by appropriate design at
the local scale (that is, *passive* solar power) can be regarded as
one means of reducing "intrinsic" energy requirements, though
some might prefer to see it simply as a means of meeting these
requirements using "free" ambient energy. However regarded,
passive solar design can lead to significant savings in conventional fuel at little or no economic or environmental cost. But
it has some important implications for spatial structure arising
from the advantages of a north/south building orientation and
the need to avoid overshadowing, which in turn affect layout
and development density.

Research suggests that these criteria are not so stringent as
to require unattractive repetitive layouts and/or very low density housing, as some critics had originally feared. Advantage
can be taken of solar gain with up to a forty degree variation
from a north/south axis (Doggart 1979, Turrent et al, 1981),
and densities of up to thirty-five dwellings per hectare present
few difficulties for passive solar design (O'Cathain and Jessop
1978). Some work even suggests that with design ingenuity,
passive solar energy could be compatible with densities of up to
fifty dwellings per hectare (Turrent et al, 1981). The most
significant constraints are likely to be the size and shape of
urban infill sites, which may severely limit the scope to choose
appropriate orientation and layout for exploitation of passive

solar energy (and, indeed, to take advantage of other micro-climatic factors). This has the interesting implication that passive solar energy might best be exploited on green field sites at or beyond the urban fringe, though in other respects such a pattern of development appears to be energy intensive.

In conclusion, therefore, certain structural factors at the local level are efficient in that they maximize solar gain; there are wider implications for densities, which should not be too high; and there may be difficulties in achieving the structural requirements with in-fill development. Subject to these constraints, there seems little reason why the principles of passive solar design and other microclimatic criteria should not be applied in a substantial proportion of new development.

At the wider urban and regional scales, research has focused on reducing intrinsic energy requirements by reducing the need to travel. The single most important structural factor in the relationship between urban form and transport energy requirements is the physical separation of activities, determined in part by density and in part by the interspersion of different land uses. The lower the physical separation, the lower travel needs are likely to be, though an efficient spatial structure alone will not guarantee transport energy savings.

In theoretical work, there is a fairly clear negative correlation between urban density and energy use for transport (Clark, 1974; Edwards and Schofer, 1975; Roberts, 1975). Although this relationship emerges less clearly from cross-sectional analyses of different geographical areas in the real world (Keyes and Peterson, 1977; Keyes 1982), Keyes, having reviewed a number of such studies, is able to conclude that:

> Otherwise comparable households who live in low density urban areas or on the periphery of large metropolitan areas tend to travel further, faster and much more frequently by auto than their counterparts in high density cities.

One way to reduce travel needs would therefore be to bring homes, jobs and services together in a high density urban center to   achieve a high level of accessibility to facilities without much need for movement. In its extreme form, exemplified by Dantzig and Saaty's multi-level "Compact City" (Dantzig and Saaty, 1973), this concept is unattractive (Steadman, 1977; Van Til, 1979), but the concentration of development in the more conventional, relatively compact center emerges as an energy efficient spatial structure in a number of comparative analyses based on models of real or hypothetical urban areas (Clark, 1974; Edwards and Schofer, 1975; Fels and Munson, 1975; Rickaby, 1987; Roberts, 1975). There must, however, be limits: above a certain size of center, there will be problems of congestion and loss of accessibility and, of course, high densities will limit the scope to make use of ambient energy, such as passive solar power.

An alternative way to reduce the physical separation of activities is then to decentralize some jobs and services and relate them to residential areas, either *within* a single large settlement, to produce Mathieu's (1978) "archipelago pattern" or Romanos' (1978) "decentralized concentration", or to form spatially separate units which may or may not retain functional links with the original center. Many theoretical exercises have found decentralization of employment and service opportunities to be relatively efficient in terms of travel and energy requirements, including comparative analyses of alternative urban forms (Hemmens, 1967; Rickaby, 1987; Schneider and Beck, 1973; Stone, 1973), attempts to model responses to energy constraints (Albert and Banton, 1978; Romanos, 1978) and comparison of alternative incremental development patterns (Clark, 1974; Owens, 1981). All of this work suggests that relatively small, semi-autonomous settlements (which may be sub-units of a larger urban area) are efficient in terms of travel requirements. Stone (1973), for example, found that per capita travel costs increased steadily between theoretical settlements of 50,000, 100,000 and 250,000 population; others have proposed that "pedestrian scale" clusters of between 10,000, and 30,000 people would be viable and energy efficient.

However, there are major uncertainties about the potential energy advantage of this kind of spatial structure. These arise from the simple fact that travel is a derived demand, and that reducing travel and transport energy requirements may (though will not invariably) involve costs in terms of amenity or in terms of access to a range of jobs and services: what really matters is how individuals trade off these different costs against each other. If energy costs restrict mobility, a pattern of "decentralized concentration" will be efficient because people will use the jobs and services which are close to them, but clearly with some sacrifice of choice. If travel costs pose only a minimum deterrent, this pattern may be more energy intensive than centralization, because of the potentially large amount of cross-commuting and other travel. This complication accounts for some of the discrepancies between theoretical and empirical work, and for the sensitivity of the results of many theoretical analyses to assumptions about the deterrent effect of distance or cost, including the cost of energy.

For example, whilst theoretical work shows a clear decline of transport energy efficiency with urban size (Stone, 1973), results of empirical work are ambiguous, with some analyses confirming the negative energy efficiency/size correlation (Bellomo et al, 1970; Keyes and Peterson, 1977; Vorhees, 1968) whilst others suggest that more energy is used for transport as size of settlement decreases (Maltby, Monteath and Lawler, 1978; Stewart and Bennett, 1975). In the U.K., for example, per capita energy use in transport in small urban areas is nearly thirty percent greater than that in provincial conurbations. Similarly, some theoretical comparisons of alternative development patterns suggest that decentralization is a relatively efficient pattern in energy terms if low mobility is assumed, but less efficient than centralization if mobility is high (Fels and Munson, 1975; Owens, 1981; Stone, 1973).

A recent analysis by Rickaby (1987), using an integrated land use and transport model (TRANUS) to compare six hypothetical development patterns for an archetypal city region in the U.K. confirms the complexity of the energy/spatial structure relationship, and concludes that both centralization and decentralized concentration would be more energy efficient than a continuation of current trends: the latter option saved less energy but is preferred on the grounds that the savings involved a lower cost:benefit ratio. Rickaby suggests that a robust pattern might be one in which "the existing urban area is surrounded by a cluster of spatially separate but economically dependent subcenters". He assumed that growth would continue to be linked to the main center and did not consider any "clean break" options.

It is probably fair to conclude that no single ideal configuration emerges from all of this complexity. Both centralization and "decentralized concentration" are potentially energy efficient but involve different sets of costs. The form which emerges most consistently as robust involves a pattern of subcenters providing access to a reasonable choice of jobs and services without the need for long journeys: journey mode is clearly another important factor which is considered in the next section. The problem is that results from all the models depend upon assumptions about lifestyles and about the way in which people value mobility and choice, assumptions which inevitably limit the practical policy value of any conclusions.

Structural Requirements of Efficient Energy Supply and Transport Technologies

So far, we have dealt with ways in which spatial structure is related at different scales to intrinsic energy requirements. But in identifying energy efficient forms, account must also be taken of the influence of spatial structure on the viability and competitiveness of energy supply and conservation options, and of efficient transport systems. Major energy savings can in theory be achieved by meeting intrinsic energy requirements efficiently, but in order to do this it may be necessary to plan new development from the outset to be structurally compatible with a desired energy supply and conservation strategy. *In principle,* spatial structure could be planned to accommodate the most efficient energy supply system (or combination of supply systems and conservation measures), and an efficient transport system. This does not necessarily imply a uniquely efficient spatial structure: in different geographical areas different supply systems (natural gas, or solar energy, for example) may be feasible or non-viable for non-structural reasons - the point is that spatial structure should permit the best possible combination. This means, as Lundqvist (1987) suggests, that it is important to integrate local technology/conservation choices with urban and regional energy production and distribution factors.

Examples of systems which are not equally viable in all urban forms are public transport and district heating (DH) networks, the latter sometimes incorporated into combined heat and power (CHP) systems, which provide both electricity and hot water and are highly (up to 80-90 percent) efficient in their use of primary fuel. These examples are considered in some detail below. Active solar energy provides a further example of a supply system with spatial requirements but, if used on a modest scale, these requirements are rather less demanding than the criteria for passive solar power discussed earlier. Used on an extensive scale, active solar energy may imply low gross densities, to provide sufficient area for solar collectors to provide heat and electricity.

Linear programing and other models have been designed to optimize heat supply/conservation within a given settlement structure (existing or planned) (Bergman, 1976; Lundqvist, 1985; Wene and Ryden, 1988), and at least one research group is attempting to combine such procedures with land use and transportation models in the development of an integrated set of models for strategic urban energy analysis (Lundqvist 1989, 1987). In one sense, this is a move towards the integration of land use and energy planning, but the complexities and uncertainties involved in an integrated set of models of this kind may limit its direct application in planning practice.

Combined Heat and Power Systems

The potential for the introduction of CHP/DH depends (among other considerations) on the density of development and on the degree of mixing of different land uses, but the relative economics of CHP/DH and more conventional heating systems also depend upon the discount rate, assumptions about real fuel prices and the type of area being considered. For example, in the case of an existing small city, with a ten percent discount rate (over a sixty year period) and assuming constant real fuel prices, a U.K. Working Group found the break even density to be more than 250 dwellings per hectare (assuming a power station fifteen km from the edge of the city) (Combined Heat and Power Group, 1977). Reducing the discount rate to five percent, or assuming that real fuel prices will double every eighteen years, reduces the break even density to twenty-five dwellings per hectare or about thirty dwellings per hectare respectively, which would make CHP economically viable in large areas of existing development in the U.K. In a green field case, the break even density was about seventy-five dwellings per hectare with a ten percent discount rate and constant real fuel prices, coming down to less than twenty-five dwellings per hectare or thirty-five dwellings per hectare by modifying the discount rate or fuel price assumptions as above.

Clearly the economics of CHP/DH are most favorable in areas of higher density, especially if conversion of existing built-up areas is being considered; but the possibility that it will become economically viable to connect quite large areas to such schemes in the future cannot be ruled out. Other structural factors are important too: a mixture of land uses helps to spread the electricity and heating loads, and certain built forms (for example, row housing) facilitate the routing of mains (though this factor is less significant for a green field site). However, though the viability of energy conserving CHP/DH systems is influenced by spatial structure, and especially by built form, density and interspersion of land uses, it is difficult to define precise criteria such as specific threshold densities below which systems would not be economic in the future. In feasibility studies in the U.K., a figure of about forty-four dwellings per hectare in existing urban areas has been adopted, but this figure, and any figures for green field sites, are bound to change with other variables because the relationship between spatial structure and the viability of CHP/DH is dynamic.

In general, the criteria which will facilitate the introduction of CHP/DH at some stage are moderately high densities, built forms which facilitate internal routing, linear layout and mixing of land uses. The interesting questions from a planning perspective are whether or where CH/DH should be integrated with new development or redevelopment from the outset, or whether attention should at least be given to those elements of spatial structure which will affect the viability of the introduction of such a system in future.

Efficient Transport

It is frequently argued that a shift from private vehicles towards public and non-motorized transport would reduce fuel consumption, as well as conferring social and environmental benefits which are already widely recognized (Adams, 1981; Hillman et al, 1973). It is also accepted that certain land use patterns are better suited to the efficient and economic operation of public transport than others. Hence the intuitively attractive argument that appropriate land use planning policies could contribute to energy conservation by providing the right conditions for an energy efficient modal shift in transport. It is easy to demonstrate that public transport is potentially more energy efficient than private transport, with rail systems occupying a position somewhere between that of buses and private cars, though whether it is *actually* more efficient depends on load factors: energy consumption per passenger mile is clearly greater for a nearly empty bus than for a full car. A shift from private to public transport could result in significant, but not enormous, savings (Maltby, Monteath and Lawler, 1979).

Modifying spatial structure is one longer term measure which might be used to promote public transport (more immediate possibilities include fare subsidies, traffic management and restrictions on the use of private vehicles). Relative concentration of homes and facilities maximizes accessibility to the transport route and encourages a high load factor (Roberts, 1975; Jamieson, Mackay and Latchford, 1976), whereas conventional public transport is particularly inefficient in dispersed, low density areas typical of residential suburbs (Keyes and Peterson 1977).

There are also significant *shape* factors involved at the intra-urban scale. For example, a linear form, involving broad bands of urban development could combine high densities along a bus or light rail route with moderate overall densities, compatible with a high quality environment (Barton, 1987; Steadman, 1980). Relevant planning policies might therefore include discouragement of dispersed, low density suburbs, some degree of concentration (though not necessarily *centralization* of facilities, relation of new development to transport routes and the maintenance of moderately high densities *along* these routes. Such policies could be applied to green field developments and to redevelopment, growth and infilling in existing settlements.

As with the reduction of travel needs however, it is all too easy to overlook the fact that appropriate spatial structures provide a necessary but not a sufficient condition for the successful operation of public transport, the viability of which depends on many interrelated factors including car ownership, socio-economic characteristics of the population, past investment in infrastructure, and public policy towards transport in the area concerned.

Public transport, with some exceptions like light rail and subway systems, has experienced accelerating decline in recent years. In the U.K., adult patronage fell by an average of thirty percent between the mid-1970s and the early 1980s. It is difficult to see why modifying the physical environment should succeed in rejuvenating public transport when other measures (traffic management schemes, subsidies and attempts to restrain private cars) have been largely ineffective. Indeed, if the only advantage of a modal shift towards public transport were in terms of energy consumption, then it would arguably be better to devote attention to traffic management and improving the energy efficiency of vehicles. However, it seems very likely that, in coming years, the social and environmental costs, including gross problems of pollution (both local and global) and serious congestion will work generally in the same direction as considerations of energy efficiency and give new impetus to more radical approaches to transport policy. Then, in theory, land use planning could make a modest but significant contribution to the more efficient use of energy resources by encouraging urban form compatible with energy efficient and environmentally sensitive public transport systems.

Summary of Theoretical Work

It is difficult to summarize the results of a large body of theoretical, and empirical, research on the energy/spatial structure relationship for a number of reasons. First, the diversity of approaches makes comparison between different studies problematic. Second, many of the assumptions in modeling are difficult to justify and the results need careful qualification. Third, what is an "energy efficient form" may depend upon factors specific to particular locations, such as climate, rate of change in the built environment or socio-economic characteristics of the population. Finally, much will depend upon the extent to which land use and energy planning are genuinely *integrated* as opposed to energy considerations being "tacked on" to the planning process: if land use planners are involved in decisions about heat supply, for example, opportunities to plan an energy efficient and flexible built environment will be more significant than if land use and energy supply decisions are unrelated.

Some spatial characteristics do, however, emerge as energy efficient. Built forms with a low surface area to volume ratio, low physical separation of activities and sensitivity to microclimatic factors can all reduce intrinsic energy needs. A suitable structure which emerges from many studies is one involving relatively compact urban sub-units though very high densities are *not* required, and indeed may be inimical to energy conservation (Owens, 1986a). Ideal forms at the local scale depend to some extent on the nature of the energy supply system: for example, higher densities (perhaps making use of linear forms) are best for district heating (and public transport) networks, while lower densities make the use of solar energy more viable (though there is sufficient flexibility here for solar design not to conflict with an overall preference for compactness). Generally speaking, the location and gross density of new development should be influenced by microclimatic and physical separation considerations; its form at a more local scale should ideally be determined in conjunction with detailed planning for energy supply and conservation technologies.

An important question is how much difference energy efficient structures would make in terms of actual energy savings. Theoretical differences between spatial structures compare favorably with potential savings from more conventional energy conservation measures (Table 3.1). But in view of the many uncertainties and constraints, such savings probably represent an upper limit. In practice, change is likely to be incremental, energy demand may not be as elastic as the models assume, the starting point may not be the worst case, and the optimum structure will not often be achieved, except perhaps at the local scale. Nevertheless, the magnitude of potential savings suggests that energy is an issue with which planners should be explicitly concerned. Some have already accepted this, and in the following section examples of energy conscious planning are briefly outlined, together with the factors which seem to encourage or inhibit the inclusion of energy considerations in the land use planning process.

Energy Conscious Planning: Practice

Although there remain many uncertainties about the potential to improve energy efficiency though land use planning, the powerful logical case for incorporating an energy dimension into the land use planning process is reinforced by evidence that opportunities exist to do so. While it is unlikely that planning policies *in isolation* could have a significant impact on energy demand, it is equally unlikely that a comprehensive energy conservation policy would be successful if it did not encompass the land use planning field. However, the mere existence of opportunities for energy conscious land use planning is not enough: while some planners have been eager to grasp these opportunities and to develop energy integrated planning policies, others (almost certainly the majority in Europe and North America)

Table 3.1
Energy Implications of Structural Variables

Structural Variable	Mechanism	Energy Implications
Shape	travel require-ments	variation of up to about 20%
Interspersion of activi-ties	travel require-ments (especially trip length)	variation of up to 130%
Combination of struc-tural variables (shape, size, land-use mix, etc)	travel require-ments (trip length and frequency)	variation of up to 150%
Density/built form	surface area: volume ratio affects energy requirements for space heating	200% variation between different built forms
Density/clustering of trip ends	facilitates running of public transport system	energy savings of up to 20%
Density/mixing of land uses	facilitates intro-duction of energy-efficient CHP/DH systems	efficiency of pri-mary energy use improved by up to 100%
Density/siting/ orien-tation and landscaping	maximises poten-tial to use 'free' ambient energy sources	can reduce conven-tional energy con-sumption by at least 20%

Source: Owens, 1986b.

have effectively ignored them. What are the conditions which encourage planners to take the energy issue on board? And what are the constraints which have militated against the integration of energy considerations into the majority of land use planning exercises? These important questions are addressed in this sec-tion in the light of practical experience at different scales.

National Commitment: The Scandinavian Example

In some cases, as in the Scandinavian countries, energy considerations have been integrated into the land use planning process within the framework of a strong national commitment to energy efficiency. In Denmark, for example, land use planners have been closely involved in the division of the country into areas where CHP/DH can be introduced (eleven percent of final energy consumption is already supplied by DH), areas which would be better served by North Sea gas and areas where space heating must be provided by other means. Kommunes (districts) are required to map present and future energy needs at local level, and the county council draws up a heating plan, including details of areas in which particular heat supply methods will receive priority, for ministerial approval. Councils may control the type of heating in new buildings within specified geographical areas (Christensen and Jensen-Butler, 1980; International Energy Agency, 1981).

Emphasis in Scandinavia tends to be on the relationship between energy supply systems and spatial structure and, as noted above, methods currently being developed in Sweden may make this kind of integration even more sophisticated in future. It has probably been stimulated, perhaps even necessitated, by a commitment to communal heating on a fairly large scale. However, broader energy related considerations have also been taken into account in some areas. The plan for the Aarhus region of Denmark for example, involves not only energy supply considerations, but includes policies for strengthening small to medium sized local centers (20-30,000 population), integration of land uses, higher densities and direction of growth to centers where there are DH networks, though the policy of "decentralized concentration" has not been without its critics (Jensen-Butler, 1980; Owens, 1986a).

The U.S. and the U.K.—A Partial Response

Where there is no overriding national priority for energy conservation, commitment to energy conscious land use planning tends to be sporadic. In the U.S. and the U.K., for example, the pattern is one in which some planning authorities have made valiant efforts to include an energy dimension in their policies while others continue to afford it low priority or ignore it altogether.

By 1985, about twenty percent of strategic planning authorities in the U.K. (the county councils) had included explicitly energy related objectives, policies or evaluation criteria in their development plans (Owens, 1986b). The energy dimension was most often related to transport, but a few plans also had policies relating to energy considerations at the local scale, such as siting of development in relation to micro-climate. One of the most enthusiastic authorities was the Greater London Council, (GLC) which (before its abolition) included "the efficient use of energy" among the objectives of the draft revisions to the Greater London Development Plan (GLC, 1983; for detail see Owens, 1987), and devoted a whole chapter to energy issues including relevant land use policies. The fate of these initiatives now that the GLC's planning functions have been taken over by the London Boroughs is unclear.

In a 1985 survey, some U.K. planning authorities noted that they intended to give energy conservation much more explicit consideration in development plans in future (Owens, 1986b). Cornwall is one county likely to include a number of relevant policies in its revised structure plan. For example, the location of new housing is to take into account "economy in energy supply"; road improvements are to take account of energy efficiency; and bus services are to be maintained and improved partly on energy efficiency grounds. Two significant new policies are also proposed:

> In considering proposals for new residential, commercial and industrial development particular regard will be paid to the form and design of buildings, their materials, general location, detailed siting, layout, orientation, landscaping, planting and other factors affecting the consumption of energy.

and:

> Proposals for industrial, commercial and the larger residential developments will be considered with regard to the

feasibility of their incorporating combined heat and power schemes with district heating (Cornwall County Council (1988).

Integration of energy considerations into the planning process has also been very uneven in the U.S. Generally, as in the U.K., the issue has not been tackled nationally, but there are some notable examples of comprehensive, city wide conservation policies, incorporating land use planning considerations. Although it is too early to tell whether broader scale urban planning policies have been effective in reducing or containing energy demand (and it may never be possible to prove such a connection), the policies in general have undoubtedly been successful in terms of reducing residential energy demand, public involvement, demonstration and, in the words of Davis's Environment and Energy Officer, proving that "energy conservation does not have to mean self denial" (Williams, undated). Davis, California established a goal of reducing energy consumption in the city's 1973 general plan. Stringent building regulations (at first opposed by developers, but later winning their support), encouragement for passive solar design and non-motorized transport, and development control to promote a more compact city have all been important elements of the energy programme with direct links to urban spatial structure.

Portland, Oregon provides an example of a larger city-region also experimenting with land use policies to control energy demand - in this case within the framework of a mandatory State planning goal which requires that land use should be managed in order to conserve energy. One of the main objectives of the Portland Energy Conservation Demonstration Project, completed in 1977, was to examine the links between energy saving and urban form (City of Portland, 1977). An energy zone map, dividing the city into five zones based on relative energy efficiency, was produced in order to guide new development to energy efficient locations, and an energy conservation policy was adopted by the city council after extensive public consultation in 1979. It included commitments to develop land use policies using density and location to reduce the   need to travel, and to improve the efficiency of the transport system and reduce its consumption of non-renewable fuels. More specific objectives related to the location of new developments and encouragement of energy efficient transport modes. These strategies were then incorporated into the city's draft comprehensive plan.

One of the central features of the plan was a "centers and corridors" concept, which would involve guiding new development into centers of existing commercial activity and along major streets (corridors). Emphasis was on energy conservation through compact high density development, using an urban pattern which combines nucleated centers with high linear densities. In theory, less travel would be required, essential travel would be carried out by energy-efficient modes and higher density development would permit more efficient use of fuel for space heating (Sewell and Foster, 1980). During the public consultation phase, the energy related features of the plan were among the most controversial, winning strongest support from environmentalists, newspapers and heads of local government agencies, and opposition mainly from developers, industrial and union leaders and the Chamber of Commerce (Sewell and Foster, 1980). Zoning was unpopular with development interests and landowners, while the emphasis on high-density corridors was opposed by neighborhood groups. Revisions were made to break up several corridors into "development nodes" - clusters of commercial activity, surrounded by high density housing. Any plan which tries to take energy considerations into account at this scale is likely to face intensive lobbying by interest groups, the power of which must be recognized as a constraint on "pure" energy- related objectives.

The Portland experience demonstrates that it is possible to plan for greater energy efficiency in large, established urban centers, though once again it is difficult to establish how effective the policies will be in the longer term in modifying the spatial structure and in reducing energy requirements. As with Davis, the demonstration value is of great significance, and both cities have been upheld as examples of energy efficiency which might be emulated elsewhere. For example, President Carter sent letters to six hundred U.S. mayors pointing put the merits of Portland's energy policy (Sewell and Foster, 1980), and the Urban Consortium, a coalition of thirty-seven major urban governments, has developed a program which is attempting to consolidate the advantages of both Davis and Portland approaches (Lee, 1984).

Green Field Sites

The best opportunities for energy integrated planning, as for land use planning in general, exist when development is on a clean slate, as in the case of new settlements or other extensive areas of growth. An unusual chance to apply energy efficient planning principles from the local to the city scale has arisen in Argentina, where plans are now being developed to build a new capital city, eight hundred kilometers south of Buenos Aires. One objective is to make the new capital a model of energy efficiency and various studies - for example, bioclimatic studies of the area - are now being undertaken (de Schiller and Evans, 1988) which will lead to general recommendations for design at the regional, urban and building design scales.

In the U.K., the lack of *physical* constraints represented by a green field situation is sometimes reinforced by the status of development corporations, which are usually granted stronger powers than conventional planning authorities. A particular source of inspiration for improving the energy efficiency of new development in the U.K. has been the work of the Milton Keynes Development Corporation (MKDC).

Milton Keynes was planned in the 1960s as a low density city, providing for high mobility and accessibility by private car (Milton Keynes Development Corporation, 1970). Paying virtually no attention to possible future energy constraints, the original plan typified the neglect of energy considerations in the land use planning of the postwar decades. By the late 1970s, when the city was approximately half complete, the possibility of a more energy conscious approach to planning the remainder began to be taken seriously. In 1983, one area of the city was designated the "Milton Keynes Energy Park", to be "an urban area   planned from the outset with priority given to policies of energy efficiency" (Milton Keynes Development Corporation, 1983).

The Energy Park is an area of some 150 hectares southwest of the city center, incorporating a range of land uses. It could be thought of as an urban sub-unit of the kind which could form the basis for energy efficient urban structures, but emphasis is on energy efficient design and management at the fine grain of urban development rather than on wider energy/spatial structure relationships. Nevertheless, like the energy conscious cities in the U.S., the Energy Park has proved valuable in demonstrating what can be achieved, and it has gained widespread publicity and recognition. Developers and the public have responded positively, costs of energy conscious design have been small, and energy savings promise to be significant. Perhaps its most important contribution has been to help to legitimize incorporation of energy considerations in the development of the built environment.

Similar, but somewhat more comprehensive energy related objectives have subsequently been adopted by the Cardiff Bay Development Corporation (CBDC). The CBDC was established in 1986 to promote urban regeneration in the waterfront area of Cardiff, in South Wales. Since Cardiff had recently been designated an "Energy Action City", in which business and local authorities come together in a coordinated effort to improve energy efficiency, the CBDC was urged to adopt energy efficiency as part of its regeneration strategy. Subsequently, the published strategy included the objective that: "the emerging and developing principles of energy conservation should be incorporated in the design guidelines and development control processes" (Gurney 1988), and the project was seen to provide a "unique opportunity to consider the efficient use of energy at an urban scale, rather than on an individual building basis, as part of an urban renewal plan" (Gurney 1988).

Both the energy impact of alternative planning policies and the planning implications of various energy efficiency measures will be considered by the CBDC during the planning of the bay area.   Although emphasis will be on microclimate, layout, built form and energy supply infrastructure, the energy plan "may... be extended to take into account the influence of transport systems" (Gurney, 1988).   Significant economic, environmental and community benefits are expected to accrue from the Energy Plan - the important point being that energy conservation is being seen, as in the successful U.S. cities, in a positive rather than a negative, sacrificial light.   It will be interesting to see whether recognition of the land use planning dimension by the CBDC will spread to the city as a whole, and to other U.K. cities which have followed Cardiff's example in adopting the "Energy Action" idea, but generally without including land use planning considerations.

Initiatives like the Milton Keynes Energy Park and the Cardiff Bay Project may well stimulate interest in other areas where rapid growth or redevelopment is taking place.   Strategic planning proposals for Cambridgeshire, for example, include plans in principle for two or three new villages (population 20-30,000) which are stimulating keen competition among developers.   This could provide an ideal opportunity for planners to make it known that they will regard energy conscious proposals in a favorable light, and they can point to experience elsewhere to show that energy efficiency need involve no sacrifice of other planning and design objectives at this scale (Cambridge Friends of the Earth, 1987).

Encouraging Factors and Constraints

The most interesting question which arises from a brief and selective review of energy conscious planning in practice is why it is adopted so enthusiastically in some places and not in others.   Some of the international differences can be explained by climatic and resource factors: countries with long experience of the need for energy efficiency in a cold climate (such as Sweden) or a poor endowment of indigenous energy resources (like Denmark) have had an impetus for energy conservation in the built environment, though clearly this impetus has to be translated into action by national policy commitments, so cultural and political differences are also important.   Some of the factors which Lee (1980) found to be significant in inducing certain American cities to establish comprehensive energy efficiency programmes may be more generally applicable. They were:

(i)   Strong leadership, and willingness of elected officials, especially Mayors to take political risks;

(ii)   A tradition of open government and local resource management;

(iii)   A conviction that energy efficiency is in the long term economic interest of the city (rather than these objectives being seen as in conflict);

(iv)   Extensive public participation, to legitimize the energy issue;

(v)   Additional impetus provided by a perceived "crisis" (energy shortages or nuclear embargoes, for example), reinforcing the view that energy efficiency will improve the quality of life.

Constraints which still militate against the adoption of energy conscious policies by the majority of planning authorities have been examined in the British context, though again they are likely to be applicable elsewhere (Owens 1986a, 1986b). Two constraints have been particularly important in the 1980s, since they tend to provide the framework for the others. First, the sense of energy "crisis" has disappeared almost entirely: not only is Britain currently well endowed with indigenous energy resources (coal reserves, for example, may last for three hundred years), but oil prices have fallen as dramatically as they rose in the 1970s, removing the financial incentive (though not the need) to use resources efficiently. Secondly, there has been a reaction against government intervention and planning in general, reinforced in rhetoric and legislation during nearly ten years of Conservative administration: it has even been suggested that the strategic (county) level of land use planning should be removed altogether. Energy conservation is seen largely as an objective to be achieved through market forces, and deregulation is in vogue: in this climate, land use planning for energy efficiency faces major philosophical and practical obstacles.

More specifically, a survey of strategic planning authorities in England and Wales in the mid-1980s revealed a number of important real or perceived barriers to energy integrated planning (Owens 1986b).

First, there had been little direction from central government, and many authorities were uncertain about the legitimacy of incorporating energy considerations into strategic planning: their doubt was reinforced by the fact that energy related policies were deleted from some plans when they were submitted for approval by the Secretary of State for the Environment, on the grounds that they were "non land use" policies.

Other important constraints were lack of resources (many planning departments were already seriously overstretched), lack of education and information on energy issues, physical and institutional inertia (including the significant problem of inherited commitments), and a feeling that policies would not be effective, even if they could be formulated and implemented. Finally, there was a problem with the perception of energy as an issue which might have relevance to the land use planning process. Planners tended to see it either as a discrete issue, but taking lower priority than issues like housing and employment, or as a ubiquitous consideration which was therefore very difficult to deal with. In practice, energy may need to be dealt with both as an issue in its own right (eg energy supply issues) *and* as a resource, which, just like financial resources has to be considered at all stages of the planning process.

Summary

When the diverse experience of energy conscious planning in different countries and at different scales is added together, it amounts to a not inconsiderable progress in fifteen years since the first energy crisis of 1973. Perhaps it is too soon to expect the extensive cooperation between authorities and consolidation of experience, which could provide a solid basis for future action, though exchange of ideas is certainly beginning to occur and to bear fruit. However, there is still vast potential for improvement and a need for a more concerted effort, and, in particular for commitment at national level - to overcome the constraints which have hitherto prevented many land use planning authorities from acknowledging the energy issue in any meaningful way.

The Next Steps

It is paradoxical that, while one conclusion of this review is that there remains considerable theoretical uncertainty about the energy/spatial structure relationship and about energy efficient land use patterns, another is that some land use planning authorities have made significant progress in incorporating energy considerations into their planning procedures, and in planning for efficient energy supply and conservation.

A major problem in theoretical work, especially as the scale of analysis increases, centers on the limits to prediction in systems which are not deterministic. However, if we were deterred by our inability to predict the future, and by uncertainty about ideal policies, we would probably not indulge in planning as a legitimate activity at all. Enough is known about energy efficiency at the local scale for policies to be put successfully into practice, especially if spatial planning and energy system planning can be coordinated, and robust policies can be identified at the urban and subregional scales, though the policy which is most appropriate may differ from place to place. So while it may not be possible to *generalize* about what planners should so, it is increasingly clear that they should do *something:* where energy considerations have been ignored completely in the past, almost any reasonable attempt to include them should result in an improvement over the current situation.

One factor which emerges fairly clearly from the review of practical experience is that energy conscious planning can be implemented at the neighborhood scale if planners, developers and architects cooperate: but for this to become the norm, and for policies to be extended to cover urban and regional levels of planning, a substantial political commitment to energy conservation through land use planning, at least at city or region level, but preferably at national level too, is essential.

There seem to be three priorities for research on energy and land use planning in future. One is to advance the understanding of the relationship between the energy system and the spatial organization of society. In particular, more work on the interaction between energy trends and evolving urban and regional structure is required: for example, we know very little about the influence of counterurbanization on travel patterns. Emphasis should be on trying to understand the social and economic bases for relationships between land use and the energy system, rather than on ever more sophisticated model structures which might still be based on unjustifiable basic premises.

In a more practical sense, it is important that results of theoretical work are communicated and made accessible to land use planners, and that experience of energy efficient planning practice is widely disseminated. This should involve intranational and international cooperation, and a comparative study of energy related planning in selected areas could produce very useful information about achievements, specific policies and constraints. It is often assumed that experience is transferable form one location to another, and one objective of any comparative study should be to subject this assumption to more critical examination than it has received to date.

Finally, it is important to monitor the effectiveness of land use planning policies adopted in the interest of energy efficiency. This is already feasible at the building (and perhaps the neighborhood) scale, where energy sensitive developments can be compared with controls but much more difficult at the urban scale where it may not be possible to isolate the effects of *land use* (and transport) from all the non-spatial policies likely to influence energy demand. Criteria for success, based on the interaction between energy, social and environmental objectives need to be developed.

While not refined in detail, the basic principles for energy efficient land use planning already exist. There are some hopeful signs that they will be more widely adopted as success stories stimulate interest elsewhere and as energy efficiency is increasingly identified as a positive asset for any location. Perhaps the only really significant stimulus, however, can come from crises and, as we enter the 1990s, the increasing urgency to deal with global environmental problems may become the incentive for energy conscious land use planning which unfulfilled threats of physical scarcity have hitherto failed to provide.

REFERENCES

Adams, J., 1981, *Transport Planning: Vision and Practice,* London: Routledge and Kegan Paul.

Albert, J.D. and H.S. Banton, 1978, "Urban Spatial Adjustments Resulting from Rising Energy Costs," *Annals of Regional Science* 12: 64-71.

Barnes, D. and L. Rankin, 1975, "The Energy Economics of Building Construction," *Building International* 8: 31-42.

Barton, H., 1987, *The Potential for Increasing the Energy Efficiency of Existing Urban Areas through Local Planning Policy,* M.Phil. Thesis, Department of Town and Country Planning, Bristol Polytechnic, U.K.

Beaumont, J.R., M. Clarke and A.G. Wilson, 1981, "Changing Energy Parameters and the Evolution of Urban Spatial Structure," *Regional Science and Urban Economics* 11: 287-315.

Beaumont, J.R. and P. Keys, 1982, *Future Cities: Spatial Analysis of Energy Issues,* Chichester, UK: Wiley.

Bellomo, S.J., R.G. Dial, and A.M. Vorhees, 1970, "Factors, Trends and Guidelines Related to Trip Length," *National Cooperative Highway Research Programme Report 89,* Washington DC: Highway Research Board.

Bergman, L., 1976, *An Energy Demand Model for the Swedish Residential Sector,* Document D4 1976, Swedish Council for Building Research, Stockholm, Sweden.

Berry, B.J.L., 1976, "The Counterurbanization Process: Urban America since 1970," in *Urbanization and Counterurbanization,* Urban Affairs Annual Review No. 11, Sage, Beverly Hills, CA.

Bloomfield, D.P., 1986, *The Use of Thermal Models for the Production of Design Guidelines,* paper presented at International Climatic Architecture Conference, Louvain-La-Neuve, Belgium, (available from Building Research Establishment, Garston, Watford, Herts, U.K).

Building Research Establishment, 1975, *Energy Conservation: A Study of Energy Consumption in Buildings and Means of Saving Energy in Housing,* Current Paper 56, Building Research Establishment, Garston, Watford, U.K.

Cambridge Friends of the Earth, 1988, *Notes on a Seminar on Energy and Environment in New Settlements in Cambridgeshire,* The Bath House, Gwydir Street, Cambridge, U.K.

Carpenter, S.M. and M.C. Dix, 1980, *Perceptions of Motoring Costs and Responses to Cost Changes,* Working Paper 123, Oxford, Oxford University Transport Studies Unit.

Champion, G., 1989, "Counterurbanization in Britain," *Geographical Journal* 155: 52-59.

Cherry, G.E., 1982, *The Politics of Town Planning,* London: Longman.

Christensen, B. and Jensen-Butler, C., 1980, *Energy, Planning of Heating Systems, and Urban Structure,* Aarhus, Denmark: Geographical Institute, University of Aarhus.

City of Portland, 1977, *Energy Conservation Choices for the City of Portland* (11 volumes), Washington DC: U.S. Government Printing Office.

Clark, James W., 1974, *Defining an Urban Growth Strategy which will Achieve Maximum Travel Demand Reduction and Access Opportunity Enhancement,* Research Report 73, (7 UMTA WA 0003, 74), Seattle: Department of Civil Engineering, Washington University.

Coelho, J.D. and Williams, H., 1978, "On the Design of Land Use Plans through Locational Surplus Maximization," *Papers of the Regional Science Association* 40: 71-85.

Combined Heat and Power Group, 1977, *District Heating Combined with Electricity Generation in the United Kingdom,* Discussion document prepared by the District Heating Working Party (Energy Paper No. 20), London: HMSO.

Cornwall County Council, 1988, *Energy Considerations in the Structure Plan,* Truro, Cornwall, U.K.

Corsi, T.M. and M.E. Harvey, 1977, "Energy Crisis Travel Behavior and the Transportation Planning Process," *Transportation Research Record* 648: 30-36.

Dantzig, G.D. and T.L. Saaty, 1973, *Compact City: A Plan for a Liveable Urban Environment,* San Francisco, CA: Freeman.

Dendrinos, D.S., 1979, "Energy Costs, The Transport Network and Urban Form," *Environment and Planning A* 11: 655-664.

De Schiller, S and M. Evans, 1988, *Healthy Buildings in a New City: Bioclimatic Studies for Argentina's New Capital,* Mimeo from Faculty of Architecture and Urban Design, University of Buenos Aires, Argentina.

Dix, M.C. and P.B. Goodwin, 1982, "Petrol Prices and Car Use: A Synthesis of Conflicting Evidence," *Transport Policy Decision Making* 2: 179-195.

Dix, M.C. and P.B. Goodwin, 1981, "Understanding the Effects of Changing Gas Prices: A Synthesis of Conflicting Econometric and Psychometric Evidence," *Proceedings of the PTRC Annual Meeting,* Warwick, England, July.

Doggart, J.V., 1979, *Eastern Flank - Energy Issues,* Unpublished discussion paper, Milton Keynes Development Corporation, Milton Keynes, U.K.

Downs, A., 1974, "Squeezing Spread City," *New York Times Magazine,* March 17: 38.

Edwards, J.L. and J.L. Schofer, 1975, *Relationships Between Transportation Energy Consumption and Urban Structure: Results of Simulation Studies,* Minneapolis, MN: Department of Civil and Mineral Engineering.

Fels, M.F. and M.J. Munson, 1975, "Energy Thrift in Urban Transportation: Options for the Future," in Robert H. Williams, (ed), *The Energy Conservation Papers: A Report to the Energy Policy Project of the Ford Foundation,* Cambridge, MA: Ballinger.

Franklin, H.M., 1974, "Will the New Consciousness of Energy and Environment Create an Imploding Metropolis?" *American Institute of Architects Journal* (August): 28-36.

Greater London Council (GLC), 1983, *Draft Alterations to the Greater London Development Plan,* London: GLC.

Grot, R.A. and R.H. Socolow, 1973, *Energy Utilization in a Residential Community* (Working Paper W-7), Princeton: School of Engineering, Princeton University Center for Environmental Studies.

Gurney, D., 1988, "Energy in the Built Environment - Cardiff," paper presented at a Conference on *Energy in the Built Environment,* Department of Town and Country Planning, Bristol Polytechnic, Bristol, U.K.

Heggie, N., 1988, "Low Energy Housing: A Developer's View," paper presented at a conference on *Energy in the Built Environment,* Department of Town and Country Planning, Bristol Polytechnic, Bristol, U.K.

Hemmens, G., 1967, "Experiments in Urban Form and Structure," *Highway Research Record* 207: 32-41.

Hillman, M. et al, 1973, *Personal Mobility and Transport Policy,* PEP Broadsheet 542, London: Political and Economic Planning.

International Energy Agency, 1981, *Combined Heat and Power in IEA Countries,* Paris: IEA.

Jamieson, G., W. Mackay, and J. Latchford, 1967, "Transportation and Land Use Structures," *Urban Studies* 4: 201-217.

Keeble, D., 1986, "The Changing Spatial Structure of Economic Activity and Metropolitan Decline in the United Kingdom," in H.J. Eivers, J.B. Goddard, and H. Matzerath, (eds), *The Future of the Metropolis,* Berlin: Walter de Gruyter.

Keplinger, D., 1978, Site Design and Orientation for Energy Conservation," *Ekistics* 269: 177-180.

Keyes, D.L., 1982, "Reducing Travel and Fuel Use Through Urban Planning," pp. 214-232 in Burchell, R.W. and Listokin, D. (eds), *Energy and Land Use,* New Brunswick, NJ: Center for Urban Policy Research, Rutgers University.

Keyes, D.L. and G. Peterson, 1977, *Urban Development and Energy Consumption* (Working Paper No. 5049), Washington, DC: Urban Land Institute.

Lamm, J.O., 1986, *Energy in Physical Planning: A Method for Developing the Municipality Master Plan with Regard to Energy Criteria* (Document D14:1986), Stockholm: Swedish Council for Building Research.

Lee, H., 1980, *The Role of Local Governments in Promoting Energy Efficiency* (Discussion Paper E-80-12), Cambridge, MA: Energy and Environmental Policy Center, John F. Kennedy School of Government.

Loudon, A. and P. Cornish, 1975, "Thermal Insulation Studies," *Building Research Establishment News*, No. 4, p. 4.

Lovins, A., 1977, *Soft Energy Paths*, Harmondsworth, UK: Penguin.

Lundqvist, L., 1989, "A Model System for Strategic Metropolitan Energy Studies" in L. Lundqvist, L-G. Mattson, and E.A. Erilson, 1989, *Spatial Energy Analysis: Models for Strategic Decisions in an Urban and Regional Context*, Aldershot, UK: Gower.

Maltby, D., I.G. Monteath, K.A. Lawler, 1978, "The U.K. Surface Passenger Transport Sector: Energy Consumption and Policy Options for Conservation," *Energy Policy* 6: 294-313.

Marche, R., 1980, *Rapport Intermediare*, Groupe de Travail "Demande Vogageurs," Cooperation Center Organismes Nationaux pour l'Etude des Transports Interregionaux. Copy available from Division Transport Interurbaine, Institute de Recherche de Transports, 2 Avenue du General Malleret-Joinville, 94114 Archueil Cedex, France.

Mathieu, H., 1978, *The Role of Urban Planning in Relation to Overall Adaption to the New Energy Context: Some Broad Lines of a Possible Strategic Orientation*, paper presented at the First International Conference on Energy and Community Development, Athens, Greece; Copy available from Secretariat du Plan Urbain, 74 Rue de la Federation, 75015 Paris.

Milton Keynes Development Corporation, 1970, *The Plan for Milton Keynes*, MKDC, Milton Keynes, U.K.

Milton Keynes Development Corporation, 1983, *Milton Keynes Energy Park: Summary Development Proposal,* MKDC, Milton Keynes, U.K.

Mogridge, M.J.H., 1984, Review of J.R. Beaumont, and P. Keys, (1982), *Future Cities: Spatial Analysis of Energy Issues* (Chichester: Wiley), in *Progress in Human Geography* 8: 591-593.

O'Cathain, C. and M. Jessop, 1978, "Density and Block Spacing for Passive Solar Housing," *Transactions of the Martin Center for Architectural and Urban Studies* 3: 137-163.

Owens, S.E. 1989, "Models and Urban Energy Policy: A Review and Critique," in L. Lundqvist et al, *Spatial Energy Analysis: Models For Strategic Decisions in an Urban and Regional Context,* Aldershot, UK: Gower.

_____, 1986a, *Energy, Urban Form and Planning,* London: Pion.

_____, 1986b, "Strategic Planning and Energy Conservation," *Town Planning Review* 57: 69-86.

_____, 1981, *The Energy Implications of Alternative Rural Development Patterns,* PhD Thesis, University of East Anglia, Norwich, U.K.

Rickaby, P.A., 1987, "Six Settlement Patterns Compared," *Environment and Planning B, Planning and Design* 14: 193-223.

Roberts, J.S., 1975, "Energy and Land Use: Analysis of Alternative Development Patterns," *Environment Comment* (September): 2-11.

Romanos, M.C., 1978, "Energy Price Effects on Metropolitan Spatial Structure and Form," *Environment and Planning A* 10: 93-104.

Schneider, J. and J. Beck, 1979, *Reducing the Travel Requirements of the American City: An Investigation of Alternative Urban Spatial Structures,* Research Report 73, Washington, DC: U.S. Department of Transportation.

Sewell, W.R.D. and H.D. Foster, 1980, *Analysis of the United States Experience Modifying Land Use to Conserve Energy,* Working Paper No. 2, Lands Directorate, Environment Canada, Ottawa: Ministry of Supply and Services, Canada.

Steadman, Philip, 1980, *Configurations of Land Uses,*

Transport Networks and their Relation to Energy Use, Center for Configurational Studies, Open University, Milton Keynes, U.K.

Stewart, C.T. Jr and J.T. Bennett, 1975, "Urban Size and Structure and Private Expenditures for Gasoline in Large Cities," *Land Economics* 51: 365-373.

Stone, P.A. 1973, *The Structure, Size and Costs of Urban Settlements,* Cambridge, UK: Cambridge University Press.

Talarcheck, G.M., 1984, "Energy and Urban Spatial Structure: A Review of Forecasting Research," *Urban Geography* 5: 71-86.

Thrall, G.I., 1982, "The Effect of Increasing Transportation Cost upon Urban Spatial Structure: An Analysis Using the Geographical Consumption Theory of Land Rent," *Urban Geography* 3: 121-141

Turrent, D., J. Doggart, and R. Ferraro, 1981, *Passive Solar Housing in the U.K.: A Report to the Energy Technology Support Unit, Harwell,* London: Energy Conscious Design.

U.K. Department of Energy, 1977, *Report of the Working Party on Energy Elasticities,* Energy Paper 17, London: HMSO.

Van Til, J., 1979, "Spatial Form and Structure in a Possible Future: Some Implications of Energy Shortfall for Urban Planning," *Journal of the American Planning Association* 45: 318-329.

Vorhees, A.M., 1968, *Factors and Trends in Trip Lengths,* Report 48, Washington, DC: National Cooperative Highway Research Program.

Wene, C.O. and B. Ryden, 1988, "A Comprehensive Energy Model in the Municipal Energy Planning Process," *European Journal of Operational Research* 33: 212.

Williams. W., undated, *The Davis Energy Program,* CA: City of Davis.

Williams, J.S., W. Kruvant, and D. Newman, 1979, "Metropolitan Impacts of Alternative Energy Futures" pp. 35-77 in C.T. Unseld, D.E. Morrison, D.L. Sills, and C.P. Wolf (eds), *Sociopolitical Effects of Energy Use Policy,* Washington, DC: National Academy of Sciences.

Wood, L.J. and T.R. Lee, 1980, "Time-Space Convergence: Reappraisal for an Oil Short Future," *Area* 12: 217-222.

The Land Use Focus
of Energy Impacts

M. J. Pasqualetti

Reducing the environmental impacts of energy development is one of the dominant, daunting, and vexing problems of
our time. It is a problem that consists of such a complex ecology of stimulus and interaction that it has largely defied our
efforts toward mitigation. We approach energy impacts a piece
at a time, looking here at air emissions and there at water pollution, aesthetics, noise, subsidence, or radioactivity. Perhaps,
if we could identify a single, central theme common to the
diversity of energy impacts, we would be better able to understand and meet the collective challenge. I propose land use to
serve this function.

If land in all its forms of sand, dirt, rock, mountains, val-
leys, and plains is the predominate natural ingredient of planet
Earth, then the use of this land is likely the predominate
human activity. Inasmuch as energy resources are acquired primarily on land, it is not surprising that land use would be an
important ingredient in energy development, especially in terms
of the environmental impact of such activity (Pasqualetti,
1981b). I address the environmental relationship between
energy development and land use by asking, What is the role of
land use in the environmental impact of energy development?
This paper reviews several case studies of the land use connection in conventional and alternative energy resource development over the past twenty years. If land use turns out to be a
fundamental factor, it should be possible to suggest land use

planning   and management techniques leading to a better understanding and reduced environmental impact of energy development.

Three biases should be stated at the outset. First, being a Westerner, many of my examples come from the western part of the U.S. This should not influence the findings because the emphasis of energy development over the past twenty years has been shifting to the western states anyway, and this trend is likely to continue. The second bias is a disciplinary one; as a geographer, I naturally emphasize spatial considerations of human influence on the land. Again, this is a logical extension of the theme being emphasized. The last bias is an exclusionary one: I am emphasizing impacts at the local, personal level. Thus, I do not include the large scale and global concerns of acid precipitation and carbon dioxide.

Some Obvious and Some Hidden
Land Use Impacts of Fossil Fuels

Coal and oil, the two most important fossil fuels, have obviously different histories of development and potential for impact. Of the two, coal has the longer, more apparent, and more extensive ties to environmental impact, but even the late-comer oil is attracting substantial criticism for its environmental threat.

Coal

Although coal is plentiful and is often looked to both as the "post-oil" fuel and as a "transition fuel" to a solar econ-omy, there are many public concerns about its continued and expanded utilization. These include air pollution, acid mine drainage, surface scars, aesthetic degradation, odor, subsidence, and mine fires. Mostly, these impacts stem from the fact that it is a bulky and messy fuel to mine, transport, and burn.

Even though impacts are given various labels, each has a land use component. One of the best examples of the aspect of land use in air pollution comes from the coal-fired power plants where   Utah, Arizona, Colorado, and New Mexico come together (Figure 4.1) (Devine et al, 1981). The Four Corners Power Plant near Farmington, New Mexico was one of the greatest single polluters in the country for about twenty years. The pollution plume from this single station is said to be the first sign of human activity Apollo astronauts could discern on returning from the Moon. By itself the pollution from this power plant rivaled that coming from a major city.

Complaints about Four Corners pollution centered mostly on the high volume of particulates it was pumping into the atmosphere. Although original pollution control devices cut these pollutants to some degree, they were relatively ineffective, and the nearby residents began complaining. They pointed out that they were constantly beneath the pall of the power plant, and that the health and aesthetic impacts were hard for an out-sider to comprehend.

Siting of power plants nowadays is approached from two directions, first by weighting traditional factors and second by excluding areas of strong (and legal) incompatibility (Hamilton and Wengert, 1980). The Four Corners power plant was sited where it is because that location satisfied all the conventional requirements: water from the San Juan River, coal from the San Juan Basin, labor from the Navajo Reservation, and a large unpolluted airshed into which the power plant could dilute its pollutants. Sites near the areas of demand (Los Angeles and Phoenix) had been excluded because their existing levels of pol-lution would no longer allow major new sources. The urbanites received immaculate electricity, and the Four Corners residents received air pollution they quickly came to detest despite the payroll to which they were attracted originally. The Four Corners power plant became the symbol for a policy of "outsit-ing" or "pollution exporting" which came to be common in later years as sites were chosen for the Navajo station at Page; the Cholla station near Holbrook; the San Jaun station near Farm-ington; the Craig station at Craig, Colorado; and the Coronado station near St. Johns, Arizona. All these power plants transmit their electricity elsewhere, while their emissions remain local.

Figure 4.1
The Four Corners Region

Perhaps in no other part of the contiguous U.S. are there more existing and potential conflicts between energy development and land use than in the Four Corners Region. These conflicts stem from the co-location of the nation's greatest concentration of protected lands (only some of which shown) and a huge concentration of its present and future energy resources (including gas, oil, coal, oil shale, uranium, solar, wind and geothermal).

The problem of particulate pollution from these power plants is traditionally viewed simply as a result of the commonly high ash content of western coals (20 percent in the case of the Four Corners plant). The usual response is to install some type of control equipment such as electrostatic precipitators (in the case of particulate control).

Two other perspectives on this pollution emphasize land use, one in terms of the area of demand, and the other in terms of the area of the power plant itself. Because neither Los Angeles nor Phoenix is in compliance with federal air pollution standards, power plants serving them can not be sited nearby. This condition is a function of land use density and topography. In this case, urban land use has affected power plant location and the quality of the rural lifestyle.

Land use is important at the location of the plants in question because of the high aesthetic values of the area. Since the construction of the Four Corners power plant, visibility has dropped sharply, an impact that has been particularly alarming to those accustomed to long, unobscured vistas and pristine atmospheric conditions at such nearby places as Mesa Verde National Park and Shiprock. Degradation of a relatively untouched environment tends to attract more notice. Rural land conditions are thus affecting power plant location and design, a new emphasis that has been particularly felt in the last few years.

Perhaps the best example of this new sensitivity is found in the case of the siting of the Kaiporowits coal-burning power plant. As initially proposed in the 1960s this huge generating station was to be located a few miles north of Page, Arizona on a site close to local coal and the water of Lake Powell (Anderson, 1975). This proposal became a rallying point for those concerned about the environmental quality in this scenic area because the operation of a power plant was viewed as wildly at odds with wilderness the values of the land. As a result of strong opposition to the original site, an alternative was chosen. The new site was a few miles east of the headquarters to equally beautiful Capitol Reef National Park, and it attracted even more negative attention than the original (McLellan, 1975).

The final resting place for the power plant, by now renamed the Intermountain Power Project or IPP, was at Lyndyl, Utah, hundreds of miles west of the picturesque Colorado Plateau (Zillman, 1986). The were no canyons, plateaus, volcanic necks, domes, arches, natural bridges, deep blue lakes, or red slickrock areas around Lyndyl: only uneconomic farming and a large airshed. Consequently, and most important of all, there were also no land use objections to its construction, and the recently completed facility now sends electricity south to Los Angeles. The factors involved in choosing the final location of the IPP demonstrated the rising importance of land use in power plant siting.

Another land use issue of coal development is reclamation of mined land and its potential for rehabilitation to former conditions. The Navajo mine which supplies the Four Corners power plant is a strip mine, and like many other strip mines in the western states, its reclamation is more difficult because of low regional rainfall. Nevertheless, reclamation is mandatory nowadays and can cost millions of dollars per year for a large mine. The laws that today require reclamation were passed in an attempt to avoid repeating the devastation of Appalachia (Caudill, 1962).

The call for reclamation strengthened at about the same time as the search for coal, particularly strippable coal, expanded into western states. As coal mining moved westward, reclamation became more and more difficult. Whereas areas in such states as Illinois and Indiana are often reused successfully for agriculture (Land, 1983), the potential for complete resumption of pre-mining land use activities in the west is much more limited. One example of this limitation is found at the coal mines on Black Mesa, Arizona. The mesa is higher (over 7,000 feet) and drier (less than ten inches) than the sites of most other coal mines, and the low rainfall makes it virtually impossible to return it to pre-mined physical or cultural condition (Churchill, 1986). In cases such as this, the land use cost of coal is obvious.

The land use cost of underground mining is not as obvious. The underground mines in eastern Pennsylvania offer examples of three additional examples of land use conflict. These problems include subsidence, mine fires, and culm banks. Subsidence results from older underground mining where structural support is inadequate to prevent the effects of underground collapse from reaching the surface. Cars and even houses have been swallowed completely because of subsidence in several communities such as Scranton, Wilkes Barre, and Coaldale (Wilson and Jones, 1974). Environmental guidelines and land use policy such as those developed by the Appalachian Regional Commission, have been implemented in these areas in an effort to reduce the risk to local residents (Appalachian Regional Commission, n.d.; U.S. GAO, 1979).

A second problem in this area of Pennsylvania coal is mine fires. Mine fires beneath Centralia have received the most media attention because of several near-fatal accidents and because the city wants the federal government to compensate and relocate them. As the extent of the fire has grown, many areas have become too dangerous for habitation, recreation or any other activities. A common method of controlling such fires in populated areas includes complete removal of all dwellings and other structures, removal of the coal involved in the fire, flooding, and a long period of monitoring of the cleared land (U.S. Department of the Interior, 1971). This procedure has been implemented in many nearby communities such as Mt. Carmel and Scranton.

A further problem from coal mining in this area is the disposal of spoils. These heaps of shale and slate, locally called culm, were created mostly several years ago, from underground mining when the unburnable materials were picked out of the coal as it was brought to the surface. Hundreds of square miles of culm banks have accumulated over the years, and it is only recently that any possible practical use for them has been suggested (Devlin, 1987). It was debris of this type that broke loose in Aberfan, Wales in the early 1970s, killing over a hundred school children. Apart from such potential instability it is an eyesore and its existence affects land use patterns.

In these three cases of subsidence, mine fires, and culm banks the underlying source of the attention and concern is the surface land use. If people were not living above the subsiding areas or the mine fires, the actual and potential impacts would be minimal because neither mine fires nor subsidence are particularly dangerous in uninhabited areas. The mine fires on Black Mesa, Arizona and Smoky Mountain, Utah for example, pose virtually no threat at all because no one is living in these locations. It is the land use that constitutes most of the problem and requires preventive and remedial actions and planning controls.

Oil

The most publicized environmental impacts of oil development come from exploration (especially in virgin territories) oil spillage (especially near shore), the construction and operation of oil pipelines, the existence of the various structures and equipment, power plant siting, and the derived impacts which come with associated jobs and workers.

Oil spills have increased as rising demand has pushed oil development offshore and multiplied tanker shipments across the world's oceans (Alvarez, 1986). Some of the larger spills have come from groundings, the most publicized being the cases of the Torrey Canyon off Lands End, England in 1967 and the Amoco Cadiz off the Brittany coast in 1975 (Conan, 1982; Dawson, 1980). In contrast to the attention groundings have received abroad, the primary worry in the U.S. has been over offshore development (Hagar, 1988; LeBlanc, 1987). Nowhere has this concern been focused more consistently than the California coast (Palmer, 1983).

The event which brought the impacts of offshore oil development to the public eye most strongly in the U.S. was the blowout on Union Oil's Platform A, five-and-a-half miles out in the Santa Barbara Channel in 1969 (Steinhart and Steinhart, 1972). Although there have been larger blowouts (see Torrey, 1980), the Santa Barbara spill brought the environmental hazards of offshore oil development to the forefront of American public consciousness like no event before or since. It was much more than an ecological disaster (Kronman, 1986); it was an event which the concentrated media of Los Angeles flashed around the world in words and pictures. Everyone could see the famous resort beaches at Santa Barbara and Carpentaria coated with oil. They perceived that oil wells and beaches did not mix, and it was that realization which set in motion a tradition of dogged opposition to any further offshore development, especially along the scenic Pacific coastlines of California and Oregon.

The human use of the coast stimulated much of this opposition; the spill itself was only a part of the problem. Future protests resulted mostly from the vivid pictures of public marinas, waterfront restaurants, pleasure boats and beaches caked in oil, pictures that are absent on vacant beaches in remote areas. Developers themselves tacitly approach offshore development as terrestrial projects when they adopt and talk about "leasing" offshore "tracts" (McManus, 1988). Even California's main coastal regulatory authority, the California Coastal Commission, is principally a land use body.

At about the same time as the Santa Barbara oil spill was gaining the attention of the world, a consortium of oil companies was confirming a nine billion barrel oil discovery at Prudhoe Bay, Alaska. In order to market the oil, they needed a 700 mile pipeline from Alaska's North Slope to relatively ice-free Valdez in order to get the oil from that oil-rich but difficult area to the hungry "Lower 48".

The original plans called for the pipeline to be largely underground, but strenuous objection ensued, first to the idea of *any* pipeline and then to its construction specifications and placement. After many years of discussion, much of the pipeline was elevated to keep the radiated heat of the oil from melting the permafrost, and also to allow free movement of animals beneath the line itself.

Although the arguments against developing the field and constructing the pipeline had to do with disrupting the native populations, animals and vegetation, this was indeed a battle of land use between those who would see the area remain wild and those who would bring in industry.

One of the main arguments against the pipeline was that it would establish precedent for further activity of a similar type in the future. Not surprisingly, the existence of the Alaska pipeline *is* an important element in plans for development each of Prudhoe Bay in the Arctic National Wildlife Refuge (Williams, 1988). Those favoring the development point to the fact that a pipeline is already there. Opposition to these proposals is strong (Anderson, 1987; Cook, 1986; Exxon, 1985; Udall, 1987), and it centers on land use, specifically habitat preservation (Stanfield, 1986), and protection of grazing lands of the indigenous caribou herds (Holmes, 1987; Kizzia, 1987; Minard, 1987).

The wilderness argument against oil development has the strongest logic in areas such as Alaska which are almost totally untouched by man, but similar arguments are being made in many other less wild areas, particularly in the Overthrust Belt of the Rocky Mountain region (Arrandale, 1981; Devine et al, 1981; Runge, 1984). The threats are being examined most carefully by the local public and advocacy groups, especially regarding projects nearest national parks (Borrelli, 1987; Forsgren and Oliveira, 1987; Glover, 1988; O'Dell, 1986; Stottlemyer, 1987). Again it is a case of oil development vs. preservation maintenance and it is difficult to reconcile these divergent uses of the land (Forsgren and Oliveira, 1987). Public reactions to proposals which threaten such protected (and unprotected) open lands, even in light of "Project Independence" arguments, have been similarly disapproving (Langenau et al, 1984; Laycock, 1988; Sumner, 1982).

Although most of the conflicts between environmental quality and energy development have taken place in relatively empty areas of the western states (Dritschilo et al, 1986), there are areas of high population density which have supplied oil for decades, often with little public notice. For example, oil has been pumped from beneath Los Angeles since the first field, the Los Angeles City Field, was found in 1892. For the next several decades, the Los Angeles area had much of the appearance of an oil boom town, particularly around Signal Hill and Wilmington. Historical photographs show that it looked every bit the gusher area as East Texas and Louisiana.

Large scale oil development in southern California continues even today, but its visual impact is greatly different. There is now a conscious sensitivity to aesthetic intrusion and competing land use. The explanation for this lowered impact is a result of community interest in establishing land use regulations which require that development companies adhere to set standards. These standards mostly address matters of directional drilling and aesthetics (sight and noise) (City of Los Angeles, 1969).

The development companies have responded to these standards in a variety of ways. Drilling rigs on the property of Beverly Hills High School are muffled. Those offshore in Long Beach harbor are hidden on artificial islands which have palm trees, waterfalls, fountains and decorative floodlights. Hundreds of oil wells in exclusive Beverly Hills are camouflaged by vegetation, equipment design, and Hollywood facades. This has allowed oil production to proceed while meeting citizen sensibilities. The impacts from these drilling projects were seen as a land use problem and they were handled with land use controls.

Such approaches to multipurpose land use in the Los Angeles have not always been successful. Occidental Petroleum has been trying to obtain development permits for the 60-million barrel field it controls beneath affluent and coastal Pacific Palisades for two decades (Williams, 1988). They have assured neighbors and regulatory authorities that they will do whatever is necessary to minimize the impact; these efforts have included numerous plans to camouflage the drilling sites. Opponents to the plan have been trying to "protect the beach" (Boyarsky, 1988). The division between the two camps became so political that the matter went before the voters in November 1988.

The Land Use Cost of Hydropower

When David Brower, as Executive Director of the Sierra Club, was in the field near the site of a proposed hydroelectric dam one day, he was asked by a developer, "You environmentalists are always *against* everything; aren't you ever *for* anything?"   He replied, "When you are *against* a dam, you are *for* a canyon." It is a difference in opinion and perspective which has been expressed many times, in many ways, by many people over the years.

In large measure, opposition to dams is based on disagreements over land use, especially the long term nature of the impacts. In such cases, the decisions of one generation affect many generations to come; future populations cannot decommission a dam as they can a power plant. The dam is in place, and there are usually no real options other than to leave it there. It is because of such essentially irreversible changes on the land that dams evoke such strong emotions.

This pattern of reaction started just after the turn of the century with plans to dam Hetch-Hetchy Valley of Yosemite National Park. Hetch-Hetchy was considered by many, including the noted conservationist John Muir, to be even more spectacular than its famous neighbor to the south (Muir, 1962 (1912)). Construction of the dam began a pattern that would last for decades. After Hetch Hetchy, the Bureau of Reclamation and the U.S. Army Corps of Engineers impounded virtually every major stream in the U.S. (Reisner, 1986). Until recently there were relatively few effective objections to these projects. Part of the reason for the small public reaction was that many of the biggest dams were in areas that we only poorly knew.

The impacts of dams are particularly vulnerable to different viewpoints. Although dams are usually viewed as water impoundment devices, they are also land inundation devices. The loss of land is not their purpose, but it is a result of their existence. Away from the reservoir itself, the nearby land may change tremendously, as we have seen in the east more than in the west. On the Tennessee River in Kentucky, for example, the Land Between the Lakes is a heavily used recreation area now that the dams are in place. The land use now is completely different than before the TVA existed. It may well be that the changes in land use in such places are viewed positively when compared to pre-dam conditions; the literature is inconclusive on the subject. Clearly, however, land cannot at once be preserved and flooded.

Also unavoidable is the fact that the best sites for hydro-electric generation are those locations which have either a high volume of water or a high amount of head, or both. Thus, many of the best sites are sure to be some of the most spectacular canyons, and this inevitably leads to conflict, if not about the area of land actually flooded, then about the complete transformation of a landscape. In the case of Glen Canyon Dam on the Colorado River, for example, a true wilderness area hardly anyone knew has been converted to a reservoir attracting millions of visitors a year. Concurrently, changes in land use make a wilderness experience now to match what was possible before a dubious possibility.

Some say that with so many people using the Glen Canyon area, it is serving a greater purpose than it did as wilderness. Others point out that the dam submerged arguably the most spectacularly scenic canyon in the world, creating in its place a totally artificial environment called Lake Powell, a reservoir 200 miles long, with over 2,000 miles of shoreline and 250 square miles of surface, not a little of it covered with floating mats of raw sewerage, wood, paper, and aluminum cans.

Many have lamented the loss of the canyon, perhaps none so eloquently or beautifully as Elliot Porter in his photo-essay on Glen Canyon *The Place No One Knew* (Porter, 1988 (1963)). Still today, reaction to this environmental transformation often becomes heated, and there has been relatively serious anarchistic talk about blowing the dam up (Abbey, 1975; McPhee, 1971; Stegner, 1985). Many preferred the landscape the way it used to be, and they are the watchdogs who are ever alert for similar threats elsewhere such as in the Grand Canyon where several dams have been proposed.

Despite the fact that dams change stream characteristics and ecology, increase evaporative losses, and destroy the potential for white water adventure, a major question with all of them is whether their land use cost is too high (Karpan and Karpan, 1988; Thompson, 1973). Many argue that the price was far too great at Glen Canyon, that few people will have ever seen what existed before the lake was created. They also argue that despite the fact that the potential for loss was obvious, no public opinion polling was conducted and no cost-benefit analysis was done to examine the potential value of the land now submerged. Even though Lake Powell itself attracts more visitors now than Glen Canyon did before the dam was constructed, numbers alone may not be the most valid measure of the area's worth.

There is a further land use aspect of hydroelectric dams that takes on a more personal meaning. In several areas of North America such as along the Columbia River and the Tennessee River, thousands of people were relocated to make way for the reservoirs. As a consequence of these and many other impoundments around the world, thousands of people have been forced to relocate (Ackermann et al, 1973). Old lands were abandoned and new lands settled.

The Increasing Land Use Cost
of Nuclear Power

There was strong public distrust of nuclear power even before the accidents at Three Mile Island and Chernobyl (Hohenemser, Kasperson, and Kates, 1977). This distrust focuses on the risks of power plant operation, the transportation and storage of its waste, and the inequities of both. All these objections are related directly to land use and siting.

The most serious objections and apprehensions to the operation of nuclear facilities occur when the power plants are in populated areas. For this reason, there is tendency to use more isolated sites for power plants than twenty years ago. As examples, the San Onofre plant (commissioned 1967) is alongside an interstate highway and between two heavily used public beaches near the town of San Clemente, California in the metropolitan southern California, while the other southern California nuclear generating station, Diablo Canyon (commissioned 1985), is largely out of sight in relative isolation, close only to the comparatively rural community of San Luis Obispo.

Nevertheless, even in relative isolation, its location was the subject of substantial public opposition.

The most important siting criteria for nuclear power plants are seismic stability and condenser water supply. Several other factors, such as air pollution, common in the siting of conventional power plants, are not directly considered. Not only do nuclear stations not emit common air pollutants, but their fuel is compact and does not require continuous supply lines or large storage areas. Together, these factors mean that nuclear power plants, considered apolitically, are significantly less disruptive from the standpoint of land use than other types of comparably sized power generation facility.

Despite these advantages, the tendency for nuclear power plant siting is toward more isolated areas, larger parcels of land, lower density usage. It is the concern about the risks brought about by incompatible land uses that has encouraged these power plants away from cities (Openshaw, 1986). The most recently licensed nuclear power plant in the United States, the desert plant called Palo Verde, exemplifies these newer standards most completely (Pasqualetti, 1983b).

Even in a large country such as the U.S., however, it is not always easy to find acceptably isolated sites. Thus, although no new power plants have been approved since 1979, research on alternative siting procedures has continued. Possible alternatives include sites adjacent to existing facilities (U.S. GAO, 1980), reusing sites after dismantlement of present equipment (Pasqualetti, 1987), clustering of reactors in mega-sites (Hemdal, 1979), constructing power plants on artificial islands offshore, and putting the power plants underground (Teller, 1979).

All these suggestions are meant to reduce land use conflict, whether it be direct incompatibility (as over the transfer of land from agriculture to industrial usage) or conflict with public sensitivities (as when people simply object to the location of the power plant itself). In either case, the siting question is basically one of technology meeting the public. Thus, although part of the move toward greater power plant isolation is related to safety, part is a matter of social psychology.

The most critical short term matter of social interest is public health. This concern was illustrated as the radioactive plume radiated outward from the Chernobyl power station following the 1986 accident. The initial concern focused on the nearby residents. The secondary concern was for the water supply and the surrounding agricultural land. The third concern was for the cities and agricultural land further downwind from the accident. The final concern was for the international impacts.

There are two spatial perspectives on these concerns, one as seen from the source of the problem and one as seen from the receiver. The second perspective is essentially one of land use sensitivities in the receiving area, and it is this one that has received the greatest international coverage (Drakulick, 1987; Egger, 1987; Handl and Pfau, 1987; Hawkes et al, 1986; Salter, 1987; Shapar and Reyners, 1987; ApSimon and Wilson, 1986). It is the second which is usually the perspective of the public.

The interest in nuclear accidents thus focused on the land use in the receiving areas. Had the accident occurred in remote Siberia and had the early (and therefore more dangerous) plume not passed over populated areas, the danger (and worry) would have been severely diminished. Instead the level of worry was sufficient to bring about evacuations--which occurred because of the residential land use nearby.

The evacuations were different in character, if not impact. When the evacuation advisory was issued in the wake of TMI, only 2500 preschool children and pregnant women were expected to be affected. Instead, an estimated 144,000 persons, or 39 percent of the population, spontaneously evacuated their homes in an area as far as fifteen miles from the plant (Zeigler, Brunn, and Johnson, 1981). At Chernobyl, more than 92,000 were evacuated by the government within a nineteen mile radius. These evacuations focused a level of unfavorable attention on the incidents at both reactors that would have been absent had the facilities been in unpopulated locations. Thus, land use, through the actual movements of people and the publicity these movements created, can affect public opinion of nuclear power.

In addition to direct impacts on people, the Chernobyl accident produced strong concern about the surrounding agricultural lands. One Soviet official estimated the cost to crops and health to be in the hundreds of billions of dollars (Keel, 1987). The dangers to populated areas and crops were this great because there were so many people and crops near the plant. Had the surrounding lands been unpopulated or used less intensively, neither concern would have been severe.

The evacuations, economic loss and attention which these accidents produced were functions of the nearby use of the land as much as they were functions of the risk inherent in nuclear power. After the Three Mile Island mishap, for example, attention to land use considerations increased at other stations in the United States. For example, more demanding emergency evacuation plans were henceforth required as a condition of licensing a plant. As a consequence of these new regulations, it has been impossible to license the Shoreham plant on Long Island because incompatible land use prevents the creation of an approvable evacuation plan (evacuees would find themselves moving *toward* the plant in order to reach ultimate safety traveling off the island) (Johnson and Zeigler, 1984). Thus, the $2.5 billion plant was denied a license and was sold to the state of New York (Peik, 1988). The basic cause of the problem was a surrounding land usage which was incompatible with the existence of the power plant.

Waste handling also links nuclear power with land use. Currently the U.S. has no civilian repositories for the disposal of high level nuclear waste (i.e. spent fuel rods and some liquids), and there are only two facilities receiving low level waste. Ultimately, the high level waste is likely to be placed in a repository being developed in Yucca Mountain, Nevada, and the low level wastes will be handled through several state waste "compacts" under consideration (Monastersky, 1987; U.S. DOE, 1982).

The siting and preparation of high and low level waste facilities has taken much longer than expected (Shelley et al, 1988; Solomon and Shelley, 1988). The difficulties in the U.S. and abroad have been over land use, with NIMBY (Not In My

Backyard)   the operative acronym.   Severe objections were encountered at many of the final proposed sites in the U.S., but perhaps the clearest case of land use conflict arose from the sites suggested for Davis and Lavender Canyons on the edge of Canyonlands National Park. A strong and lively campaign was launched to defeat these two proposals, including petitions, lectures, articles in the press, and testimony in Congress. The debate received such publicity that a television production entitled "Nuclear National Park" was prepared and aired on many PBS televisions stations. The core of disagreement was the incompatibility of intense nuclear waste storage activities next door to protected, public wilderness.

Although the Canyonlands sites were eventually withdrawn from consideration, several others remained, each one to be "characterized" in terms of geological and socioeconomic appropriateness. Later, these sites were also dropped, with the exception of Yucca Mountain, the most isolated of them all (Davis, 1988). The primary reason for dropping the other finalists was the land use conflict each had provoked.

Now that the Yucca Mountain site and some state-compact sites have been chosen, the next step is to approve the transportation routes (FitzSimmons, 1987). This task may not be as difficult as the siting itself because the officially preferred routes are interstate highways and they fall under federal control. When these highways pass near or through urban areas, however, objections are still possible. Lonely roads, like lonely dump sites, encounter fewer people and less opposition.

Equity issues have become increasingly important in the debate about the development of nuclear power and other resources (e.g. Churchill, 1986; Kasperson, 1983; Miller, 1987). One of the objections to waste disposal sites, for example, has been that the impacts of the existence and operation are borne almost entirely by facility neighbors, and little by those receiving the benefits of the electricity from the power plants themselves. The equity argument affects other steps in the fuel cycle as well, such as power plant siting itself. One of the most recent examples of this question was the siting of the Palo Verde Nuclear Generating Station near Phoenix, Arizona. Since over   fifty percent of the electricity is transmitted out of the state, more than half the power goes to users assuming none of the risk yet receiving all of the benefits (Pasqualetti, 1983b). These and other examples are matters of geographically matching risks with land use.

To summarize,   whether it is a matter of power plant siting, locating waste dumps and transport routes to reach them, measuring and absorbing the impacts of nuclear accidents, or assessing the equity of risk, location and land use are key considerations.

The Crucial Role of Land Use
in Alternative Energy Development

The last thing an alternative energy developer wants is an environmental   conflict.   Unfamiliar technological challenges, resistant utility infrastructures, and skeptical lending institutions are already barriers enough. Unfortunately, as with conventional fuels, each new resource has its own idiosyncratic environmental problems which must be overcome before development can be successful. The non-fossil "Big Three" of alternative energy development (solar, geothermal, and wind) have environmental problems common to land use.

Solar

Developers of each of the two types of direct solar energy (photovoltaics and solar collectors) have encountered land use difficulties. This is ironic given the fact that of all the earth's energy resources, solar energy is the most ubiquitous. It is everywhere naturally, and there is little need for the traditional considerations of mining, processing, transportation or, seemingly, siting.

The land use problems which solar energy characteristically encounters are very different from other energy resources. The most publicized land use problem of solar energy, usually associated with photovoltaics (pv's), is a result of its low energy concentration; large arrays are necessary to satisfy even relatively small demands. Although panels of photovoltaic cells have long been   economically justified for isolated usage, large arrays, occupying huge areas, are usually considered necessary to generate significant electricity levels. This means that if electricity is to be generated in the customary scheme of centralized power stations, large tracts of land must be found for the deployment of the devices. An estimate in a widely circulated article in *Newsweek* magazine reflected this common perception when it calculated that using solar pv's to offset the amount of electricity produced by nuclear power plants would require covering an area the size of West Virginia, and that to generate all the electricity the U.S. needed would require covering an area equivalent to the State of Oregon (Winston, 1979).

This type of land commitment would discourage all but the most strident solar advocate, but the figures by themselves are misleading. A paper by Pasqualetti and Miller (1984) compared the amount of land required by various types of solar devices to that which is required to generate electricity from by coal in Arizona. The land requirements for the entire fuel cycle of coal, from mining through ash disposal, were included. Calculated in this manner, solar was found to require just 15-20 percent more land than coal. Even if this relatively small extra land use burden was undesirable, it could be more than offset by the other much lower environmental costs of solar energy. Of course, the land use problem of solar devices is largely moot because it makes much more sense to place them on the roofs of existing and/or planned structures. In such a case, the new land commitment for solar would be small.

In addition to the possible commitment of raw land, the other major spatial consideration of solar energy development lies in city form and function. Cities with lower profiles are more amenable to distribution of solar devices because they have a more favorable roof-to-floor-space ratio. Thus a city such as Phoenix which has a relatively flat profile has a structural advantage for solar power installation to add to its high naturally high insolation.

Other aspects of city form and function incorporate characteristics at the scale of the neighborhood and individual home. Because the most ideal direction of tilt of a solar array in the northern hemisphere is to the south, the deployment of solar devices is enhanced when the principal axis of a house is east-west. Ordinances can be implemented to effect such a land use policy in much the same way that solar access can itself be protected.

Thus, the connections between solar energy and land use have to do with the amount of land, the form and function of cities, architecture, solar access, and planning. All these have to be considered and balanced against the obvious advantages of availability and low cost.

Geothermal

Two case studies in California, the Imperial Valley and The Geysers, illustrate the close ties geothermal energy has to the land (Figure 2). In both cases, environmental factors have played a significant role in shaping the timing, cost, and scale of development. Although these factors have often been discussed separately (and under a variety of headings), land use has always been the key influence.

The conflict between land use and geothermal development has been perhaps most obvious in the Imperial Valley, a 500,000 acre agricultural oasis resulting from irrigation water imported by gravity canals from the Colorado River to the East. Inasmuch as this arid region realizes about 120 inches of evaporative loss per year, salt accumulation in the soils is a potential threat. Excess irrigation water is applied to the fields in order to keep the salts from rising to root level. Underground tiles and canals have been installed to carry the excess water north to the Salton Sea. Any pollutant or any disruption to either the supply of irrigation water or the drainage of the waste water would threaten the $800 million yearly agricultural output of the Valley. Geothermal development posed such a threat.

The 1970s brought several research teams to the Imperial Valley to characterize the geothermal resource and to estimate the environmental impacts of its development (Layton, 1980;

Figure 4.2
Large Geothermal and Wind Sites in California

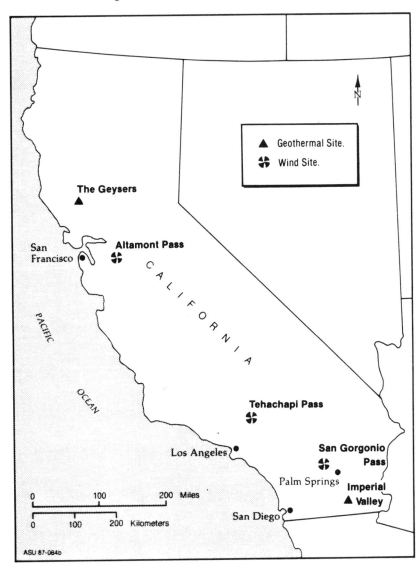

Both large geothermal and wind sites in California are immobile, and this characteristic puts extra emphasis on land use where they are developed.

Rose and Edmunds, 1979). The principal environmental concerns were ground subsidence, induced seismicity, water pollution, air pollution, and noise (Kercher, 1982; Layton, 1979; Pasqualetti 1980; Pasqualetti and Rose, 1979). Subsidence was of primary concern because of its potential to disturb the gravity irrigation and drainage network. In addition, hydrogen sulfide and caustic geothermal brines threatened the crops directly, noise from the steam would have been excessive and disturbing, and induced seismicity would have added to the frequency of tremors along this the most active area of the San Andreas Fault. From the perspective of land use, not one of these problems would have posed a severe limitation to geothermal developers had the agriculture been absent.

In the Mayacama Mountains five hundred miles to the northwest, California's other major geothermal area, The Geysers, is now the largest development of its kind in the world. For years, development efforts were threatened by protest about the obnoxious odor of hydrogen sulfide. Complaints from downwind resorts and their guests virtually stopped all expansion at The Geysers in the early 1970s. The problem was discussed in terms of air pollution, but it was equally a case of incompatible land use between the industrial developments upwind and the recreational developments downwind.

The juxtaposition of these land uses resulted in another environmental problem a decade later. Ironically, it was a consequence of the abatement of the hydrogen sulfide. Although the problem of air pollution had been resolved through the installation of control devices, the raw chemicals used in this equipment and the waste products that were produced both had to be hauled over the winding and steep road network at The Geysers with which they were not familiar. The problems began when the hauling trucks were involved in accidents that contaminated the environment and resulted in several deaths.

Although the difficulty was considered one of hazardous waste, it resulted from a site specific energy resource being developed in a wet and hilly environment having narrow roads and many recreational homes and resorts. A flatter topography or   a less competitive land use would have eliminated most of the problem (Pasqualetti and Dellinger, 1989).

Further relationships between geothermal development and land use, such as the efforts to develop the resource in the wilderness of Yellowstone National Park or the urban setting of several western cities, are discussed in other papers (Pasqualetti, 1980, 1983a, 1986).

Wind

Large wind farms became a reality in the U.S. between 1984 and 1985 with the help of state and federal subsidies. The world's three largest areas of wind development are in California in Altamont Pass near San Francisco, in Tehachapi Pass northeast of Los Angeles, and in San Gorgonio Pass near Palm Springs (see Figure 4.2). There are thousands of turbines in each area (Gipe, 1988; Shea, 1988). Although there has been some opposition to the wind turbines at each site, it tends to be strongest in areas of greatest population density (Thayer, 1987).

Most of the opposition has been over aesthetics, as has been evident in San Gorgonio Pass. San Gorgonio Pass lies between the highest mountains in southern California and is the gateway to the scenic Colorado Desert. More significantly, it is also the corridor to affluent resort communities such as Palm Springs (Figure 4.3). The City of Palm Springs filed suit over the development of the wind farms, claiming that their existence marred the entryway to the famous resort (Paris, 1985). Such complaints, along with those of several private citizens, particularly those living in the unincorporated areas near North Palm Springs, have compelled the authorities to place several restrictions on developers.

The basic problems encountered in San Gorgonio Pass are those of land use (Pasqualetti and Butler, 1987; Throgmorton, 1987). Like geothermal energy, wind energy is site specific and it is only feasible to develop it for electricity where it is most concentrated. It cannot be moved to less contentious power plant sites. This automatically puts a burden on the existing land use. If that area is already developed, as is much of the

Figure 4.3
San Gorgonio Pass Wind Energy Area

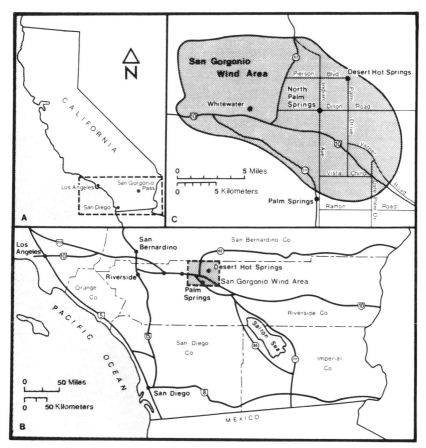

Land use conflicts have been particularly noticeable in the San Gorgonio Pass Wind Energy Area because of the open space and resort land use which competes with the deployment and operation of the wind farms.

San   Gorgonio Pass area, the intrusion is greater. When the wind turbines are in more isolated, less intensely utilized areas, such Tehachapi Pass, the objections to them are substantially reduced.

Land Use Emphasis and Change

The emphasis on land use is one perspective on the environmental conflicts of energy development. For example, instead of viewing the problem as one of air pollution coming from a power plant, the problem may be viewed as one of land use sensitivity to pollutant deposition. This perspective is actually already in place in the planning departments of many utility companies. When, for example the Phoenix-based utility company, The Salt River Project, was in the initial stages of finding a location for the Coronado Generating Station, they excluded all the national park lands right from the beginning. Was this a problem of air pollution or of land use? These lands were not eliminated because the power plant equipment did not meet all the emission standards; these sites were eliminated because of incompatible land use.

When the Kaiporowits generating station was suggested for a site near Page, Arizona it was opposed not for a lack of fuel or water, but because the site was viewed as incompatible with the existing wilderness use of the land. Its secondary location near Capitol Reef National Park was defeated on similar grounds of land use incompatibility. The suggested siting of the nuclear waste repository near Canyonlands National Park was opposed not because it was geologically unsound, but rather because it was incompatable with the nature of the adjacent park. The same type of argument can be advanced in the discussion of off-shore development near Big Sur, geothermal development in Yellowstone National Park, oil development in the Arctic National Wildlife Refuge, or wind development near in Palm Springs.

Land use is becoming a key element in all aspects of energy development, from original facility siting to the viability of alternative energy systems. In proposed developments, it is being used as an anticipatory mechanism to oppose or reject projects. Especially in such cases, it is becoming powerfully effective in steering public opinion and resource development.

The land use conflicts which arise over energy development most often arise from threatened change. If offshore oil is developed, the shoreline will change. If "x" resource is developed, the wilderness will be degraded. If "y" resource is used, the urban environment will have to change to accommodate it.

Actual changes come in different forms. Sometimes the change is from the pristine, as in the Arctic Wildlife Refuge. Other times the change is from a fully human landscape, as in the Imperial Valley. Sometimes the change is one of sight, as near Palm Springs. Sometimes it is one of odor, as at The Geysers. Sometimes it is unseen, as in the changes which may accompany nuclear waste disposal. Other times the change threatens human life, as in coal mines fires in Pennsylvania. Each of these changes has a land use component.

Land use is particularly important in its effect on alternative energy development. This is true because land use is such a critical element to each type, and because this element must be considered in addition to the gauntlet of unfamiliarity, unsteady infrastructure, untried economic viability, and possible changes in lifestyle. Considerations of land use are the most important environmental consideration in the development of these resources.

The Benefits of the Land Use Perspective

Now that we have made the point that land use is an important ingredient in the conflicts of energy and environment, we need to ask about the benefits of this perspective. One benefit is that it simplifies how we address the problems of environmental impact because it consolidates and distills these disparate problems (air, water, noise, aesthetics, subsidence, seismicity) to one focus (Figure 4.4). More significantly, the land use perspective suggests different solutions to the conflicts which

Figure 4.4

The Land Use Focus of Energy Impacts

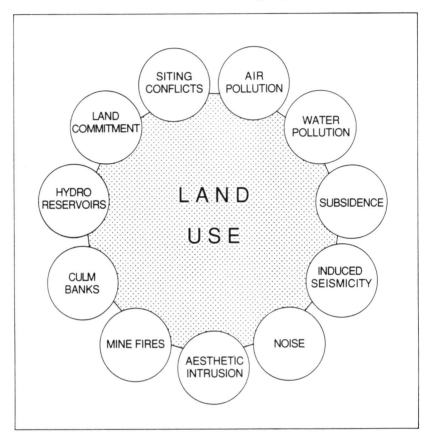

arise   because it attributes a different emphasis on the impact itself. Particularly with respect to alternative energy development, it identifies new limiting characteristics.

Perhaps the most noticeable and important effect of the land use emphasis is that it stresses a more passive concept of environmental conflict by changing the emphasis of problems from originator to receptor. Instead of seeing the problem in terms of air pollutants wafting away from a power plant, the problem becomes more of a matter of where the pollutants arrive, be it city, cropland, wilderness, or open ocean.

Other examples of perceptual differences may be taken from coal, oil, and uranium. Instead of always viewing coal strip mining as a process which devastates the land, the impact could be more accurately measured in accordance with what the pre-mining landscape looked like, the purpose to which it had been put, and its potential for reclamation. Instead of oil well drilling being considered inherently evil wherever it is suggested, the measure of possible damage should be made in terms of the sensitivities of the area of its development. Instead of a nuclear power plant always posing threats to continued good health, its particular threats should be considered at least partly to be functions of nearby population density and agricultural land use.

The principal impact of a land use perspective is a shift from a resource specific to site specific environmental emphasis. This means that some of the burden of energy impacts also shifts, from the energy resource itself to the use of the land. This also means that the environmental problems we are encountering with increasing regularity during energy developments are not the result of inherently "bad" or polluting resources, but rather that we are on a limited earth, with limits placed on us as to the compatibility of different types of land use. All human activity simply does not fit together geographically in a manner which is always, or even usually, acceptable.

Conclusions

Virtually all energy/environment problems originate in conflicting land use. This is true despite the fact that most environmental concerns of energy development are defined in terms of some other resource such as air or water, or some other environmental quality such as aesthetics or wilderness. Land use is the underrecognized common link among the various types of environmental impacts. It is the genesis of most negative public opinion about proposed development, and it plays a particularly important role in the acceptability of many forms of alternative energy.

A land use perspective on the environmental impact of energy development produces a change of emphasis about the individual sources of energy as well as the importance of the sites used for its exploitation. It is a particularly significant consideration for alternative energy choices such as geothermal and wind because these resources are immobile. In areas common to such resources and an existing or planned alternative land use, the choice has to be made between the relative advantages of their development and the development of another (perhaps more environmentally objectionable) resource somewhere else.

For solar energy, on the other hand, the land use consideration is less significant not only because the land commitment is not as anomalous as commonly believed, but more importantly because such solar devices are best deployed in a distributed manner anyway; that is one of their prime advantages.

For the traditional fossil fuels, the land use perspective not only attributes responsibility for environmental impacts more fairly, it also illustrates that the problems of using these resources cannot be avoided merely by changing location. This is especially true in the contexts of acid precipitation and the build-up of carbon dioxide.

Many of the environmental concerns about nuclear power are little changed when viewed from the perspective of land use. While it is true that more isolated plants pose fewer immediate threats, such isolation does little to the long term impacts of accidental emissions, nor to the apprehensions and dangers associated with waste handling, the connection to weapons, or ethics.

All this discussion leads to several conclusions. First, there will always be areas of potential conflict between development and maintenance of the status quo. We need to decide how we wish to deal with these conflicts. We have ostensibly done so with regard to some areas such as national parks, but we have equivocated with other lands.

Second, and in contrast, we need to identify those locations where resources are particularly plentiful so that we can decide whether we would like to hold them in a special category of protection for later exploitation. These areas would be "resource reserves" whose future land use would be designated in much the same way (albeit for different purpose) as wilderness lands (Pasqualetti, 1981a).

Third, we need to develop a greater sense of "regional responsibility". We need to admit that we cannot avoid environmental impacts simply by moving equipment around until we sneak below some variable level of public sensibility or notice. We need to meet the challenge of supplying ourselves responsibly. That means that there must be a greater emphasis on regional generation of electricity (the needs for supply reliability notwithstanding). Geothermal energy and wind power should be developed where they exist in greatest abundance, even if it costs more than importing electricity from elsewhere. Coal-burning power plants should be constructed closer to areas of demand, even if the coal has to be moved greater distances (the air pollution is more of a public concern than the coal movement). Non polluting sources such as solar should be developed everywhere.

This approach has implications for resource poor areas. Perhaps such regions that do not have great resources to develop should not be inhabited to such a concentrated degree. Why should some locations of great demand continue growing at the expense of environmental quality hundreds of miles away? Economic arguments should perhaps be given a lower priority in energy supply decisions, with a greater attention to the quality of the land itself. These are some of the lessons of the land use focus of energy impacts.

REFERENCES

Abbey, E., 1975, *The Monkey Wrench Gang,* New York, NY: Avon.

Ackermann, W.C., G.F. White, E.B. Worthington (eds), 1973, *Man-Made Lakes: Their Problems and Environmental Effects,* Washington, DC: American Geophysical Union.

Alvarez, A., 1986, *Offshore: A North Sea Journey,* London: Hodder and Stoughton.

Anderson, Alun, 1987, "Oil Explorers Make Waves In Alaskan Tundra Reserve," *Nature* (May) 327/7: 9.

Anderson, Orson L., 1975, *Utah Coal for Southern California Power: The General Issues,* Lake Powell Research Bulletin No. 13, Los Angeles: Institute of Geophysics and Planetary Physics, University of California.

Appalachian Regional Commission, n.d., *The Development of Environmental Guidelines for Land Use Policy, Applicable to Flood-Prone and Mine-Subsidence-Prone Areas in Pennsylvania,* Report ARC-73-185-2563, Washington, DC: Appalachian Regional Commission.

ApSimon, Helen and Julian Wilson, 1986, "Tracking the Cloud from Chernobyl," *New Scientist* (July 17): 42.

Arrandale, Tom, 1981, "Western Oil Boom," *Editorial Research Reports* (May 29) 1/20: 391.

Borrelli, Peter, 1987, "Oilscam," *The Amicus Journal* (Fall).

Boyarsky, Bill, 1988, "Westside Crude," *Los Angeles Times Magazine,* September 25, p. 9.

Caudill, Harry M., 1962, *Night Comes to the Cumberlands,* Boston, MA: Atlantic-Little, Brown.

Churchill, Ward, 1986, "American Indian Lands: The Native Ethic amid Resource Development," *Environment* (July/August) 28/6: 13.

City of Los Angeles, 1969, Chapter 1--Article 3--Specific Plan--Zoning (Title Amended by Ord. No. 138,800).

Conan, G., 1982, "The Long Term Effects of the Amoco Cadiz Oil Spill," *Phil. Trans. R. Soc. Lond.*, B 297: 323.

Cook, W.J., 1986, "Quest for a New Oil Bonanza Strikes Sparks," *U.S. News & World Report*, Dec. 8.

Davis, Joseph A., 1988, "The Wasting of Nevada," *Sierra* 73/4: 30.

Dawson, J., 1980, *Superspill: The Future of Ocean Pollution*, London: Jane's Publishing.

Devine, M.D., S.C. Ballard, I.L. White, M.A. Chartock, A.R. Brosz, F.J. Calzonetti, M.S. Eckert, T.A. Hall, R.L. Leonard, E.J. Malecki, G.D. Miller, E.B. Rappaport, and R.W. Rycroft, 1981, *Energy From The West*, Norman, OK: University of Oklahoma Press.

Devlin, Joe, 1987, "Pennsylvania Culm Power," *Alternative Sources of Energy* (September) 93: 20.

Drakulick, Slavenka, 1987, "Hard Rain Falls On Yugoslavia," *The Nation* (February 14): 177.

Dritschilo, William, Paul M. Merifield, David Kay, John Sarna, Michael N. Weinstein, and Terry C. Sciarrotta, 1986, "Energy and Arid Lands: Potential Impacts of Intensive Energy Deployment in Desert Regions of Southern California," *Environmental Conservation* (Spring) 13/1: 7.

Egger, Daniel, 1987, "West Germany Pours Hot Milk," *The Nation* (March 28): 392.

Exxon, 1985, "Checking on Alyeska's Animals, *Exxon USA* 24/4: 6-11.

FitzSimmons, Ann, 1987, *Have Waste, Will Travel: An Examination of the Implications of High-Level Nuclear Waste Transportation*, University of Colorado Natural Hazard Research Report 59.

Forsgren, Dean and Oscar Oliveira, 1987, "Oil and Gas in Wilderness Areas: The Need for Compromise," *Western Wildlands* (Fall) 13/3: 16.

Gipe, Paul, 1988, "Windpower Around The World," *Alternative Sources of Energy* (May/June): 38.

Glover, James, 1988, "An-Wars and Other Conflicts," *American Forests*, May/June.

Hagar, Rick, 1988, "Increased Activity Expected in Permian Basin, Gulf of Mexico," *Oil and Gas Journal* (March 14): 40.

Hamilton, Michael S. and Norman Wengert, 1980, *Environmental, Legal and Political Constraints on Power Plant Siting in the Southwestern United States: A Report to the Los Alamos Scientific Laboratory,* Fort Collins, CO: Colorado State University Experiment Station.

Handl, J. and A. Pfau, 1987, "Feed-milk Transfer of Fission Products Following the Chernobyl Accident," *Atomkernenergie-Kerntechnik* 49/3: 171.

Hemdal, John F., 1979, *The Energy Center,* Ann Arbor, MI: Ann Arbor Science Publishers.

Hawkes, Nigel, Geoffrey Lean, David Leigh, Robin McKie, Peter Pringle, and Andrew Wilson, 1986, *The Worst Accident in the World,* London: Pan Books.

Hohenemser, C., R.E. Kasperson, and R.W. Kates, 1977, "The Distrust of Nuclear Power," *Science* 196: 25-34.

Holmes, John, 1987, "More Oil Rigs among the Caribou?" *Insight* 3/6: 56.

Johnson, J.H. Jr., and D.J. Zeigler, 1984, "A Spatial Analysis of Evacuation Intentions at the Shoreham Nuclear Power State," P. In M.J. Pasqualetti and K.D. Pijawka (eds), *Nuclear Power: Assessing and Managing Hazardous Technology,* Boulder, CO: Westview Press.

Karpan, Robin and Arlene Karpan, 1988, "Should the Souris be Dammed?" *Canadian Geographic* (February/March) 108/1: 12.

Kasperson, R.E. (ed), 1983, *Equity Issues in Radioactive Waste Management,* Cambridge, MA: Oelgeschlager, Gunn and Hain.

Keel, Paul, 1987, "Moscow says Chernobyl cost 200bn." *The Guardian* (Thursday, September 17).

Kercher, J.R., 1982, "An Assessment of the Impact on Crops of Effluent Gases from Geothermal Energy Development in the Imperial Valley, California," *Journal of Environmental Management* 15(3): 213.

Kizzia, Tom, 1987, "Confrontation in the North," *Defenders* (Sept/Oct): 10.

Kronman, Michael, 1986, "California's Fish and Oil: Conflict or Coexistence?" *Sea Frontiers/Sea Secrets* (July/August) 32/4: 260.

Land, George W., 1983, "Energy Use and Production: Agriculture and Coal Mining," *Landscape Planning* 10: 3.

Langenau, Edward E. Jr., R. Ben Peyton, Julie M. Wickham, Edward W. Caveney, and David W. Johnston, 1984, "Attitudes Toward Oil and Gas Development among Forest Recreationists," *Journal of Leisure Research* (Second Quarter): 161.

Laycock, George, 1988, "Wilderness by the Barrel," *Audubon* 90(3): 100.

Layton, D.W., 1980, *An Assessment of Geothermal Development in the Imperial Valley of California, Volume 1: Environment, Health and Socioeconomics; Volume 2: Environmental Control Technology,* Washington, DC: U.S. Department of Energy, DOE/EV-0092.

_____, 1979, *Water-Related Impacts of Geothermal Energy Production in California's Imperial Valley,* NTIS Report UCRL-82871, July 5.

LeBlanc, Leonard, 1987, "Target: Giant Fields," *Offshore* (January): 36.

McLellan, Jack, 1975, "Kaiporowits: The Crossroads," *Sierra Club Bulletin* (August/September): 7.

McManus, Reed, 1988, "Love It Or Lease It," *Sierra* 73/4: 16.

McPhee, J., 1971, *Encounters with the Archdruid,* New York, NY: Farrar, Straus and Giroux.

Miller, C. 1987, "Efficiency, Equity, and Pollution: The Case of Radioactive Waste," *Environment and Planning A* 19: 913.

Minard, Lawrence, 1987, "All Caribou are not the Same," *Forbes* 139, March 9.

Monastersky, R., 1987, "The 10,000 Year Test," *Science News* 133: 139.

Muir, John, 1962 (1912), *The Yosemite,* Garden City, New York: Doubleday.

O'Dell, Rice, 1986, "Alaska: A Frontier Divided," 28(7): 11.

Openshaw, Stan, 1986, *Nuclear Power: Siting and Safety,* London: Routledge and Kegan Paul.

Palmer, Mark J., 1983, "A Slick Proposition: Why We Oppose OCS Leasing," *Sierra* (July/August) 68/4: 27.

Paris, Ellen, 1985, "Palm Springs and the Wind People," *Forbes* (June 3): 170.

Pasqualetti, M.J., 1987, "Decommissioning as a Neglected Element in Nuclear Power Plant Siting Policy in the US and UK," in Andrew Blowers and David Pepper (eds), *Nuclear Policy in Crisis: Politics and Planning for the Nuclear State,* London: Croom-Helm.

_____, 1986, "Planning the Development of Site Specific Resources," *Professional Geographer* 38: 82.

_____, 1983a, "The Site Specific Nature of Geothermal Energy: Its Effects on Land Use Planning," *Natural Resources Journal* 23: 795.

_____, 1983b, "Nuclear Power Impacts: A Convergence/Divergence Schema," *Professional Geographer* 25: 427.

_____, 1981a, "Geothermal Energy, Site Specificity, and Resource Reserves," *GeoJournal,* Supplementary Issue 3: 49.

_____, 1981b, "Energy and Land Use," in John Lounsbury, L. Sommers, and E. Fernald (eds), *Land Use: A Spatial Approach,* Dubuque, IA: Kendall-Hunt Publishers.

_____, 1980, "Geothermal Energy and the Environment: The Global Experience," *Energy: The International Journal* 5: 111.

Pasqualetti, M.J. and Edgar Butler, 1987, "Public Reaction to Wind Development in California," *International Journal of Ambient Energy* 8/3: 83.

Pasqualetti, M.J. and M. Dellinger, 1989, "Hazardous Materials from Site Specific Energy Development," *Journal of Energy and Development* (in press).

Pasqualetti, M.J. and B.A. Miller, 1984, "Land Requirements for the Solar and Coal Options," *Geographical Journal* 152: 192.

Pasqualetti, M.J. and Adam Rose, 1979, "The Environmental Impact of Geothermal Development," in Adam Rose and Stahrl Edmunds (eds), *Geothermal Energy and Regional*

Development: The Case of Imperial County, New York, NY: Praeger.

Peik, Ronald A., 1988, "Dr. Beckmann on the Shoreham Sale," *New American* (July 4): 13.

Porter, E., 1988 (1963), *The Place No One Knew: Glen Canyon on the Colorado,* Salt Lake City: Peregrine Books.

Reisner, Marc, 1986, *Cadillac Desert: The American West and its Disappearing Water,* New York: Penguin Books.

Rose, Adam and Stahrl Edmunds (eds), 1979, *Geothermal Energy and Regional Development: The Case of Imperial County,* New York, NY: Praeger.

Runge, Carlisle Ford, 1984, "Energy Exploration on Wilderness: 'Privatization' and Public Lands Management," *Land Economics* 60: 56.

Salter, Mary Jo, 1987, "Italy: Living with Fallout," *Atlantic* (January): 30.

Shapar, Howard K. and Patrick Reyners, 1987, "Nuclear Third Party Liability: The Challenge of Chernobyl," *Nuclear Engineering International* (July): 25.

Shea, Cynthia P., 1988, "Harvesting the Wind," *World-Watch* (March-April) 1/2: 12.

Shelley, F., B. Solomon, M.J. Pasqualetti, and G.T. Murauskas, 1988, "Locational Conflict and the Siting of Nuclear Waste Disposal Repositories," *Environment and Planning C* 6: 323-333.

Solomon, B. and F. Shelley, 1988, "Siting Patterns of Nuclear Waste Repositories," *Journal of Geography* 87: 59.

Stanfield, R.L., 1986, "Alaska Face-Off: Crude Oil vs. Habitat," *National Journal* 18/50: 3028.

Stegner, Wallace, 1985, *The Sound of Mountain Water,* Lincoln, NE: University of Nebraska Press.

Steinhart, Carol and John Steinhart, 1972, *Blowout,* Belmont, CA: Duxbury Press.

Stottlemyer, Robert, 1987, "External Threats to Ecosystems of US National Parks," *Environmental Management* 11/1: 87.

Sumner, David, 1982, "Oil and Gas Leasing in Wilderness-- What the Conflict is About," *Sierra* (May/June): 28.

Teller, E., 1979, *Energy from Heaven and Earth,* San Francisco, CA: W.H. Freeman.

Thayer. R. L. Jr., 1987, "Altamont: Public Perceptions of a Wind Energy Landscape," Center for Design Research, Department of Environmental Design, University of California, Davis.

Thompson, Robert H., 1973, "Decision at Rainbow Bridge," *Sierra Club Bulletin* (May): 8.

Throgmorton, James A., 1987, "Community Energy Planning: Winds of Change from the San Gorgonio Pass," *Journal of the American Planning Association* 53: 358.

Torrey, Lee, 1980, "Black Tide from the Bay of Campeche," *New Scientist* (January 24): 243.

Udall, James R., 1987, "Polar Opposites," *Sierra* 72(5): 40.

U.S. Comptroller General. General Accounting Office, 1979, *Alternatives to Protect Property Owners From Damages Caused by Mine Subsidence,* CED-79-25, Washington, DC: U.S. General Accounting Office.

U.S. Department of Energy, 1982, *Status Report: Low-Level Radioactive Waste Compacts,* DOE/NE-0045, Washington, DC.

U.S. Department of the Interior, 1971, "Three Mine Fire Control Projects in Northeastern Pennsylvania," Bureau of Mines Information Circular/1971: I.C. 8524: 22.

U.S. GAO (Government Accounting Office), 1980, "Existing Nuclear Sites can be used for New Powerplants and Nuclear Waste Storage," EMD-80-67.

Williams, Bob, 1988, "Oxy Eyes Drilling Resumption in Delayed California Project," *Oil and Gas Journal* (Apr. 11): 21.

Wilson, Richard and William J. Jones, 1974, *Energy, Ecology, and the Environment,* New York: Academic Press.

Winston, Donald C., 1979, "There goes the Sun," *Newsweek* (December 3): 35.

Zeigler, D.J., S.D. Brunn, and J.H. Johnson, Jr., 1981, "Evacuation from a Nuclear Technological Disaster," *Geographical Review* 71/1: 1.

Zillman, Donald, 1986, "Contolling Boomtown Development: Lessons from the Intermountain Power Project, Part One" *Land and Water Law Review* 21/1: 1.

Nuclear Waste Landscapes:
How Permanent?

Diane M. Cameron and
Barry D. Solomon

In this paper we explore the time dimension in nuclear waste disposal, with the hope of untangling future land use issues for a full range of radioactive waste facilities. The longevity and hazards presented by nuclear reactor irradiated (spent) fuel and liquid reprocessing waste are well known. Final repositories for these highly radioactive wastes, to be opened early in the 21st Century, are to be located deep underground in rural locations throughout the developed world. Safety concerns will be addressed by engineered and geological barriers containing the waste canisters, as well as through geographic isolation from heavily populated areas. Yet nuclear power plants (as well as other applications of atomic energy) produce an abundance of other types of radioactive wastes. These materials are generally known as "low level" wastes (LLW) in the United States, though their level of longevity and radioactivity can vary dramatically. For example, both iodine-131, with a half life[1] of 8.5 days, and iodine-129, with a half life of

Author's Note: The authors thank Barry Cullingworth, Gerald Jacob and Lowell Ungar for their helpful comments on an earlier draft of this essay. All opinions and conclusions expressed, however, are solely those of the authors and not of the U.S. League of Women Voters Education Fund or the U.S. Environmental Protection Agency.

seventeen million years, can occur in LLW. Consequently, the U.S. Nuclear Regulatory Commission (NRC) divides LLW into Classes A, B, and C, based upon the concentrations of long and short lived radionuclides.

The paper is organized as follows. The first section reviews the various categories and sources of radioactive wastes and controversies surrounding their current management schemes. We also clarify the often misused terms of waste storage, disposal and management. The following sections comprise the heart of the paper, where we discuss current knowledge on time frames for performance assessments of repositories and long term control strategies. The contrasting perspectives of different stakeholders is given, along with real world experience with HLW storage and LLW disposal facilities. The divergent views of participants in the nuclear waste debate will shed light on waste policy outcomes. We then delve into the trade-offs of waste storage versus disposal from a time perspective, which lead to the conclusions of the paper.

There is much debate over proper disposal practices for nuclear wastes, which reflects different viewpoints on the nature of the environmental hazards involved. While some argue for below ground disposal of all radioactive wastes, others view indefinite, above ground waste storage as desirable. These differences have not been resolved by federal legislation, which has encouraged several options for radioactive waste management. Moreover, the Low Level Radioactive Waste Policy Amendments Act (LLRWPA) of 1985 encourages states to act quickly to "solve" this extremely long term problem by 1993 (Colglazier and English, 1988). Any solution to the nuclear waste problem, including LLW disposal, is indeed a paradox:[2] We must make decisions in the present about wastes which will continue to be hazardous in the far distant future.

The debate over proper disposal practices for various types of nuclear waste includes debate over time related issues: over what time frames should various nuclear waste disposal options be assessed, their performances characterized? How urgent is the present need to find permanent disposal sites for the range of nuclear waste types? What has past experience taught us about either extreme delay, or hasty actions, in nuclear waste decisionmaking? The first question, on the appropriate time frames for nuclear waste repository performance assessments, will be treated in this paper from a range of interest group perspectives. The second question, on the degree of urgency of the need for a nuclear waste solution, is also related to the time perspectives of different stakeholders.

At one extreme, nuclear industry representatives and their friends in the U.S. Department of Energy (DOE) and Congress have been arguing for over a decade that the nuclear waste disposal "problem" must be "solved" as soon as possible, in order for future growth of the nuclear power industry to proceed unhindered by a bottleneck at the long neglected back end of the fuel cycle. As Assistant DOE Secretary Theodore Garrish told a 1988 Congressional panel, progress in the construction of new nuclear power plants is contingent upon progress in waste repository construction (Spence, 1988). Although Mr. Garrish is a senior government official, there are others in DOE and other federal agencies as well as in the National Academy of Sciences who see the need for a cautious approach to repository siting, uninfluenced by any perceived "crisis" situation. On the other extreme end of the nuclear waste arena, some environmentalists have argued that the unresolved technical questions surrounding nuclear waste disposal necessitate a halt in the current disposal programs pending further technical research and resolution of outstanding geological problems (Friends of the Earth, 1987; Resnikoff, 1987b). This environmentalist viewpoint is at least partly informed by the knowledge that nuclear wastes present hazards on the order of thousands of years and thus their very longevity requires sufficient time to develop a careful approach.

In addition to these stakeholder groups interested in nuclear waste issues, the viewpoints of the "general lay public" must be considered regarding nuclear waste management time frames and their impact on land use. Although the lay public is an amorphous, diverse group, its collective opinions are an important driving force in setting and changing nuclear waste policy and in accelerating or halting its pace of implementation (Wiltshire, 1986; Monti, 1987; Freudenburg, 1987). Public concerns have been addressed in depth by the Panel on Social and Economic Aspects of Radioactive Waste Management of the National Academy of Sciences (National Research Council, 1984). Sources of the lay public's anxiety over nuclear wastes include: their association with the manufacture and use of nuclear weapons, the record of government and industry secrecy in all matters nuclear, past mistakes in nuclear waste management, and lack of public control over complex technologies. The public perception of the unusual longevity of the radioactive elements contained in nuclear wastes is another probable cause for public anxiety over questions of nuclear waste management.

Despite the role of time perspectives in influencing the public debate, time related issues are rarely overt factors in public discussions on nuclear waste policy. Decisions about where and how to store, treat, and dispose of nuclear waste have historically been made to meet other objectives: *immediate protection* from radiological hazards, *appeasing* public opponents or public anxieties over waste related hazards, *eliminating the political liabilities* that result from these public anxieties, and *removing* the waste from densely populated areas. Historically, recognition of the unusual longevity of the radiological hazards of the waste has rarely been a key factor in nuclear waste management decisions, and political expediency has tended to dominate all other competing objectives. The nuclear waste anxieties of Congress in 1987, which resulted in the 1987 Nuclear Waste Policy Amendments Act (NWPAA) (regarded as a debacle by then Governor and now U.S. Senator Richard Bryan of Nevada, and a *deus ex machina* by the nuclear industry), reveal the dominance of short term political imperatives over long term scientific concerns in the nuclear waste arena.

While it is indeed true that some toxic organic compounds and heavy metals have long biological half lives, and that the total volume and biotoxicity of these non-radioactive toxins far exceeds the total volumes and biotoxicity of nuclear wastes, this comparison is rarely made by concerned lay people. Indeed, several of the more biologically recalcitrant toxic organic compounds have been shown to be degraded on the order of 10^1 to 10^2 years, orders of magnitude below the decay time of irradiated fuel nuclides. In contrast, heavy metals such as lead, cadmium, and mercury do not decay, and therefore present a potential biological hazard in perpetuity. Nevertheless, though some non-radioactive toxic chemicals have very long half lives in the environment, the lay public usually views radionuclides as presenting a much longer term hazard than non-radioactive toxic chemicals.

The urgency of the nuclear waste problem, the current state of the art in waste storage and disposal technology, and social equity considerations are all value laden perspectives on the nuclear waste debate that differ according to an interest group's value system. Perspectives on the degree of urgency, disposal technology and social equity criteria are in turn dependent upon how a nuclear waste stakeholder perceives the time frame in which decisions should be made and implemented, and the time frame in which their effects are felt.

The long term impacts of nuclear waste facilities on the environment and land use are virtually impossible to predict. Furthermore, even determining the present geohydrological characteristics of a complex waste site can be impossible (Shrader-Frechette, 1988). It is thus unclear over how long a period radioactive waste repositories will present a potential hazard to people and the environment, though numerous radioisotopes in the waste stream have half lives over 10,000 years. Consequently, the U.S. Environmental Protection Agency (EPA) has established standards for transuranic (TRU) and high level wastes (HLW) that set radionuclide release limits for 10,000 years after repository closure (Campbell and Cranwell, 1988). While radiation was discovered about 94 years ago by Wilhelm Roentgen, data on the environmental behavior of such wastes go back just 45 years, to the beginning of "disposal" of military wastes from the Manhattan Project. Thus, forecasting the ultimate environmental fate of repository wastes in accordance with EPA standards would be roughly like making a

1,000 year forecast with an econometric model based on five years of baseline data!

Table 5.1
Location of Commercial LLW Facilities
in the United States

State	Site	Site Acreage	Operating Period
Kentucky	Maxey Flats	300	1963-1977
New York	West Valley	25	1963-1975
Illinois	Sheffield	20	1967-1978
South Carolina	Barnwell	280	1971-1992
Washington	Richland	110	1965-
Nevada	Beatty	90	1962-1992
California	Ward Valley*	TBD	1991-2020
Texas	Hudspeth County*	TBD	1991-2020
Illinois	Martinsville*	TBD	1993-2022
North Carolina	TBD	TBD	1993-2012
Michigan	TBD	TBD	1993-2022
New York	TBD	TBD	1993-2022
New Jersey	TBD	TBD	1993-2022
Connecticut	TBD	TBD	1993-2022
Colorado	TBD	TBD	1993-2022
Nebraska	TBD	TBD	1993-2022
Pennsylvania	TBD	TBD	1994-2023
Massachusetts	?	?	?

*   - Proposed.
TBD - To be determined

Despite these scientific uncertainties, many observers agree that nuclear wastes should be disposed as soon as possible in surface facilities or deep geologic repositories. About twelve new LLW repositories are expected to be built in the next four or so years in the United States, where three operating and three   closed commercial LLW sites exist (Table 5.1).   In addition, a military TRU waste facility is scheduled to open in 1989 at the Waste Isolation Pilot Plant (WIPP) near Carlsbad, New Mexico, and site characterization work continues for the proposed HLW repository at Yucca Mountain, Nevada.   The U.S. landscape is thus to be dotted with radioactive waste facilities, at a much greater number than in any other country.

Categories, Definitions
and Controversies

Radioactive wastes are created at each stage of the nuclear fuel cycle, with the main concern in the United States being placed on the so called LLW and HLW produced by commercial nuclear reactors.   This simple dichotomy of waste classes is neither fully reflective of the relative hazards of the wastes, nor is it followed in Europe and Canada, where LLW is additionally divided into short and long lived intermediate level wastes. Whether the U.S. classification system for LLW has been helpful in facilitating safe waste disposal is questionable.   Nonetheless, the U.S. waste disposal policies have led to a system of LLW and HLW repositories, along with a special facility for military TRU wastes.

The official definitions of HLW and TRU are straightforward.   HLW is defined in the 1982 Nuclear Waste Policy Act (NWPA) as either (a) the highly radioactive material resulting from the reprocessing of spent nuclear fuel, or (b) other highly radioactive material (such as unreprocessed spent fuel) that requires permanent isolation (Wood et al, 1987).   TRU waste is officially defined as material that is "contaminated with alpha-emitting transuranic radionuclides of atomic number higher than 92, half lives greater than twenty years and concentrations greater than one hundred nanocuries per gram" (DOE, 1987b). These definitions enable managers of the nuclear weapons and nuclear power industries to segregate the wastes into convenient categories for disposal either at the future geologic repository or at   WIPP.

Low level waste, in contrast, has no clear, positive definition; instead it is defined by exception as "what it is not": it is not spent fuel, reprocessing residues, or uranium mill tailings. The 1980 Low Level Radioactive Waste Policy Act (LLRWPA) also refers to Greater than Class C (GTCC) wastes, as defined by NRC's 10CFR61, and stipulates that, whereas the states are given disposal responsibility for Classes A, B, and C LLW, the federal government is given responsibility for disposal of GTCC wastes. There are four major commercial sources of GTCC wastes: (1) nuclear power reactors; (2) nuclear fuel testing facilities; (3) sealed source manufacturers and users; and (4) manufacturers of radiolabeled chemical compounds. Of these, forty-five percent of the current total GTCC volume is contributed by nuclear reactor wastes, which include activated metals from reactor internals (e.g., core shroud, lower core barrel, lower grid plate), and some ion-exchange resins and sludges. The current GTCC volume of 14,000 cubic feet is projected to increase twelvefold by the year 2020, primarily because of nuclear reactor decommissionings (OTA, 1988). The major decommissioning isotopes of concern for long term isolation are Ni-59, Ni-63, and Nb-94, with half lives of 75,000 years, 100 years, and 20,000 years respectively (Knecht, et al, 1987; DOE, 1987b). Nevertheless, the annual volume of LLW produced is over one hundred times that of GTCC's annual production (OTA, 1988).

It is thus in the realm of the so called LLW where controversy and confusion exists over whether a given waste material is sufficiently "low level" to warrant disposal in existing shallow land facilities or even municipal landfills. Alternatively, engineered above ground vaults are now being planned by the LLW compacts and the individual states. The crux of the dilemma in categorizing nuclear wastes is that most waste materials are highly variable, containing a plethora of radionuclides with wide ranges of half lives and curie concentrations; nuclear wastes are generated according to the vagaries of the power plants, weapons factories, hospitals, and other industries that make them, and resist clear cut categorization because they fall along a continuum in their mix, concentration, and longevity of radionuclides. NRC's 10CFR61 regulations give guidelines for Classes A, B, and C LLW; these categories are based upon concentration ceilings for a list of specified radionuclides (NRC, 1982). Key points of debate over LLW definitions relate to the fate of nuclear wastes that fall below Class A or above Class C in radionuclide concentration. Other points of contention include the extent to which the NRC should consider half life and non-radioactive contaminants, as well as radionuclide concentration in its nuclear waste definitions. The problem of nuclear waste definition is not a trivial exercise in semantics; the category into which a given waste material falls is crucial because it determines both the cost that the generator will incur in providing for its disposal or storage, and the potential environmental and health risks to which present and future generations will be exposed.

In 1987 the NRC issued a proposed rule that would remove from HLW classification wastes that are either "highly radioactive" or "in need of permanent isolation", but not both (Fehringer and Boyle, 1987). Some of these wastes would be designated as GTCC. As we will discuss below, however, the NRC ruled in May 1988 that GTCC wastes should be disposed in an HLW repository, so that in practice GTCC wastes are to be treated as though they were HLW (Helminski, 1988d). Other problems of definition remain, including the issue of "Below Regulatory Concern" wastes, which will be discussed in a later section of this paper.

Up to this point we have been purposely loose with our use of the terms "waste storage", "waste disposal" and "waste management". These terms are, of course, also used outside the nuclear arena. Our vagueness reflects the lack of scientific or political consensus about the long term handling of radioactive wastes, which we believe will be in a state of flux for at least the next two decades. We offer the following definitions, not so much as a reflection of current policy than as a guide to future developments.

Nuclear waste storage is the practice of containing radioactive wastes, of any activity level and in liquid or solid form, within an engineered barrier with the intent of moving the wastes to another location at some specified time. A storage site is thus presumed to be temporary, and accessibility (retrievability) of the wastes is a key design feature. The eventual disposal site may be in the same vicinity at, for example, a much greater depth, but this will not normally be the case. A waste storage facility may be underground or at the surface, and will often be used to consolidate waste packages arriving from different locations. Another distinguishing feature of a storage site is that it will always require institutional controls, including security and monitoring measures, to ensure waste containment. The designation of a facility as a waste storage site will not always be made at the beginning of its development, and a storage site can be converted to a waste disposal facility for either technical or political reasons.

Nuclear waste disposal is the emplacement of radioactive wastes in a repository intented to be permanent. The repository will usually rely on geological and engineered barriers to contain the wastes over a time period that will far outlast all human controls. These barriers need to be stronger than those found in a waste storage facility, and will be underground or possibly beneath the seabed. It is quite possible again, however, that a political decision would be made to convert a storage facility into a nuclear waste disposal site (and the technical basis for this decision would be questionable). We explore these isssues later in the paper.

Nuclear waste management is the practice of short term containment and treatment of radioactive wastes for the express purpose of cooling, vitrifying, compacting, and/or reducing its volume. Other management functions include packaging, transporting, and incinerating nuclear wastes. Waste management usually takes place at a nuclear power station or reprocessing plant, but is also possible at a specialized waste facility. While the difference between waste storage and management is fuzzy, the latter is usually shorter term, involves lower quantities of wastes, and includes active waste treatment technologies. Following waste management, the radioactive materials may be shipped to a storage or disposal site. Examples of waste storage and management facilities include the closed West Valley (NY) reprocessing plant, and the storage facilities at the Idaho National Engineering Laboratory, Hanford Reservation (WA), and the Savannah River Plant, or 'SRP' (SC) where the liquid HLW is not ready for permanent disposal.

Long Term Control Strategies:
Current Thinking

Scientists

The time frame required for nuclear waste isolation is determined in part by consideration of the decay time necessary for radioactive wastes to become non-hazardous (Milnes, 1985; Brookins, 1984). The term "non-hazardous" is commonly applied to an amount of HLW that has decayed to the point where its toxicity equals that of an equal volume of unrefined uranium ore. Using updated radiobiological data from the International Commission on Radiological Protection, it has been estimated that HLW falls below the ingestion toxicity of an equal mass of uranium ore after 10,000 years (Merz, 1987). Toxicity, or hazard index, is also expressed in terms of the volume of dilution water required for a given mass of dissolved spent fuel, after a given decay period, to be "drinkable". Merz (1987) makes a persuasive case that accident and release scenarios and event forecasting can be accomplished with a reasonable degree of confidence for a 10,000 year time period. The bench mark of 10,000 years for probabilistic risk assessment of HLW disposal is based upon the geologic reasoning that another epoch of glaciation is highly likely in North America within the next 10,000 years. Another reason is that 10,000 years is at a turning point for the decay of spent fuel radioisotopes, before which the toxicity and heat drop precipitously and after which they decline more slowly.

However, scientists and policy analysts in several countries with advanced nuclear waste disposal programs in Western Europe disagree with the 10,000 year cut off time for risk analyses of HLW geologic disposal. For example, a group of French scientists has attempted to derive a preliminary model of glaciation and subsequent melting for a 100,000 year time frame (Peaudecerf et al, 1985). Other European scientists have used up to 10^6 to 10^7 year time frames in modelling risk scenarios for nuclear waste disposal options (Parker et al, 1987).

Scientists often disagree on the ability of disciplines such as seismology and climatology to provide reliable forecasts of future natural events that may cause a breach of containment at nuclear waste disposal sites (Shrader-Frechette, 1988). A geologist has commented that "besides the many different kinds of scientists and engineers, at least one clairvoyant would be needed to help with guesses about future geologic and other changes that could be hazardous" to the integrity of nuclear waste repositories (Hunt, 1983). The strength of a given prediction depends on the robustness of the model on which it is based; and it is the risk assessment and hazard assessment models which are the source of debate within the scientific community over nuclear waste management options. Lovins (1978) has emphasized the weaknesses inherent in basing nuclear waste risk estimates on models that are hypersensitive to even small changes in base assumptions. Small "nickel and dime" changes in input numbers can cause enormous changes in estimates of climate and groundwater parameters, and radiation exposures.

The long time line required for nuclear waste management has an important geologic implication: any geologic event is possible at a given site. Over a period of 10,000 to 100,000 years, a given site could experience any of the following events: earthquake, glaciation, change in climate resulting in changes in surface and groundwater regimes, and vulcanism. In the case of the Yucca Mountain site, all of these events are assigned relatively high probabilities of occurrence during the 10,000 to 100,000 year time frame. A maxim amongst solid and toxic waste managers is "all landfills leak"; and this is true as well for HLW repositories; the question is not whether a repository will leak, but when (Hunt, 1983).

The subjective nature of scientific judgements in designing and interpreting the results of forecasting models for nuclear waste disposal is rarely admitted in DOE documents, but is sometimes revealed in academic conferences and journal articles. Peaudecerf et al (1985) acknowledge and justify the subjective nature of expert judgement in interpreting nuclear waste models; they call their modelling system, which combines deterministic and probabilistic models, the "Geoforecasting Approach" and note that subjective engineering judgement can and does produce reliable forecasts. This expert judgement however must be based on sufficient historical knowledge; for example, knowing the Quaternary history of a proposed nuclear waste site is key to predicting its geologic future over 10^4 to 10^5 years.

Examples of scientific debates over the validity of a given model for predicting the geologic future of a proposed nuclear waste facility are found at Yucca Mountain and the Waste Isolation Pilot Plant (WIPP), New Mexico. At Yucca Mountain, in 1987-88, scientists disagreed over the likelihood of an earthquake resulting in significant groundwater table changes (the "Szymanski affair"), and the probability of a major volcanic eruption (Helminski, 1988a; Davis, 1988). At WIPP, geologists and a National Research Council panel have debated the extent and effect of brine pockets in the Salado formation salt beds, the existence of breccia pipes, and fracture flow in aquifers above the repository. These debates have explicit time dimensions; in the case of the volcanic eruptions, the discussion is over the age of a volcanic cone near Yucca Mountain; previously thought to be 300,000 years old, a geologist now claims its age to be approximately 20,000 years (Helminski, 1988c). This revised estimate of the cone's age may call for a revision in the forecast of future volcanic activity near the site.

Goble (1983) has discussed the mismatch between geotechnical and social/institutional time scales in controlling nuclear waste facilities. As he observes, most of the technical time scales relevant for nuclear waste isolation (radioactive decay time, breakdown of canisters and leaching of radionuclides, groundwater transport) extend from twenty years up to millions of years. Most key social factors (the lifespan of government institutions and private corporations) tend to fall within the time frame of an individual human life: twenty to one hundred years. This mismatch between the technical and human time scales poses serious problems in establishing and maintaining a system which will contain nuclear wastes for 10^4 years or more.

The mismatch between human life spans and long term scientific experiments was also described by Darwin (1956: 968), who discussed the existence of a "sound barrier" at forty years, beyond which any scientific experiment is impractical because the researcher cannot see the results of his or her experiment. "The technologist is not a conservative like the craftsman," writes Darwin, "and he is always trying to cheat the human time scale and to accelerate the rate of change." Perhaps the "accelerated" timescale of technologists (engineers and technical managers) accounts for the optimistic pronouncements that are so often made by officials in government and the nuclear industry, that a given facility or packaging technique "has solved" or "will solve" the nuclear waste problem (Ralph M. Parsons Company, 1985). Because technologies such as nuclear power and microelectronics have been developed within the lifetimes of many current officials in the nuclear industry, they expect to see the same rate of change and speed of success applied to nuclear waste isolation, and apply their own short (10-50 year) time scales when declaring the nuclear waste problem to be "solved". Except for transmutation of radionuclides, which is considered to be impractical and prohibitively expensive (Lipschutz, 1980), there is no way to shorten the half lives of the radionuclides contained in nuclear wastes; therefore any statement that the nuclear waste "problem" has been "solved" in a ten to fifty years time scale is not realistic. This thinking on nuclear waste time frames within the U.S. government and nuclear industry will be further explored in the section below.

Government and Industry

Technical, environmental and institutional requirements at radioactive waste facilities have been established by the NRC, EPA and DOE, pursuant to federal legislation. Options on these matters within the nuclear industry are thus constrained by the federal government. In addition to requirements for LLW, TRU, and HLW, disposal requirements for uranium mill tailings have also been defined, as part of the DOE's Uranium Mill Tailings Remedial Action Project. Mill tailings are to be "disposed" at production sites, mostly in the western states, using a cover layer of compacted clay riprap designed to contain and isolate the radium slurry for at least two hundred years. Environmental isolation systems have been completed at sites in Shiprock, New Mexico and Canonsburg, Pennsylvania (Thiers and Wathen, 1987). Radium-226, however, has a half life of 1,600 years; indeed, some analysts consider disposal of uranium mill tailings to be the most serious long term problem in radioactive waste management (Goble, 1983: 170; Kasperson et al, 1983: 360).

The nuclear industry's main preoccupation with waste has been HLW disposal. The Atomic Industrial Forum assumes that the eventual HLW repository will isolate the spent fuel from the environment for at least the required 10,000 years (Russ, 1984: 24). The industry is in fact fairly confident that the HLW will be effectively isolated from the environment for a much longer period.

The HLW repository is to be designed so that the waste is retrievable to the surface for the initial fifty years after the start of waste emplacement. Despite the 10,000 year safety standard, the EPA requires in 40CFR191 institutional control of the repository for only a hundred years after site closure. These post-closure standards, however, are being reconsidered by the EPA following a July 17, 1987 decision by the U.S. Court of Appeals for the First Circuit.

The WIPP facility for TRU waste disposal is regulated by the same EPA standards that cover the HLW repository, though its authorizing legislation (Public Law 96-164) exempts WIPP from NRC licensing. Thus, as with HLW, WIPP must be designed to effectively isolate nuclear wastes from the environment for 10,000 years, following the fifty year retrievability and the one hundred year institutional control periods.

This, of course, presumes that the project continues following an initial five year test phase.

Facilities for LLW disposal are generally perceived as less hazardous and easier to site than HLW repositories. The NRC's requirements in 10CFR61 for LLW disposal also include a 100 years period of institutional control, along with 500 years of protection through special packaging for Class C waste (with the highest concentration of long lived radionuclides occurring in LLW). In addition, Classes B and C wastes must be processed to retain their shape and size for three hundred years. The nuclear industry promotes the concept that virtually all LLW is short lived and very low in hazard. A pamphlet from the Atomic Industrial Forum (AIF) for example, states that less than one percent of commercial LLW shipped for disposal in 1985 was Class C (Russ, 1986: 15). This statement is misleading because although Class B and C wastes comprise less than five percent of the volume of commercial, reactor generated LLW, they include greater than seventy-five percent of the total LLW radioactivity (Lawroski, 1987; Sierra Club, 1985). Moreover, the AIF pamphlet identifies cesium-137, with a half life of thirty years, as a typical example of LLW from nuclear fission. The report also claims that almost all LLW decays to harmless levels relatively quickly, and after three hundred years becomes only as radioactive as natural soil (Russ, 1986: 6).

It is true that most current LLW volumes are comprised of very short lived Class A radioactive "trash", but concentrated liquids and ion exchange resins (Class B) are much higher in radioactivity. The latter, for example, are considered by the NRC to be hazardous for over 100,000 years (NRC, 1986). Furthermore, non-fuel reactor components (e.g., fuel channels, control rods), activated with niobium-94 and nickel-59 are also hazardous for over 100,000 years (Resnikoff, 1987b:12). Finally, the AIF report on LLW ignores commercial reactor decommissioning wastes. This additional category of wastes, though not yet buried at LLW disposal sites, will eventually present by far the most radioactivity of all sources in the LLW stream, though again the volumes are relatively small (Manion, 1980). Neutron activated components in reactor internals contain nickel-59 and niobium-94, as well as short lived radionuclides such as cobalt-60 (5.27 year half life). The discrepancy between NRC requirements for LLW disposal and the long term environmental hazard presented by a small volume of the LLW stream stems from two factors: the U.S. government has historically given an inadequate definition for LLW; defining it as "what it is not"; and the nuclear industry and the NRC have given only minor consideration to decommissioning in LLW policy, focusing instead on existing waste streams (Solomon and Cameron, 1984). These government and industry policies have resulted in a rather misleading view of LLW as homogeneous, consisting mainly of short lived radioisotopes, and amenable to easy categorization.

Environmentalists and Grassroots Activists

Environmentalists and anti-nuclear advocates are not a monolithic group; likewise, the nuclear waste policies and proposals put forward by different environmental organizations vary widely. For example, whereas the Natural Resources Defense Council and the Union of Concerned Scientists favored President Carter's 1978 policy of encouraging India and other countries to send their spent fuel to the United States, Friends of the Earth and Mobilization for Survival opposed the policy (Robinson, 1978). Certain generalizations, however, can be made about common underlying assumptions which inform many environmental advocates' claims about the disposal of radioactive wastes.

A principle shared by most environmentalists is "the polluter should pay"; in the context of the nuclear waste issue this means that the nuclear power industry should bear the full burden of managing nuclear wastes, including maintaining responsibility for on-site spent fuel storage until a permanent geologic repository is ready. Many environmentalists and anti-nuclear activists also see all types of nuclear wastes as presenting unacceptable public health risks due to potential radiation releases during their storage, transport, and land disposal. Because many environmentalists are pessimistic about the ability of the nuclear industry and government to isolate radioactive wastes from   the environment, they advocate a formal moratorium on new nuclear power plants and a phase-out of existing reactors in order to stem the further production of commercial radioactive wastes.

In contrast to most federal officials and industry spokespeople, whose technological optimism does not allow much room for retrospection on past nuclear waste containment failures, environmentalists tend to focus on those failures in their critique of current nuclear waste policy. While spent fuel storage and nuclear waste transport has a record of few major mishaps and accidents, only LLW has thus far been shipped in any appreciable volumes on the nation's highways and railways. For virtually all other links in the nuclear fuel cycle, the nuclear industry and the agencies who regulate it have dismal historical management records. The well known history of LLW disposal at West Valley (NY), Maxey Flats (KY), and Sheffield (IL), as described below, is riddled with documented radionuclide leaks and negligent burial practices. The history of federal policy on HLW disposal is likewise a well known account of negligent management, over-optimistic pronouncements on "the state of the art" capability in disposal technology, and outright deception of the public in matters of soil and groundwater modelling and public exposure to waste related radionuclides (Lipschutz, 1980; Carothers, 1988).

Although environmentalists look to the past in forming their critique of current nuclear waste management schemes, they also "take the long view" in determining how far into the future they believe the wastes will present a serious public health hazard. The time frame for most environmentalists is usually based on the time lines of botany and geology, ranging anywhere from five to a thousand years (Colglazier, Dungan and Reaven, 1987). Many environmental advocates and local rights activists focus on the obligation of the present generation to confront and resolve environmental problems so that they are not foisted off onto future generations (cf Kasperson, Derr and Kates, 1983). But this principle conflicts with the view held by many environmentalists that the present level of knowledge of nuclear waste-host rock interactions is too low to justify geologic isolation of HLW (or land disposal of any category of nuclear wastes). These views (and contradictions) will be further elaborated later.

American Indians

Many American Indians live in rural villages on reservations, especially in the Great Plains and Western States, and this means that many Indians are potentially affected by nuclear waste management policies that favor transport or disposal in sparsely populated regions. Indian tribes are sovereign governments with which the DOE must negotiate over such issues as hunting and fishing rights and access to federal property with Indian cultural significance, nuclear waste impacts on tribal resources, and nuclear waste shipment notification and emergency response.

Nuclear issues tend to be politically sensitive for many Indians; historically, hazards resulting from the front end of the nuclear fuel cycle have caused radiation exposure and contamination problems in Indian communities. Navajos who worked in uranium mines, Colorado Indians who built homes and schools out of uranium mill tailings, and Lakota who have seen the Badlands of South Dakota become a target area for uranium exploitation, have raised the awareness of Indians towards nuclear issues in general and nuclear wastes in particular. The 1982 NWPA mandated that Indian tribes are "equal players" in the protection of the environment, and established for tribes potentially affected by a HLW repository an oversight role in DOE's waste program (Gover, 1987). Indeed, potential repository states have sometimes formed alliances with tribes (e.g. Washington State and the Nez Perce tribe), in waging a legal and political battle against DOE's site characterization program at the potential HLW repository site at Hanford.

It remains to be seen whether the greater role for tribes in overseeing nuclear waste disposal operations under NWPA will result in a conceptual shift in national nuclear waste management programs: adoption of the long range vision and planning approach   traditional among tribes. A tradition among the Seneca is that a chief must be able to see and plan for seven generations beyond the present. This tradition is meant to ensure the long term survival of the tribe. If a generation is taken to be thirty years, then seven generations is 210 years. Even though this period is double that of the current require- ment for institutional control at a nuclear waste repository, it is still far shorter than the federal government's 10,000 years horizon   for "sufficient" decay of HLW radionuclides. Yet perhaps the traditional Indian long range view of resource and tribal planning, as well as the empathetic Indian view of animals and ecosystems, could inform and enrich the current debate on nuclear waste policy. American Indian cultures have seniority over European cultures in the Americas, having existed in some cases for a thousand years or more; and indeed one writer has observed that Indian culture encourages a 10,000 year time frame on environmental issues such as nuclear waste disposal (Colglazier, Dungan and Reaven, 1987).

Real World Experience

Given its short, forty-five year existence, nuclear waste management is an industry still in its adolescence. This obser- vation is verified in that the only nuclear waste disposal experi- ence to date is with LLW; TRU and HLW have merely been stored in temporary containers. Several basic lessons can be learned from past nuclear waste management experience, lessons both political and technical. The poor experience with HLW stored in tanks at Hanford, West Valley and the Savannah River Plant serves up the lesson that the federal government tends to be overly optimistic in its projections of the state of the art and the speed of development of new waste treatment technologies. The leaking of single shelled tanks at these three sites, and the inability to remove the extremely radioactive sludges that resulted from waste liquid neutralization in the tanks (League of Women Voters, 1985), is still unresolved and barely mitigated. Current estimates of the cost of complete removal, solidification, and disposal of waste at the Hanford HLW storage site exceed $40 billion. Demonstration of HLW vitrification only began in 1987 at the SRP, well behind the progress in France at Marcoule. Perhaps a generalizable lesson from this HLW experience is that waste storage facilities are a lot less "temporary" than their designers and managers had originally intended, and therefore any nuclear waste storage facility should be built according to the following principles: (1) the waste form, package, tank, container, or storage cask should be designed for at least double the projected lifetime; or (2) the waste form, package, and container should be designed for ease of retrieval and repackaging, and to minimize worker exposure, and this retrieval should be accomplished with proven technology.

Some insight may be gained on the expected performance and longevity of LLW repositories through an examination of existing repositories, if consideration is given to differences in physical geography, geology and waste engineering. Of the five LLW sites that were opened in the United States in the 1960s, three were prematurely closed because of rapid migration of radionuclides, among other reasons. Of the latter group, Maxey Flats is by far the largest and contains the most radioactivity (Shrader-Frechette, 1988). The site operator, the Nuclear Engineering Company (now U.S. Ecology) was granted a twenty-five years lease by the Commonwealth of Kentucky, but closed the site a decade early (cf. Table 5.1). Maxey Flats had many problems: complex geology, heavy rainfall, permeable trench caps, and poor management among them. Tritium, abundant in the waste trenches, was migrating about fifty feet per year (O'Donnell, 1983), while plutonium surprisingly showed subsurface movement, and cobalt-60 and manganese-54 were found in a trench seep just before site closure. The site is now undergoing remedial action and is planned for decommissioning by the State, which assumes that the land could be released to unrestricted use in one hundred years (Commonwealth of Kentucky, 1984).

A LLW facility opened in West Valley, New York the same year that Maxey Flats went into operation. Sited on a swamp thirty miles southeast of Buffalo, West Valley exists next to the only commercial reprocessing plant ever to operate in the United States. The LLW facility consisted of two sets of burial trenches, northern and southern. But the West Valley site met the same fate as did Maxey Flats: water infiltrated through the trench caps, and eventually rose by five feet per year until it broke back through the caps. This so-called bathtub effect occurred because the trench caps were more permeable than the trench bottoms and walls (Resnikoff, 1987a: 189). Since site closure in 1975, the State of New York has conducted remedial work at the site. Concern has been expressed at West Valley about migration of tritium, plutonium, americium, cobalt, strontium and iodine-129. Site cleanup is further complicated by the presence of the closed reprocessing plant.

The Sheffield LLW facility is yet another case of failed waste engineering in the humid eastern half of the country. Located fifty miles north of Peoria, the problem at Sheffield was the proximity of the trench bottoms to the water table. Unfortunately, no detailed inventory of trench contents is available at this site. After space was filled up at this twenty acre site, the operator (Nuclear Engineering Company) applied for a 168 acre expansion in 1976, which was turned down by the State of Illinois. Since then, tritium migration has been accelerating immensely, and it is now moving east at a rate of a half-mile per year (Resnikoff, 1987b: 37). The State finally settled a ten year old lawsuit with U.S. Ecology in May 1988, whereby site maintenance and clean-up responsibilities have been resolved. U.S. Ecology must now recap all the trenches, replace the site boundary fence and some monitoring wells, maintain the site for ten years, and pay the State $2.5 million over the next ten years (when the State of Illinois assumes management for the site).

Barnwell is the other LLW site in the humid East, and is the nation's largest commercial nuclear waste facility. Since it is located on permeable sand and clay fifty-five miles southwest of Columbia, South Carolina, Barnwell has largely escaped the environmental problems that have beset the other eastern LLW facilities. Migration of tritium and other radionuclides is believed to be minor there. Barnwell will close at the end of

1992, after twenty-two years of operation, when a new LLW site in neighboring North Carolina is scheduled to open.

The Richland and Beatty sites are located, respectively, in semi-arid and arid regions of the West. This one fact has made radioactive waste disposal much easier at these western sites than in the East. Both western sites have sand and gravel soil. Richland is scheduled to remain open into the next century, which will make it the longest operating repository. Beatty is scheduled to close when an LLW facility opens in Colorado, presumably in 1993.

There is also experience with LLW facilities outside the United States, principally in Britain and France. The Drigg site in northwest England is the oldest, having begun operation in 1959, and will probably operate until early in the next century. Drigg is comprised of primitive trenches and has a high rate of water infiltration. Lack of good knowledge of the radionuclides in the waste there makes it very difficult to determine the hazardous lifetime of the site, though many observers have deplored the crude disposal practices at Drigg. The French facility, at Centre de la Manche, was first opened in 1969. The site will be filled in the early 1990s, after about twenty-five years of operation. An earth mounded concrete bunker is used at this site, which provides much better containment in the humid climate. The intermediate level wastes are disposed in concrete monoliths below the ground, and covered by LLW in earth covered tumuli. The various barriers at La Manche are expected to maintain the integrity at the site for at least three hundred years (Devgun and Charlesworth, 1987). Other LLW sites have operated in West Germany, East Germany, the USSR and Sweden. New LLW sites are under development in France, West Germany, Switzerland, Finland, Japan and Canada (Solomon and Shelley, 1988). The Canadian facility, at the Chalk River Nuclear Laboratories, will be an engineered shallow-land repository. After site closure, 100 year institutional control and 500 year containment periods will take effect (Devgun and Charlesworth, 1987). These time frames for LLW disposal in Canada are thus the same as those in the United States.

The next section will draw on past nuclear waste management experience and various viewpoints of different stakeholders in the policy debates to illuminate outstanding concerns of storage, disposal, and retrieval for different nuclear wastes.

Storage Versus Disposal

High Level Wastes

All commercially generated spent fuel, as well as much of the HLW generated from nuclear weapons production is to be emplaced in a geologic repository, probably more than 1,000 feet deep. Currently the DOE is conducting site characterization of the volcanic tuffs at Yucca Mountain, Nevada, though many other sites have been considered (Carter, 1987; Marshall, 1986a). While the technology to be used for HLW and TRU waste disposal is similar, each waste facility will be structured to fit the local subterranean environment. In the case of Yucca Mountain, all of the land of the proposed site is owned by the U.S. Government, most of which is on the Nellis Air Force Base. (The U.S. government also owns the land on which the WIPP facility is located.) Two angular ramps are to be constructed at nine and eighteen percent slopes at lengths of 4630 and 6600 feet (DOE, 1988b). Four vertical shafts would also be built to access the waste emplacement area, with depths of between 1,000 and 1,500 feet. The waste canisters would be transported through the waste ramp, which would eventually be backfilled with crushed tuff.

In the wake of the 1987 NWPAA, interregional HLW repository siting conflicts no longer framed the debate over the ultimate fate of HLW. Now that Yucca Mountain has been chosen as the sole site for repository characterization, the politically salient issues concern the proper role of a Monitored Retrievable Storage (MRS) facility in the waste management system, the technical basis for an eventual license application for the Yucca Mountain site, and the hazard of cross country transport of HLW. All of these issues have important time dimensions which have often been given short shrift in government and scientific policy documents.

It is a simplification, but nonetheless illuminating, to frame the nuclear waste management problem in terms of "storage versus disposal". Virtually all other components of a nuclear waste management system (transportation, packaging, intergovernmental cooperation and conflict) depend upon decisions surrounding storage or disposal of nuclear waste. Policy decisions that favor storage over disposal, or vice versa, depend in turn upon a range of factors such as the time perspective of the decisionmaker and those stakeholders wielding influence on the decisionmaker.

From the beginning of the nuclear age up to the present, storage of HLW has been the only option practiced by the federal government as well as the utility industry. With few exceptions, spent commercial fuel has been stored on-site at nuclear reactors, and liquid HLW, whether from civil or military reprocessing plants, has been stored largely in surface tanks. Some HLW from reprocessing has been solidified via calcination at the Idaho National Engineering Laboratory, and subsequently stored there. The current situation, which has existed since the late 1970s, consists of a climate of urgency within both the commercial nuclear power industry and the nuclear weapons complex. This climate of urgency has resulted from the leaking HLW liquids from storage tanks at Hanford and SRP, which have received much attention from the media, Congress, the National Academy of Sciences, and public interest groups. These groups are pressuring DOE and the U.S. Defense Department to clean up their facilities, remove the leaking tanks and sludges, and vitrify the liquid wastes in order to stabilize them (Marshall, 1986b). This sense of urgency on the part of the utilities is because many of their spent fuel storage pools have been re-racked and are at or near their maximum storage capacity.

In contrast to the poor environmental record of military HLW storage, commercial spent fuel has been stored since the 1950s with a record almost free of accidents. Upon removal from the reactor core, on-site spent fuel storage for a minimum of ten years prior to transportation and/or disposal is wise, since the heat output of the spent fuel is reduced by a factor of one hundred during the first ten years of cooling (Milnes, 1985).

The HLW storage or disposal option that is favored by a given stakeholder group has much to do with that group's perceived urgency of the situation. Colglazier, Dungan and Reaven (1987) have described the viewpoints of different stakeholders regarding the need for an MRS. Before the passage of the 1982 NWPA, the MRS was proposed (by Senators from repository candidate states, among others), as a long term storage facility that would "buy time" for further scientific and technological research into ultimate geologic isolation. The MRS is also envisioned as providing easy access to commercial spent fuel, should the U.S. nuclear industry revive civil reprocessing. As Colglazier and colleagues note, although the pro-geologic repository faction won out with the passage of the NWPA, provisions for an MRS were part of the final Act, though the MRS concept was later altered. Instead of being seen as a long term storage alternative to a deep geologic repository, the plan developed by DOE pursuant to the NWPA proposed that the MRS be an integral part of the total HLW management system. The MRS as described by DOE would be a half-way house for spent fuel on its trip from reactor site to a permanent repository. The nuclear utilities' spent fuel storage crisis led to the altered conception of the MRS as a temporary storage depot and repackaging plant, which would be solely DOE's responsibility.

A provision authorizing the MRS was included in the 1987 NWPAA, although the NWPAA, in a seeming self-contradiction, also stipulated that a three member expert commission be formed and report back to Congress in June 1989 on the need for an MRS facility. Thus the concept of an MRS could again change, depending upon the findings of the MRS commission, or it could be deemed as unnecessary to the whole spent fuel management system, although this latter outcome is unlikely.[3]

As discussed in the section above on the viewpoints of scientists and technologists, both physical and social scientists have written extensively on the projected lifespan and required time frames for performance assessments of a deep geologic HLW repository. Very little has been written about the expected time frame of performance for the MRS, partly because of the uncertainty over whether the MRS is to be a long term storage alternative to a repository, or a short term "support facility" used in tandem with a repository program.

In its 1987 MRS proposal to Congress, DOE stated that the MRS would operate from 2003 to 2032, after which time the facility would be decommissioned (DOE, 1987a). The MRS proposal further stated that the steel and concrete walls of the spent fuel storage cask, as well as the ventilation filters, are materials that have been routinely used for spent fuel storage for over forty years. However, the proposed engineering design life of the above ground spent fuel storage casks is not noted anywhere in the three volume 1987 MRS Proposal. The MRS design life is also ignored in DOE's 1988 *Mission Plan Amendment,* which is vague about the role of the MRS and its design specifications (DOE, 1987a; DOE, 1988a).

Engineering design life is an important component in any design for an MRS, because it determines how long a facility can operate before succumbing to weathering and structural breakdown, and whether a facility's usefulness can be extended through provision of replacement parts. The 1987 NWPAA places several constraints on the MRS by tying its schedule to that of the geologic repository. One of the linkages is that if at any time construction ceases at the repository, waste acceptance at the MRS must also cease. The NWPAA also stipulates that the MRS must have a spent-fuel ceiling of 10,000 metric tons of heavy metal (MTHM) before the repository begins accepting waste and 15,000 MTHM thereafter. Since the current national inventory is about 16,000 MTHM, these ceilings are below what the nuclear industry desired.

Although many environmentalists support extended reactor-site storage of HLW for several reasons, including the dim view they take of DOE's record of HLW management and the present state of the art in disposal technology, they oppose DOE's proposal to build the MRS (Friends of the Earth, 1987). One of the oft repeated reasons for the opposition of environmentalists to the MRS is that it would be designed and constructed with the objective of a ten to twenty year storage lifetime, but would likely end up being a de facto repository, and pressed into long term (fifty to one hundred years) service as a spent fuel warehouse which would far outstretch its structural, mechanical, and institutional capacity for radionuclide containment. Another reason for environmentalist opposition to the MRS is that it would concentrate commercial spent fuel in one convenient, centrally located facility, which poses further social policy and security dilemmas. The social policy dilemmas would arise from the "temptation" to view the MRS as a spent fuel warehouse, holding a huge quantity of uranium and plutonium, which are valuable both as nuclear reactor fuel and as potential weapons material. Both uses of the spent fuel would necessitate reprocessing, which itself is fraught with environmental and national security liabilities, including problems of safeguarding, accounting, and inventorying plutonium. An MRS poses security problems even without spent fuel reprocessing, because any large quantity of surface accessible fissile materials requires severe security measures to guard against the possibility of theft or sabotage.

The concept of the MRS as a short term spent fuel warehouse is supported by many private nuclear utility companies as well as the DOE. On the part of the nuclear industry, short term objectives such as providing immediate spent fuel storage relief for nuclear utilities, and "demonstrating to the public" that nuclear wastes can be safely managed on a large scale, at times take political precedence over long term objectives such as permanent geologic isolation which incorporates long term scientific research program results. These short term objectives are at least partly the result of the public pressure from varying organizations to "solve" the nuclear waste problem. Historically, the industry has neglected the back end of the fuel cycle, regarding it as a problem that the federal government would tackle for it at some point in the indefinite future. Indeed, in the early days of the industry this view was reasonable, since the federal government owned the reactor fuel. Most nuclear utilities have stored their spent fuel in on-site "swimming pools", and regard spent fuel not as a waste material but as a future uranium and plutonium resource. As for liquid reprocessing wastes, of both commercial and weapons origin, their industry managers have tended to take a lackadaisical approach to monitoring for leaking tanks and performing remedial action when leaks were detected. This managerial negligence is true for the liquid HLW stored at the Hanford, West Valley, and SRP sites (Lawless, 1985), although during 1988 there were signs that DOE was making environmental and safety problems a top priority at SRP and Hanford (Schneider, 1988).

In addition, more positive, proactive approaches to HLW management are now being taken by some nuclear industry leaders, at least for commercial spent fuel. Virginia Power Company, for example, has been licensed by the NRC to store spent fuel in cast iron casks which are stored vertically, on a concrete pad near its Surry reactor. Carolina Power and Light has a similar dry cask storage facility for spent fuel (Resnikoff, 1987c). Other, less independently minded nuclear utility managers are anxious for any federal government initiative that will take spent fuel off their hands, and are pushing for rapid siting and construction of an MRS. This approach may actually be pragmatic from the viewpoint of nuclear utilities who surmise that development of the deep geologic repository may well be postponed indefinitely because of political and technical exigencies.

The DOE has provided a relief valve for the nuclear industry by signing contracts that obligate DOE to take title to spent fuel by 1998. DOE may have to come up with a novel way to physically "take title" to the waste, since neither the MRS nor the HLW repository are likely to be constructed by that date (Helminski, 1988e; DOE, 1988a).

Retrievability

The DOE is planning to keep the HLW repository open for a fifty year period following the start of waste emplacement in 2003, which is expected to take twenty-five years (DOE, 1988a). The justification for a fifty year retrievability period is given by the NRC obliquely in its 10CFR60 regulations. This justification consists of the statement that retrievability be maintained "throughout the period during which wastes are emplaced and, thereafter, until the completion of a performance confirmation program and Commission review of the information obtained from such a program." This statement indirectly points to one of the two main reasons for maintaining retrievability - that of ensuring that geotechnical problems have been fully identified and mitigated before the repository is permanently sealed, and ensuring that any near term (up to fifty years) catastrophic events such as an earthquake may be mitigated via swift waste retrieval in the wake of such events. The paradox inherent in this first justification of retrievability is that the very preservation of such an option may in itself create geotechnical problems - e.g. that repository seals will be left open which may allow for weathering and water infiltration. The second main justification for preservation of retrievability is that spent fuel is a uranium and plutonium resource, both for nuclear weapons manufacture and for electricity generation. Presumably, government and industry plutonium and uranium demand could change dramatically within the fifty year period between the 2003 start date for waste emplacement and the 2053 date for permanent closure of the repository seals. The dilemma in this second justification for retrievability is, as Lovins (1978) has noted, that what is retrievable for one group (the U.S. government) is presumably also retrievable for other groups: foreign governments, corporations, and terrorist organizations.

The mixing of objectives, such as accessibility and isolation in the case of nuclear waste disposal, creates major problems. Goble (1983) describes the parallel case of the Egyptian Pharoahs, who mixed the objectives of providing for regal, opulent display, and very long term preservation of their own remains and accoutrements, in the building of their tombs within the pyramids. This combination of objectives resulted in rapid and repeated plunder of the tombs, which began soon after the time of their closure. The objective of a fifty year retrieval period for the HLW and TRU repositories conflicts in several respects, both technical and social, with the separate objective of complete radionuclide containment and isolation from the surface environment.

Another objection to a fifty year period of retrievability, from an opposite perspective, is that fifty years is rather arbitrary, and perhaps a much longer period of time is needed to assess the geological stability and hydrologic suitability of a site.   It appears that DOE is attempting to create a HLW program which combines temporary retrievable storage with long term disposal, and in the process is raising serious concerns about the integrity of both the MRS and the HLW repository facilities. At the same time, it must be acknowledged that these conflicting objectives can cause problems for all levels of nuclear waste, including LLW.

Transuranic Wastes and WIPP

A traditional rule of thumb within the nuclear industry is that nuclear waste should be confined for ten half lives of the dominant radioisotope before it can be considered "non-hazardous" (Milnes, 1985). The WIPP, excavated in a salt bed near Carlsbad, New Mexico, is scheduled to begin receiving the first of approximately six million cubic feet of plutonium laden waste in 1989. Two plutonium isotopes are predominant among the transuranic wastes that will be shipped to WIPP. Plutonium-238, with a half life of 86 years, is estimated to account for 3.4 million out of the 4.0 million curies expected to be delivered to WIPP, and the canisters containing high concentrations of Pu-238 will be handled remotely (Neill and Channell, 1983). Because of the relatively short half life of Pu-238 in comparison with Pu-239's half life of 24,000 years, the latter isotope is of concern for long term environmental protection. The repository will be expected to confine the waste for 10,000 years since WIPP is subject to EPA's repository regulations in

40CFR191, which stipulate such long term performance assessments. If the "ten half lives" rule were applied to the Pu-239-contaminated waste destined for WIPP, however, the 10,000 year containment goal would fall far short of the mark, because ten half lives for plutonium-239 equals approximately 250,000 years. Assuming that the WIPP site succeeds in containing the waste radionuclides for 10,000 years, the Pu-239 would not yet have undergone even one half life of decay.

It is fortunate that no HLW are to be buried at WIPP, because the high levels of heat emitted by HLW would have had detrimental interactions with the surrounding salt; salt is known to expand when exposed to heat. In contrast, the contact-handled TRU canisters are not high heat emitters, although some of the remotely handled TRU canisters will emit heat (Lipschutz, 1980; Neill and Channell, 1983).

Both physical and human induced containment breaches are perhaps more probable at WIPP than at the proposed Yucca Mountain HLW site. The existence of pressurized brine reservoirs at WIPP is the source of ongoing controversy over the site's potential for future salt dissolution problems, and even now in some of the excavated salt rooms at WIPP there is constant brine seepage. Future mining of potash or natural gas at the WIPP site has been predicted to cause no significant public health threat by the New Mexico Environmental Evaluation Group (EEG), a group of scientists who evaluate WIPP for the State of New Mexico (Little, 1982). However, another group of scientists has raised concerns that future potential oil and gas drilling operations near the WIPP site could bring radionuclides to the surface (Scientists Review Panel on WIPP, 1988). A natural breach of containment of the plutonium canisters by the intrusion of water may also be a significant threat.

Many of the environmentalist criticisms of WIPP are based on the technical issues raised by the EEG and the Scientist's Review Panel on WIPP, composed of several University of New Mexico scientists, and by the engineers, geologists, and other scientists at the EEG. The environmentalist critique of WIPP has tended to center on the specific geologic and radiologic flaws of the facility and on transportation risks, and has tended to ignore the broader policy question of "what is the best storage or disposal option for isolating TRU wastes?". The same lack of a broader policy overview characterizes the federal government's awkward policy switches on the mission of WIPP; Congress and the DOE essentially "backed in" to the decision to "store" TRU wastes at WIPP (Carter, 1987: 176-193).

There are several key issues at WIPP that have significant time and land use dimensions; among them are the half life of plutonium-239, discussed above, and the rate of salt creep. It has been estimated that the excavated rooms at WIPP are closing at the rate of three inches per year (Chaturvedi, 1988). This rapid rate of closure will place limits on any retrieval period for the TRU canisters. Other time/land use issues at WIPP include future mining activities that may cause a breach of containment (both potash mining and salt solution mining are possible in the WIPP area), and the one hundred year institutional control period (which may be too short), mandated by the EPA regulations.

Perhaps the single most troublesome issue at WIPP is in the nature of the facility itself: the fact that WIPP is a "pilot" facility. Many critics of DOE's management of WIPP ask why DOE persists in calling it a pilot project when virtually all of the nation's TRU waste will soon be emplaced there with the goal of permanent geologic isolation. The current plan for WIPP includes a five year study phase, beginning with the date of opening, during which approximately 160,000 barrels, or fifteen percent of the total 1.1 million TRU barrels, will be emplaced for study in the repository. DOE has proposed that this five year experimental phase be completed before DOE applies for EPA certification of WIPP under the 40CFR191 regulations. In the first year and a half of this study period, the DOE has announced that it will emplace about three percent of the total number of barrels (about 30,000) for an initial study of waste/host rock interactions. This latter plan is DOE's response to the EEG and National Academy of Sciences panel recommendations that no more drums than those necessary for study and experimentation be placed underground, until crucial uncertainties about brine accumulation could be reduced (Helminski, 1988b).

The WIPP facility provides an excellent example of the land use/time nexus in nuclear waste disposal. The EPA standards under 40CFR191 require a one hundred year institutional control period for geologic repositories, during which there should be both active and passive institutional control over the facility. The active institutional controls include restricting site access, monitoring local groundwater for radionuclide content, and control and cleanup of any radionuclide releases from the site. Passive institutional control is intended to continue indefinitely into the future, and includes the long term maintenance of documents concerning the location and contents of the repository. WIPP's surface land area is divided into three concentric circles labelled Control Zones I, II, and III, which together encompass WIPP's 10,000 acres. Control Zone III, the outermost zone, provides one mile of a subsurface geologic barrier to future human encroachment of the repository (Cason, 1988). It is not clear how future salt and potash miners will be kept from drilling into the repository following the one hundred year active institutional control period.

Retrievability at WIPP is essentially the same as that being planned for the HLW repository: near term retrieval capabilities will be followed by permanent site closure and sealing of all rooms, shafts, and boreholes. Unlike the proposed HLW repository at Yucca Mountain, the WIPP site will be sealed via plastic flow of the salt itself as well as by engineered sealing components.

Low Level Wastes

Longevity of hazard is as important in LLW management as it is in HLW and TRU management. As discussed above in the sections on nuclear waste categories and real world experience, LLW as currently defined in Federal regulations contains a small portion of very long lived radionuclides, known as Class C and GTCC wastes. In addition, some of the so-called "short lived" nuclides have half lives of tens of years and present acute exposure hazards. The current LLW interstate compact system is encouraging the proliferation of radioactive waste disposal sites. An overlooked problem is that of LLW generated during the manufacture of nuclear weapons, to which the DOE began to give greater attention in 1988. All of these concerns relate to the question of the permanence of "nuclear waste landscapes": What is the longevity of the various radionuclides in the existing commercial and military LLW streams? How many new sites are being developed, and what are the hazardous lifetimes of the facilities? Can poorly managed military LLW sites be cleaned up and restored? And is storage a feasible option for the management of LLW?

Federal regulatory definitions of the separate LLW categories are arbitrary. However, since LLW is essentially a catch all category for all nuclear wastes which are neither HLW nor TRU, nor mill tailings, some further distinctions within the LLW category must be drawn, as described in the section above on "categories, definitions and controversies." Thus, the NRC has defined (and in 1986 revised) the LLW subcategories called Class A, B, C, and GTCC, as well as a subcategory at the other end of the concentration scale, "Below Regulatory Concern". Recall that in May 1988 the NRC issued its final rulemaking on GTCC waste, stating that it must now be disposed in the future HLW repository. As of July 1988, however, permission was being granted for whole decommissioned reactors to be disposed at LLW sites, as in the case of Northern States Power's Pathfinder reactor, which was scheduled to be shipped to the Hanford commercial LLW facility in 1988 (American Nuclear Society, 1988). Within Class C, there are several possible components, such as spent ion exchange resins and reactor internals, which can contain radioactive elements of very long half lives. Though Class C requirements include packages that must maintain their integrity for three hundred years, few structural or packaging materials have been in use long enough to predict such long term integrity.

On the other end of the LLW scale, there are the wastes which have been called "de minimus" or Below Regulatory Concern (BRC). The BRC wastes are those which contain radionuclides in very dilute concentrations, dissolved in organic solvents, or mixed in with large quantities of trash, solid activated carbon, diatomaceous earth, or other solid materials. Some critics have charged that NRC is moving to classify greater and greater quantities of the LLW stream as BRC in an effort to deregulate nuclear wastes (Resnikoff, 1987b; D'Arrigo, 1987a). Indeed, some LLRW disposal authorities, such as that of Texas, have already promulgated rules which will allow BRC wastes to be sent to municipal solid waste landfills. The Texas policy allows nuclides with half lives of three hundred days or less to be sent to Class I municipal landfills, and is based on a radiological risk assessment model (Rogers, Baird and Pollard, 1987). It is certainly not clear that municipal landfill disposal of short lived radionuclides is an environmentally sound practice. However, the Texas policy may be unique in that its disposal scheme is based upon nuclide longevity, a concept that we think should be applied more widely in nuclear waste management and policymaking.

Status of the Compact System

As a response to the 1979-80 political crisis over LLW disposal at Beatty (Nevada), Hanford (Washington) and Barnwell (South Carolina), Congress passed the LLW laws. These laws stipulate that states, not the federal government, must be responsible for regulating the disposal of commercial LLW generated within their borders. States are encouraged under the Acts to form interstate compacts wherein one state is chosen to host a regional LLW site, and are given strict time-tables with which to meet planning and siting deadlines or "milestones." It is now clear that the LLW law may result in an undesirable plethora of new LLW sites. Nine interstate compacts have been ratified by Congress. Seven other states are "going it alone", and if three of these states develop their own sites, as Texas and New York are now planning, there could be thirteen operating commercial LLW sites by 1993 (cf. Table 5.1).

Military LLW

In addition to the multitude of commercial LLW sites that are closed, currently operating, and on the planning boards, there are many military LLW sites in the United States which are often overlooked in discussions of LLW policy (Coyle et al, 1988). Low level nuclear waste generated during the process of manufacturing nuclear weapons is significant because its total national volume and its total radioactivity are each approximately double that of commercial LLW (Klein, 1987; DOE, 1987b). The SRP generates about one million cubic feet of solid LLW per year (Cook, 1987). In contrast to commercial LLW, military LLW receives little public scrutiny, and it is subject only to self-regulation by its sole generator, DOE; NRC has no jurisdiction over military LLW.

Some of this military LLW is contaminated with TRU material such as plutonium-239; as long as a waste contains less than 100 nanocuries per gram of transuranics the DOE considers it to be LLW. This TRU contamination can also occur with commercial LLW. At the SRP, TRU waste with less than 10 nanocuries per gram of alpha activity is disposed as LLW, and TRU waste with between ten and one hundred nanocuries per gram of alpha activity is subjected to greater confinement disposal (Cook, 1987). "Greater Confinement Disposal" consists of putting those canisters into bore holes at the SRP. Other current disposal methods for LLW at SRP include incineration and emplacement into trenches of twenty feet depth. Cardboard boxes are also used to dispose of most military LLW (Lawless, 1985). Since the beginning of the Manhattan Project, liquid nuclear wastes have been allowed to seep into the ground through discharge to unlined seepage basins or cribs; the justification used by the Atomic Energy Commission and the DOE is that the ion-exchange and sorption properties of the soil would retard the radionuclides as they leached through the soil.

The DOE does not keep detailed statistics on its liquid LLW discharges (Lawless, 1985); its justification is that liquid discharge to the "soil column" is a time worn, standard practice which is only used for liquid waste streams containing very low concentrations of radionuclides. In 1984, the DOE issued new guidelines for military LLW management; these did not restrict seepage basin use, and DOE's order for a new weapons production reactor contains a provision for a new LLW seepage pond (Lawless, 1985).

Proposals for New LLW Management Policies

In contrast to the government and nuclear industry view that LLW can be safely disposed with presently available technology, many environmentalists and nuclear critics point out that LLW is merely a catch all term for all nuclear waste which falls out of the official TRU and HLW categories, and that a small but significant portion of LLW is either highly radioactive or extremely long lived or both. Critics of the nuclear industry have developed a number of policy options in response to these LLW hazards. One recent proposal, developed at a conference of grassroots LLW activists, supports a redefinition of LLW as that nuclear waste that has a hazardous life no greater than 100 years, which is the active institutional control period required by NRC regulations (D'Arrigo, 1987b). This proposal is based on the assumption that since LLW sites are to be released for "productive" use after one hundred years (NRC, 1982), they should not contain any isotopes which present a hazard after that point.

Another grassroots policy initiative on LLW regards the storage option as preferable to disposal, given the present lack of knowledge about containment technologies and long term radiation health effects. The Coalition on West Valley Nuclear Wastes, of upstate New York, has proposed that all LLW be stored retrievably in above ground, monitored, engineered facilities (Coalition, 1988). The Coalition's proposal is based on a critique of current government LLW disposal policy: whereas federal regulations assume that LLW disposal is both permanent and inaccessible, it may in reality only be inaccessible, but not permanent given that all landfills eventually leak. The proposal also states that future generations can better protect themselves from radiologic hazards if they can have ready access to a LLW containment facility, and if they can make their own choices, given the state of technology development at that time, about storage versus disposal of LLW.

Conclusions

There are inevitable tradeoffs in deciding between permanent geologic isolation of nuclear wastes, and monitored, retrievable, temporary storage; these tradeoffs apply to TRU and LLW as well as to HLW. There will be a burden of vigilance and environmental risks placed on future generations regardless of whether nuclear wastes are disposed in deep geologic repositories or emplaced in above-ground vaults, concrete bunkers, or sealed cask "warehouses". When confronted with a set of policy tradeoffs, the ultimate decision is a judgement based upon the value system of the decisionmakers. Therefore, it is important to analyze the value system of the stakeholders who affect nuclear waste decisions (Colglazier, Dungan and Reaven, 1987). We have outlined the value systems of various stakeholders in the nuclear waste arena: scientists, government and industry representatives, environmentalists, and Indian tribes, with a particular emphasis on their time perspectives.

Time is an important dimension in nuclear waste policy that has been underemphasized in certain key categories of nuclear waste management. Among these categories are the proposed MRS facility for spent fuel storage, LLW management and disposal, and TRU waste disposal at the WIPP and elsewhere. Most of the policy decisions about nuclear waste issues are made at the federal level by Congress, NRC, DOE, and EPA, where a range of underlying values serves to guide policymaking. Such values as *immediacy* in protection against acute radiological hazards and in "solving" perceived nuclear waste crises, *political expediency* in appeasement of influential groups, and *geographic isolation* of nuclear wastes from densely populated areas, have had more influence over federal nuclear waste policymaking than has the value of *long range planning*. There are notable exceptions to this generalization. The EPA's nuclear waste regulation, 40CFR191, requires the HLW and TRU repositories to be subject to 1,000 and 10,000 year performance evaluations; and NRC's 10CFR61 regulation of LLW requires that Class C LLW packages be able to contain their wastes for three hundred years, and also requires a one hundred year institutional control period for disposal sites. Similar requirements for institutional control will be placed on the HLW and TRU repositories. However, as noted above, the LLW regulations alone do not satisfy the need for long term protection of human health and the environment, since some radionuclides in Class C LLW have half lives much longer than one hundred years.

Interregional equity is a value which played a crucial role in the passage of the LLW and original HLW laws. However, the principle that the states should be responsible for commercial LLW has been taken to its absurd extreme in that LLW sites are now proliferating like mushrooms. The present LLW policy decisions being taken by the federal government and the states will result in a national landscape dotted with nuclear waste sites, most of which will eventually leach radionuclides into the soil unless the wastes are stored retrievably. The present commercial LLW compact system has the effect of "spreading the misery", to borrow Carter's (1987) phrase (with which he criticized the NWPA program of multiple, regional HLW repositories).

Long range planning on the order of fifty to a thousand years or more is anathema to most nuclear industry managers, who see the nuclear waste problem as a political millstone which they must bury as quickly as possible so that they can get on with the business of generating electricity or manufacturing nuclear weapons. Short term, "bottom line" mindsets are not unique to the nuclear industry; even social scientists and planners do not typically design for greater than fifty year time horizons (Tonn, 1986).

Nuclear wastes require long range planning because they present long range hazards, and any nuclear waste policy must be based on the hazardous life of the waste if it is to be both responsible and realistic. To date, neither the nuclear industry, nor the federal agencies charged with regulating it, have developed comprehensive policies which take the hazardous life of nuclear waste into account. Even the NRC 10CFR60 and 10CFR61 regulations on LLW, which are based in part upon certain indicator nuclides, are an insufficient means of categorizing nuclear wastes because they fail to account for the complete range of long lived nuclides which can be present in LLW.

Indian tribes, environmental organizations, and some local rights activists have perspectives on the nuclear waste dilemma which include a concern for intergenerational equity, as well as concern for the long range integrity of natural ecosystems. The nuclear industry, DOE, NRC, and their friends in Congress have often side stepped these perspectives in setting the national nuclear waste agenda. The incorporation of these neglected perspectives into national nuclear waste policy would lead to a reexamination of nuclear power and weapons production priorities in light of the nuclear waste burden which these activities foist on to future generations. It would also lead to a nuclear waste program that categorized and sequestered nuclear wastes according to their hazardous life, an approach which is now only partially taken by federal policy. For LLW this might mean having three categories of LLW sites: one for short lived ($<$ one year half lives), one for intermediate lived (one year to 100 year half lives), and one for long lived nuclear wastes. For HLW, this policy would mean storage of spent fuel for ten to fifty years to allow for decay of short lived isotopes such as cesium-137, followed by deep geologic isolation in a host rock with low probabilities of human intrusion and chronic or catastrophic geologic events that could increase the rate of radionuclide leakage. For TRU, the same deep geologic disposal strategy is appropriate.

Federal definitions of various nuclear waste categories must change if they are to reflect the reality that a small but significant portion of "low level waste" is not short lived. In 1988 the NRC took a step in the right direction when it ruled that GTCC wastes must be disposed in the HLW repository when it begins operation. This ruling is important because many large nuclear power reactors will be decommissioned starting around the turn of the century, and much of the reactor internals will be classified as GTCC. Serious consideration should also be given to disposing of Class C wastes in the HLW repository, since they, like the GTCC wastes, can contain significant quantities of long lived radioisotopes or those nuclides which present acute exposure hazards. When many older nuclear power plants begin to be decommissioned around the turn of the century, the issue of GTCC and Class C waste disposal will become even more crucial as dismantled reactor vessels add highly radioactive metals to the waste stream.

Military nuclear waste is an underregulated problem that will continue to worsen as long as the DOE refuses to release statistics on such programs as the liquid LLW seepage basins, and refuses to subject its programs to scrutiny and regulation by an independent government agency. The long term hazards presented by military LLW are significant, especially in light of the fact that military LLW often contains alpha emitting nuclides of extremely long half lives.

With respect to the proposed Monitored Retrievable Storage (MRS) facility, DOE has not yet provided enough information in order for a full long range analysis to be made of the proposal (GAO, 1987; DOE, 1988a; DOE, 1987a). In particular, the proposed engineering design life of the MRS, including the specifications for the dry cask lifetime and the provision of spare parts for the MRS need to be provided by DOE; this information is needed in order to analyze the adequacy of DOE's plans for the facility, both for its proposed forty year operation, and for the contingency of extended operation for fifty to a hundred years if such storage ability becomes necessary.

Potential time related problems at the WIPP site are numerous and, because of the 24,000 year half life of plutonium-239, one of the dominant waste isotopes to be emplaced in WIPP's deep salt caverns. Among these potential problems are the relatively short (one hundred year) institutional control period for the site, and the existence of langbeinite and other economically valuable minerals at and around the WIPP site, (which may attract future mining activities).

Whereas salt creep is occurring in the excavated rooms at WIPP, retrievability will be nearly impossible, or at least dangerous to workers, within a few decades of waste emplacement.

Benjamin Franklin's adage "haste makes waste" seems particularly apt in describing the present state of nuclear waste policymaking at the federal level, in which virtual neglect from the 1940s until the late 1970s (League of Women Voters, 1985: 27) has been followed by decisions made in a climate of urgency and political duress by Congress and the DOE. The extremely long technical and environmental time frames required for sound nuclear waste management are severly mismatched with the relatively short political and institutional time frames used by decisionmakers (Goble, 1983). In this paper we have shown how nuclear waste management policies for all three major categories of radioactive wastes have neglected the time dimension in favor of other considerations such as political expediency and perceived urgency. Present nuclear waste management plans are creating a U.S. landscape burdened with permanent disposal facilities designed according to quite temporary objectives.

NOTES

1. Half life is a measure of the time in which it takes for a given radioisotope to decay to one-half of its original mass.

2. Deep geological disposal of radioactive wastes was acutely characterized by both environmentalist Amory Lovins and science journalist Luther Carter as a paradox (Lovins, 1978; Carter, 1983). The Paradox Basin of Utah and Colorado, which was once investigated by the U.S. Department of Energy for HLW disposal, was seen as symbolic because the geological investigations required to confirm site suitability give rise to further uncertainties of the suitability of a rock formation. We argue that radioactive waste disposal gives rise to a wide range of social, political, and scientific paradoxes and uncertainties,

though we perhaps have less confidence than Carter that these problems can be solved. See, e.g., Carter (1987).

3. None of the three MRS Commissioners, Dale Klein, Frank Parker, or Alexander Radin, are known to be opposed to the idea of an MRS as an "integral part" of a national spent fuel management system. In our opinion, however, they are conducting the MRS hearings in a thorough manner, allowing all sides of the debate to air their views.

REFERENCES

American Nuclear Society, 1988, "Late News in Brief," *Nuclear News* 31: 124.

Brookins, D.G, 1984, *Geochemical Aspects of Radioactive Waste Disposal,* New York, NY: Springer-Verlag.

Campbell, J. and R. Cranwell, 1988, "Performance Assessment of Radioactive Waste Repositories," *Science* 239: 1389-1392.

Carothers, A., 1988, "The Death of Ellenton," *Greenpeace* 13.

Carter, L. J. 1987, *Nuclear Imperatives and Public Trust: Dealing with Radioactive Waste,* Washington, DC: Resources for the Future.

_____, 1983, "The Radwaste Paradox," *Science* 217: 33-36.

Cason, J.E., 1988, Deputy Assistant Secretary, U.S. Department of the Interior, Testimony before the Subcommittee on Energy and the Environment, Committee on Interior and Insular Affairs, House of Representatives, on H.R. 2504, the "Land Withdrawal" Bill for the Waste Isolation Pilot Plant.

Chaturvedi, L., 1988, "Issues to be Resolved at the Waste Isolation Pilot Plant," paper presented at *Waste Management 1988,* University of Arizona, College of Engineering and Mines, Tucson, AZ.

Coalition on West Valley Nuclear Wastes, 1988, *Retrievability,* East Concord, New York.

Colglazier, E.W., D.L. Dungan, and S.J. Reaven, 1987, "Value Issues and Stakeholders' Views in Radioactive Waste Management," in R.G. Post (ed), *Waste Management 1987,* Vol. 1, Tucson, AZ: University of Arizona, College of Engineering and Mines.

Colglazier, E.W. and M.R. English, 1988, "Low-Level Radioactive Waste: Can New Disposal Sites Be Found?" in M.E. Burns (ed), *Low Level Radioactive Waste Regulation: Science, Politics and Fear,* Chelsea, MI: Lewis Publishers.

Commonwealth of Kentucky, 1984, *Comprehensive Low-Level Radioactive Waste Management Plan for the Commonwealth of Kentucky,* Kentucky Natural Resources and Environmental Protection Cabinet, DOE/ID/12348-TG, Frankfort, KY.

Cook, J.R., 1987, "New Low Level Radioactive Waste Storage/Disposal Facilities for the Savannah River Plant," in R.G. Post (ed), *Waste Management 1987,* Vol. 3, Tucson, AZ: University of Arizona, College of Engineering and Mines.

Coyle, D. et al, 1988, *Deadly Defense: Military Radioactive Landfills,* New York, NY: Radioactive Waste Campaign.

D'Arrigo, D., 1987a, *Comments on Nuclear Regulatory Commission 10CFR Part 60 Advance Notice of Proposed Rulemaking,* definition of "High Level Radioactive Waste," Nuclear Information and Resource Service, Washington, DC.

_____, 1987b, "NIRS Sponsors Low-Level Waste Conference," *Groundswell* (Autumn) 10/12.

Darwin, Sir C.G., 1956, "The Time Scale in Human Affairs," in W.L. Thomas, Jr. (ed), *Man's Role in Changing the Face of the Earth,* Chicago, IL: University of Chicago Press.

Davis, J.A., 1988, "The Wasting of Nevada," *Sierra* (Sierra Club) (July/August).

Devgun, J.S. and D.H. Charlesworth, 1987, "Impacts of Past Experience on Engineering a Shallow Land Burial Facility," in R. Post (ed), *Waste Management 1987,* Vol. 3, Tucson, AZ: University of Arizona, College of Engineering and Mines.

Fehringer, D. and R. Boyle, 1987, "Status of NRC Rulemaking for High Level Radioactive Waste Disposal," in R.G. Post (ed), *Waste Management 1987,* Vol. 2, Tucson, AZ: University of Arizona, College of Engineering and Mines.

Freudenburg, W., 1987, "Rationality and Irrationality in Estimating the Risks of Nuclear Waste Disposal," in R. Post (ed), *Waste Management 1987,* Vol. 2, Tucson, AZ: University of Arizona, College of Engineering and Mines.

Friends of the Earth, 1987, "An Easy Question," *Not Man Apart* (November/December) 17/6 Editorial: 2.

Goble, R.L., 1983, "Time Scales and the Problem of Radioactive Waste," in R.E. Kasperson (ed), *Equity Issues in Radioactive Waste Management,* Cambridge, MA: Oelgeschlager, Gunn and Hain.

Gover, B.K., 1987, "Indian Tribes Enter the Nuclear Waste Debate," *The Workbook:* Magazine of the Southwest Research and Information Center 12/3.

Helminski, E., 1988a, "DOE Scientist's Report Questions Viability of Nevada Yucca Mntn. Site," *The Radioactive Exchange* (Jan. 22) 7/1, E. Helminski, publisher.

_____, 1988b, "DOE Accepts NAS WIPP Panel Advice, But Not As Media Reports," *The Radioactive Exchange* (March 21) 7/5.

_____, 1988c, "Our Man in Nevada," *The Radioactive Exchange* (May 15) 7/9.

_____, 1988d, "NRC Finally Issues HLW, GTCC Redefinition in Federal Register," *The Radioactive Exchange* (May 31) 7/10.

_____, 1988e, "Amended HLW Mission Plan Raises Possibility of an 'Earlier' MRS," *The Radioactive Exchange* (July 5) 7/12.

Hunt, C.B., 1983, "How Safe are Nuclear Waste Sites?" *Geotimes.*

Kasperson, R.E., P. Derr and R.W. Kates, 1983, "Confronting Equity in Radioactive Waste Management: Modest Proposals for a Socially Just and Acceptable Program," in R. Kasperson (ed), *Equity Issues in Radioactive Waste Management,* Cambridge, MA: Oelgeschlager, Gunn and Hain.

Klein, J.A., 1987, "The Integrated Data Base Program: An Executive Level Data Base of Spent Fuel and Radioactive

Waste Inventories, Projections, and Characteristics," in R. Post (ed), *Waste Management 1987*, Vol. 3, Tucson, AZ: University of Arizona, College of Engineering and Mines.

Knecht, M.A., O.I. Oztunali, A.L. Dressen, 1987, "Characterization of Non-DOE Greater-Than-Class-C Low Level Waste," in R. Post (ed), *Waste Management 1987*, Vol. 3, Tucson, AZ: University of Arizona, College of Engineering and Mines.

Lawless, W.F., 1985, "Problems with Military Nuclear Waste," *Bulletin of the Atomic Scientists* 41/10: 38-42.

Lawroski, H., 1987, "Alternative Enhanced Low Level Radioactive Waste Burial," in R. Post (ed), *Waste Management 1987*, Vol. 3, Tucson, AZ: University of Arizona, College of Engineering and Mines.

League of Women Voters, 1985, *The Nuclear Waste Primer*, (S. Wiltshire and I. Weber) New York, NY: Nick Lyons Books.

Lipschutz, R., 1980, *Radioactive Waste: Politics, Technology and Risk*, Cambridge, MA: Ballinger.

Little, M. S., 1982, *Potential Release Scenarios and Radiological Consequence Evaluation of Mineral Resources at WIPP*, EEG-12, Environmental Evaluation Group, Health and Environment Department, Santa Fe, NM.

Lovins, A.B., 1978, *Comments on the 10/78 Draft IRG Report to the President* (TID-28817 draft), unpublished memo to the Interagency Review Group on Nuclear Waste Management, available from the Rocky Mountain Institute, Old Snowmass, Colorado.

Manion, W.J., 1980, *Decommissioning Handbook*, prepared for the U.S. Department of Energy, Washington, DC.

Marshall, E., 1986a, "Nuclear Waste Program Faces Political Burial," *Science* 233: 835-836.

_____, 1986b, "The Buried Cost of the Savannah River Plant," *Science* 233: 613-615.

Merz, E.R., 1987, "Time Period of Concern for Judging the Long Term Hazards of Geological Disposal of Radioactive Waste," in R.G. Post (ed), *Waste Management 1987*, Vol. 3, Tucson, AZ: University of Arizona, College of Engineering and Mines.

Milnes, A.G., 1985, *Geology and Radwaste,* New York, NY: Academic Press.

Monti, G.G., 1987, "The Role of the Public in Siting and Regulatory Issues," paper presented at the DOE Annual LLW Management Conference, Denver, CO.

National Research Council, 1984, *Social and Economic Aspects of Radioactive Waste Disposal,* panel on Social and Economic Aspects of Radioactive Waste Management, R.E. Kasperson, chair, Washington, DC: National Academy Press.

Neill, R.H. and J.K. Channell, 1983, *Potential Problems from Shipment of High-Curie Content Contact-Handled Transuranic Waste to WIPP,* Environmental Evaluation Group, Santa Fe, NM.

O'Donnell, F, 1983, "Insights Gained from NRC Research Investigations at the Maxey Flats LLW Shallow Land Burial Facility," *Proceedings of the Fifth Annual Participants' Information Meeting,* DOE Low Level Waste Management Program, EGG Idaho, Idaho Falls.

Office of Technology Assessment (OTA), U.S. Congress, 1988, *An Evaluation of Options for Managing Greater-Than-Class-C Low Level Radioactive Waste,* OTA-BP-O-50, Washington, DC: O.T.A.

Parker, F.L., R.E. Kasperson, T.L. Anderson, and S.A. Parker, 1987, *Technical and Sociopolitical Issues in Radioactive Waste Disposal,* Vol. 1, Safety, Siting, and Interim Storage, Stockholm: Beijer Institute, Royal Swedish Academy of Sciences.

Parsons, Ralph M. Company, 1985, *Monitored Retrievable Storage (MRS) Facility;* brochure prepared for the U.S. Department of Energy, Washington, DC.

Peaudecerf P., M. D'Alessandro, M. Canceill, J. Fourniquet, and P. Godefroy, 1985, "The Geoforecasting Approach and Long Term Prediction of Evolutive Nuclide Migration," in R. Simon (ed), *Radioactive Waste Management and Disposal,* Cambridge, UK: Cambridge University Press.

Resnikoff, M., 1987a, "Buried Forever? The U.S. Experience of Radioactive Waste Disposal," in A. Blowers and D. Pepper (eds), *Nuclear Power in Crisis: Politics and Planning for the Nuclear State,* London: Croom Helm.

_____, 1987b, *Living Without Landfills,* New York, NY: Radioactive Waste Campaign.

_____, 1987c, "Case for MRS Gets Weaker," *RWC Waste Paper* 9/182: 3-4.

Robinson, G., 1978, "Bringing it all Home," *Environmental Action* 10/14: 11.

Rogers, V.C., R.D. Baird and C.G. Pollard, 1987, "Disposal of Short Lived Radionuclide Wastes in Sanitary Landfills," in R.G. Post (ed), *Waste Management 1987,* Vol. 3, Tucson, AZ: University of Arizona, College of Engineering and Mines.

Russ, G.D., 1986, *Low Level Radioactive Waste: Building a Perspective,* Bethesda, MD: Atomic Industrial Forum.

_____, 1984, *Nuclear Waste Disposal: Closing the Circle,* Bethesda, MD: Atomic Industrial Forum.

Schneider, K., 1988, "U.S. Scales Back Plan for Burial of Atomic Waste," *New York Times,* March 11: A1, D17.

Scientists Review Panel on WIPP, 1988, *Evaluation of the Waste Isolation Pilot Plant (WIPP) as a Water Saturated Nuclear Waste Repository,* Albuquerque, New Mexico, p. 9.

Shrader-Frechette, K.S., 1988, "Values and Hydrogeological Method: How Not to Site the World's Largest Nuclear Dump," in J. Byrne and D. Rich (eds), *Planning Under Changing Energy Conditions,* New Brunswick, NJ: Transaction Books.

Sierra Club, 1985, *A "Low Level" Nuclear Waste Primer,* Sierra Club Radioactive Waste Campaign Fact Sheet.

Solomon, B.D. and D.M. Cameron, 1984, "The Impact of Nuclear Power Plant Dismantlement on Radioactive Waste Disposal," *Man, Environment, Space and Time* 4/1: 39-60.

Solomon, B.D. and F.M. Shelley, 1988, "Siting Patterns of Nuclear Waste Repositories," *Journal of Geography* 87: 59-71.

Spence, C., 1988, "OCRWM's Fiscal Year 1989 Budget Request Gets a Relatively Quiet Hearing in the House," *Oversite* March 18, No. 63: 13.

Thiers, G.R. and T.R. Wathen, 1987, "Recent Developments in Disposal and Isolation of Uranium Mill Tailings under the

UMTRA Program," in R.G. Post (ed), *Waste Management 1987* Vol. 3, Tucson, AZ: University of Arizona, College of Engineering and Mines.

Tonn, B.E., 1986, "500 Year Planning: A Speculative Provocation," *Journal of the American Planning Association* 52: 185-193.

U.S. Department of Energy (DOE), 1988a, *Draft 1988 Mission Plan Amendment*, DOE/RW-0187, Oak Ridge, TN: U.S. Department of Energy.

_____, 1988b, *Site Characterization Plan Overview. Yucca Mountain Site, Nevada Research and Development Area, Nevada*, DOE/RW-0161, Washington, DC: U.S. Department of Energy.

_____, 1987a, *Monitored Retrievable Storage Submission to Congress*, Vol. III, "MRS Program Plan," Chapter 3, Deployment Plan, Springfield, VA: National Technical Information Service.

_____, 1987b, *Integrated Data Base for 1987: Spent Fuel and Radioactive Waste Inventories, Projections, and Characteristics*, DOE/RW-0006, Rev.3, Springfield, VA: National Technical Information Service.

U.S. General Accounting Office (GAO), 1987, *Nuclear Waste: DOE Should Provide More Information on MRS*, GAO/RCED-87-92, Washington, DC: G.A.O.

U.S. Nuclear Regulatory Commission (NRC), 1986, *Technical Considerations Affecting Preparation of IX Resins for Disposal*, NUREG/CR-4601, prepared by the Brookhaven National Laboratory, Upton, NY, for the NRC.

_____, 1982, "Licensing Requirements for Land Disposal of Radioactive Waste," *Federal Register*, 47/248: 57446-57482.

Wiltshire, S., 1986, "Public Participation in Department of Energy High Level Waste Management Programs," *Tennessee Law Review* 53: 541-557.

Wood, D.E., M.H. Campbell and M.W. Shupe, 1987, "Impacts and Ramifications of Defining High Level Waste," in R.G. Post (ed), *Waste Management 1987*, Vol. 2, Tucson, AZ: University of Arizona, College of Engineering and Mines.

Economic Development, Growth and Land Use Planning in Oil and Gas Producing Regions

Robert L. Mansell

It is widely accepted that the dramatic shifts in oil prices experienced since the early 1970s have had, and continue to have, significant macroeconomic implications. In the case of both the United States and Canada, numerous studies have concluded that the upward spiral of these prices following the Arabian oil embargo in 1973 served to noticeably increase the rate of inflation, erode productivity and diminish economic growth (Perry, 1975). Similarly, the subsequent collapse of oil prices is generally recognized as making a sizeable contribution to the strong, non-inflationary economic growth enjoyed by both countries in recent years.

While these macroeconomic effects of energy price fluctuations clearly deserve attention, there is also an important regional dimension that is often overlooked. In both nations there are numerous regional economies that are heavily based on the production of oil and natural gas and, hence, which tend to be particularly sensitive to these price fluctuations, as well as the associated shifts in energy policies. Indeed, the rapid economic growth in these regions during the 1970s and the sharp reversal of their economic fortunes in recent years amply demonstrate the power of changes in oil prices to significantly and swiftly alter the regional pattern of growth and prosperity.

Given the pronounced regionalism that characterizes Canada and the United States, and the enormous social and economic costs associated with such large regional shifts, this dimension obviously has important ramifications for regional policies and planning. Not only does it point to the need for policies aimed at stabilizing the economies of these areas but, also, it emphasizes the importance of incorporating these regional supply side impacts of energy price changes in land use planning. Whereas most of the research concerning the relationship between land use planning and energy prices has focused on the demand side effects (that is, the impacts on location, transportation and housing patterns), it is apparent that in the oil and gas surplus regions it is the supply side effects which dominate. Indeed, this dimension raises serious questions about the use of traditional planning techniques in these regions. For example, with the apparent unpredictability of oil (and natural gas) prices it may simply be impossible to forecast economic and demographic variables for these areas with any reasonable degree of accuracy. Since these projections are a key ingredient to conventional planning approaches, the use of such methods is open to question and new techniques based on planning under uncertainty may be called for. Moreover, the inherent instability displayed by these economies adds another requisite for effective planning; namely, the need to allow for variability and, at the same time, to encourage and facilitate the type and rates of development necessary to bring about a reduction in this variability.

This regional dimension in the United States and Canada of fluctuations in energy prices is the primary focus in this paper. Specifically, there are two main objectives. The first is to outline the role of the oil and gas sector in regional growth and development and the mechanisms through which shifts in energy prices affect the structure and performance of the oil and gas producing regions in the two countries. The second objective is to discuss the implications for planning, and in particular, land use planning in these regions.

It should be noted at the outset that the emphasis here is on oil and gas surplus regions; that is, regions which produce more   of these commodities than they consume and, hence, where the supply side effects of energy price changes dominate the demand side effects.   Other surplus regions that produce and export significant amounts of coal and/or electricity are not considered (Miernyk et al, 1978).   Although these latter forms represent a substantial proportion of total energy supply in the two nations, they do not possess many of the characteristics which make oil and gas a unique driving force in a regional economy.[1]

Also, the focus here is limited to three representative oil and gas surplus regions.   These are the states of Texas and Oklahoma in the U.S. and the province of Alberta in Canada. Texas and Alberta, in spite of the large distance separating them and the quite different national contexts, are similar in terms of their resource base, general character, and economic performance (Mansell, 1981).   In addition, they are the dominant oil and gas producing regions within each country. There are also some notable differences.   For example the population of Texas is currently just under seventeen million compared to about 2.4 million for Alberta.   Oklahoma, with a population of 3.3 million, ranks third in the U.S. (behind Texas and Louisiana) as an oil and gas producer and is more comparable to Alberta in terms of population size.

In any event, these three cases cover a suitably broad range for the purpose of illustrating the main linkages among oil prices, economic growth and development, and land use planning in oil and gas surplus regions.   At the same time, however, it is useful to note that there are numerous other areas where these linkages and their implications are relevant.   States such as Louisiana, New Mexico, Wyoming, Kansas, Colorado and Mississippi are, or contain, important oil and gas producing regions.   Similarly, in Canada there are areas within the provinces of British Columbia, Saskatchewan and Manitoba and within the Atlantic region where the petroleum sector plays or is beginning to play a key role in the local economy.

This paper begins with a discussion of the role of the oil and gas sector in the development of a regional economy.   Here, attention is focused on the implications for the industrial structure and general character of the region. Following this is an outline of the mechanisms through which changes in oil and gas prices affect these regional economies and the nature of the impacts on economic performance and structure. The 1973-1981 experience is used to demonstrate the implications of rising oil prices while evidence from the post-1981 period is employed to illustrate the effects of falling prices.

In the next section, attention is turned to the implications for land use planning. These include the problems and challenges for planning that are associated with the unpredictability and high degree of variability exhibited by the oil and gas surplus regions. A summary is provided in the final section.

The Role of the Oil and Gas Sector in Regional Development

Initial Developmental Phase

As in many of the oil and gas surplus regions in the U.S. and Canada, the economies of Texas, Oklahoma and Alberta initially developed around an agricultural base and the evolution of a broader industrial base was impaired by a combination of economic and political factors. The main markets in the U.S. were in the densely populated northeastern states, and in Canada the dominant markets were in the central provinces of Ontario and Quebec. Consistent with profit maximizing behavior, secondary and tertiary industry tended to locate in these more populated areas, and the resulting additions to population, infrastructure and markets created opportunities for further industrialization. On the other hand, regions like Texas, Oklahoma and Alberta, with their smaller and widely dispersed populations and the great distances to the main markets, were at a significant disadvantage in attracting industry. Thus, market forces served to make them hinterland regions whose primary function was to provide raw materials to the industrial heartland.

This tendency was enhanced by political factors. In both countries national policies were aimed at promoting industrialization in the densely populated Northeastern U.S. and Central Canadian areas, primarily through high tariffs on manufactured goods. As a consequence the hinterland regions purchased their manufactured inputs at the higher prices associated with tariff protection but sold their products in unprotected and often volatile markets. Industrial development in these regions was further discouraged by regulated transportation rate structures that generally made it more profitable to locate processing activities at the market rather than at the raw material source. For example, the low rates on raw materials relative to those on manufactured products worked to reduce the locational pull for processing at the source of the raw materials.

Impacts of the Development of the Petroleum Sector

The discovery of oil and the development of the petroleum industry marked a major shift in the evolutionary path of these agrarian hinterland economies. Although oil was discovered in all three regions well before the turn of the century, it took many decades for the industry to become a substantial force. In Texas the industry came of age with the Spindletop discovery in 1901. By 1930, with many additional finds (especially in the East Texas field), petroleum had become a major factor in the Texas economy. The temporal pattern of the development of the industry in Oklahoma was similar. In Alberta, on the other hand, the turning point was not until the Leduc discovery in 1947. However, within fifteen years the petroleum industry emerged as the principal source of value added in the province.

Perhaps the most visible and commonly used indicator of the importance of a sector to a regional economy is its direct contribution to employment. Using this measure the petroleum sector would not appear to score very highly. Even in 1981, at the peak of the energy industry boom, mining (which in these regions primarily consists of the oil and gas industry) directly accounted for only 4.7 percent, 8 percent and 6.7 percent of the respective total non-agricultural employment in Texas, Oklahoma and Alberta.[2] However, one has only to observe the

dramatic   differences between these economies and their
agrarian hinterland counterparts that were not blessed with
petroleum to see that this measure masks the features which
have made this sector a dominant transforming force in the
economy.[3] As outlined by Hansen (1958) these features include:
its substantial contributions to the region's exports which, via
regional balance of payments effects, greatly increased income
and employment; its highly capital intensive nature which,
along with the specialized and technological nature of its input
requirements, generated strong backward and forward linkages
within the region, created a demand for a skilled labor force
and produced an impetus for urbanization; and, its large contributions to regional government revenues which facilitated the
rapid development of social infrastructure without the imposi-
tion of repressive levels of taxation.

It is useful at this point to expand upon several of these
features. First, it should be noted that there are few, if any,
sectors that can match the ability of the petroleum sector to
directly generate large revenues for regional governments. For
example, by 1948 gas and oil severance taxes accounted for over
thirty percent of Texas' tax revenues and over the past half
century these severance taxes have averaged twenty percent of
the State's annual tax revenues. Even more dramatic is the
situation in Alberta where, in 1981, oil and gas royalties, land
rentals, fees and bonuses accounted for 73 percent of the provincial government's total revenue.[4] Thus, many of the impacts of
the petroleum sector occur indirectly via the tax/expenditure
system rather than through its direct contributions to employment. Also important in this context is the inherent instability
of these sources of revenue and the implications for both the
variability of the regional economy and infrastructure planning.

Second, the petroleum sector ranks at or near the top in
terms of capital intensity. For example, 1986 data for Alberta
reveal that capital per worker in the oil and gas sector was
$709,000 compared to an average of just under $100,000 for the
other sectors.[5] As a consequence, the development of this sector
tends to make the region's economy heavily dependent on
investment as the engine of growth. This occurs not only

because energy investment becomes a key element of the region's aggregate demand (defined as the sum of consumption, investment, government expenditure and net exports), but also because of the development of many investment related industries (such as construction, metal fabrication, financial services and services to management) in the region. As indicated later, this reliance on the most variable component of aggregate demand has serious ramifications for the stability of the region's economy.

Third, along with these investment linkages, the petroleum sector has led to the development of many industries in the region based on the supply of production inputs (backward linkages) and the transportation, processing and marketing of output (forward linkages). Based on linkage indexes computed from input-output transactions matrices for Texas and Alberta, it is noteworthy that of the four industries with the strongest forward linkages (agriculture, mineral fuels, petroleum and coal products, and chemical and chemical products), three are related to the petroleum sector. In addition, these three industries rank among the top six in both regions in terms of backward linkages (Mansell, 1981). What emerges then is a pattern of industrial development, as predicted by the theories associated with Perloff et al (1960), that is closely tied to the resource base. In addition, it is apparent that these linkage characteristics, as well as the other features noted previously, suggest that the oil and gas industry nicely fits the classic definition of a key or 'motor' industry for the purpose of regional development. As noted by Perroux (1955), these industries tend to be characterized by large scale, where individual factors of production are separated from each other, where capital is concentrated, and where there is a high degree of specialization and technical division of labor.

In summary, it would appear that impacts of the petroleum sector on the economies of Texas, Oklahoma and Alberta generally follow those predicted by the staples or export-base theories of regional development and growth (Watkins, 1963; Chambers and Gordon, 1966; Stabler, 1968; Richards, 1985). That is, an economically exploitable staple initially attracts capital and labor to the region. This, combined with subsequent exports of the staple, generates an income and population base which, over time, leads to the development of other industries primarily dedicated to serving local markets. As explained by Norrie (1984) the end result is an economy consisting of: a large primary sector which exports most of its output to markets outside the region; an under-developed manufacturing sector; a large service sector; and an industrial structure based on processing raw materials prior to export or on providing inputs for the extractive sector.

These general characteristics are evident from the location quotients displayed in Table 6.1. These quotients measure the percentage of regional employment in each industry or sector relative to the percentage of national employment in the same industry or sector. Thus, a location quotient greater than one indicates above average specialization in that activity while a value of less than one indicates that the activity is under-represented in the region. As shown, all three regions are characterized by above average specialization in mining (primarily oil and gas), construction, transportation and utilities and trade, and relatively small manufacturing sectors. Although location quotients for agriculture are not shown for Texas and Oklahoma (due to difficulties in obtaining a consistent series of agricultural employment figures for the entire period covered), the values computed for selected years were all greater than one. For example, in 1981 and 1984 the values for Texas are 1.12 and 1.19 respectively, and the comparable values for Oklahoma are 1.61 and 1.51.

Also, as discussed in a later section, this table reveals significant and predictable shifts in the industrial structures of these regional economies. In particular, there is increased specialization in energy and energy related activities (or reduced diversity) during the period of high/rising energy prices and a reversal of this process with low/falling oil and gas prices.

Table 6.1
Location Quotients for Texas,
Oklahoma and Alberta, 1973-1985

	Texas						
	1973	1975	1977	1979	1981	1983	1985
Mining	3.11	2.99	3.21	3.31	3.79	4.49	3.93
Construction	1.24	1.38	1.50	1.51	1.53	1.56	1.41
Manufacturing	0.73	0.76	0.77	0.78	0.81	0.76	0.76
Trans/Util	1.11	1.11	1.11	1.10	1.10	1.08	1.06
Trade	1.14	1.10	1.10	1.09	1.09	1.09	1.07
Finance	1.08	1.07	1.04	1.02	0.97	1.04	1.09
Services	0.99	0.96	0.93	0.90	0.87	0.87	0.90
Government	1.00	0.97	0.96	0.96	0.92	0.95	0.98

Oklahoma

	1973	1975	1977	1979	1981	1983	1985
Mining	5.07	4.61	5.10	5.08	6.41	7.03	5.73
Construction	0.99	1.06	1.08	1.11	0.99	1.00	0.83
Manufacturing	0.67	0.71	0.70	0.72	0.75	0.69	0.73
Trans/Util	1.07	1.05	1.06	1.04	1.02	1.04	1.00
Trade	1.06	1.06	1.06	1.05	1.03	1.05	1.03
Finance	0.98	0.98	0.93	0.90	0.85	0.87	0.89
Services	0.91	0.88	0.88	0.89	0.83	0.85	0.85
Government	1.28	1.20	1.20	1.17	1.13	1.18	1.28

Alberta

	1973	1975	1977	1979	1981	1983	1985
Agriculture	2.45	2.59	1.99	1.71	1.62	1.51	1.62
Mining	2.63	2.37	2.94	3.60	3.28	3.74	3.69
Construction	1.18	1.25	1.47	1.78	1.79	1.50	1.17
Manufacturing	0.41	0.43	0.44	0.41	0.47	0.43	0.44
Trans/Util	1.00	1.00	1.00	1.06	1.01	1.05	1.05
Trade	1.09	1.06	1.09	1.04	1.03	1.05	1.03
Finance	1.06	0.89	0.97	1.01	0.97	0.98	0.96
Services	1.03	0.96	0.97	0.97	0.94	0.99	1.01
Government	0.96	1.01	0.93	0.90	1.00	1.04	1.11

Location quotients are computed using data from U.S. Department of Commerce, *Employment and Earnings, States and Areas* (various issues) and Statistics Canada, *The Labour Force*. The coefficients for Texas and Oklahoma are computed using non-agricultural employment data.

Implications for the Character of the Region

The effects of oil price changes depend not only on the structural aspects discussed above, but also on the general character of the regional economy (as defined by features such as the degree of population mobility, price and wage flexibility and adjustability of the labor force). Consequently, it is useful to briefly examine this character and the manner in which it has been shaped by the development of the oil and gas sector.

There are some striking similarities between the petroleum industry and the agricultural sector that initially dominated the economic bases of Texas, Oklahoma and Alberta. Specifically, both tend to be typified by very capital intensive production processes, a high degree of risk, externally determined prices and policies and a fairly large number of independent producing units. Thus, the development of the oil and gas industry reinforced the foundation of basically rural conservative values characterized by risk taking, rugged individualism and a strong entrepreneurial spirit. Also, like agriculture, it did not provide a broad base for organized labor. Taken together, these traits have generally meant a widespread respect for and acceptance of market forces and the need to adjust to shifts in these forces. They have also meant a history of regional governments with, at least on the surface, a non-interventionist, market bent.

There is a number of other significant characteristics of these regions, many of which can be related to the fundamental traits outlined above. One is the high degree of intraregional and interregional population and labor mobility. For example, as illustrated in Figure 6.1, variations in the rate of population growth (which primarily result from shifts in net migration) are large and they bear a strong negative relationship to changes in relative employment conditions (as measured by the level of unemployment in the region relative to that in the nation). While this mobility does help dampen the fluctuations in per capita income and unemployment rates arising from swings in the region's basic industries,[6] it also greatly complicates the land use planner's tasks.

Figure 6.1

Regional Population Change From 1973-1987 vs.
Unemployment Relative to the National Average

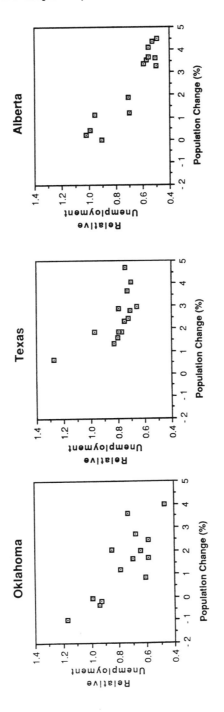

Source: Based on data from U.S. Department of Commerce, *Employment and
Earnings, States and Areas*, U.S. Bureau of the Census, *Current Population
Reports*, and Alberta Bureau of Statistics, *Alberta Statistical Review*.

Another important characteristic is the absence of many of the institutional factors which serve to reduce the volatility of prices and wages. Unlike the more industrialized regions where prices tend to be set in local or domestic markets, the prices of the key exports produced in the petroleum (and agriculture) surplus regions are typically determined in the international marketplace and subject to all of the vagaries of this market. A similar situation exists with respect to factor payments. For example, since these products are not labor intensive and since the returns to labor tend to be more of a residual than a cost based on labor contracts (which embody a significant degree of downward wage rigidity), wage and income levels in the driving sectors of these economies are subject to considerable variability. When added to the output or quantity fluctuations, the result is considerable instability of the regional economy.

In addition to their high degree of exposure to volatile international markets, these regions are very vulnerable to domestic policy shifts. Since their economies are capital intensive and largely investment driven, they are particularly sensitive to the interest rate movements associated with monetary policy. Even more important are the shifts in national energy policies. As perhaps best illustrated by the events of the 1970s, these policies tend to be shaped more by the interests of the net energy consuming regions than by the interests of the net energy producing regions. Thus, during this period they involved regulated pricing and marketing of oil and gas along with a variety of special taxes levied on the petroleum sector. More recently, with falling or depressed international oil prices, the shift has been to deregulated market pricing. Consequently, they were denied the full benefits of high/rising oil and gas prices but completely exposed to the downside of these prices. In addition to introducing an element of "policy risk" to the oil and gas surplus regions, this behavior has reinforced the sense of economic alienation that goes back to the earlier agricultural era.

Texas, Oklahoma and Alberta all have a history of discontent focused on tariffs, transportation rates, the distribution of manufacturing, monetary policy and banking. Even today there are vestiges of the political populism anchored in this discontent with federal policies and in the real or perceived abuses by big Eastern industrial and financial interests. Hence, there has been a tendency within these regions to view national energy policies as but another example of federal policies which are at their expense rather than in their interest.

It is difficult to argue that all of this alienation is based on clearly discriminatory federal policies. Part of it is no doubt simply a dissatisfaction with the results generated by a market economy and a natural response to the vulnerability and variability experienced in a hinterland economy whose fortunes are decided by factors (such as internationally determined commodity prices) that are beyond the control of the region's decision makers. However, especially in the case of energy policies, there is evidence that federal actions have tended to be more of a destabilizing than a stabilizing factor in these regional economies. For example, it is now clear that the National Energy Program introduced in Canada in late 1980 was the single most important factor in explaining the very deep and prolonged economic downturn experienced by Alberta in the early 1980s (Mansell and Percy, 1989).

It can be argued that policy responses which run counter to the interests of the energy surplus regions are systemic and, therefore, must be taken into account by the land use planner. Cheap energy is viewed within the politically powerful heartlands as an important source of comparative advantage and a prerequisite for a strong national economy. In addition, unlike labor intensive industries where the social contributions in the form of wages and employment are highly visible, the contributions of the oil and gas industry are skewed towards 'returns to capital' and typically involve widely diffused rents. Further, it is often perceived as being excessively powerful and driven by cartel determined prices. Consequently, when energy prices rise there are strong pressures on national governments to impose special taxes on the industry and/or policies to keep domestic prices below international market levels but when prices are low or falling, opposite policy responses seem unlikely even if it means a growing reliance on imported crude. This assymetry is compounded   by the long lags inherent in policy formulation and implementation which often means that by the time the energy policy comes into effect the problems it was aimed at no longer exist or are substantially different. For all of these reasons it is not unreasonable to expect that in both countries national energy policies will continue to enhance rather than reduce the variability of the energy surplus regional economies.

Oil Prices, Regional Economic Performance and Structural Change

The 1973-1981 Period

Prior to the early 1970s, real oil and natural gas prices had followed a pattern of gradual decline. In spite of this the Texas, Oklahoma and Alberta economies generally outperformed their national counterparts, albeit not by a wide margin. This situation quickly changed, however, with the oil embargo in 1973; oil prices began a dramatic upward spiral and these regional economies embarked on a growth path that was much higher than that for either national economy. This section focuses on the mechanisms through which this shift in oil prices affected the economies of these regions and the nature of the impacts.

Macro Impacts: Over the decade 1960 to 1970, the average annual rate of population growth in Texas was 1.2 times that for the United States and Alberta's was 1.1 times that for Canada (Mansell, 1981). For the period 1973 to 1981 on the other hand, this ratio moved up to 2.5 for the case of Texas and 2.9 for the case of Alberta. Oklahoma's population growth rate showed a similar increase to 1.7 times that for the United States. Over this same period the unemployment rates for Texas and Oklahoma averaged, respectively, 73 percent and 67 percent of that for the nation and Alberta's averaged 55 percent of that for Canada.[7] Data for other macro variables such as personal income and employment paint a similar picture of 'boom type' economic growth in these oil and gas surplus regions.

The substantial improvements in the performance of these regional economies are obviously related to the increases in oil and gas prices experienced over the 1970s. However, it is far from easy to completely explain this relationship, particularly since there are numerous transmission mechanisms involved, many of which involve rather indirect links between energy prices and economic growth. For example, as outlined by Miernyk (1982, 1978), Mansell (1987, 1984), Hunt (1988), Perryman (1988) and others, these mechanisms include: Leontief or input-output multipliers, Keynesian multipliers, interregional migration, investment accelerators, expenditures on public goods and interregional trade. These are discussed below.

It is now fairly evident that many of the macro impacts represented the outcome of a multiplier-accelerator process initiated by the substantial increases in energy and energy related investment that were based on rising oil and gas prices and, perhaps more importantly, on expectations of continued increases in these prices. As noted earlier, all three regions have a heavy concentration of sectors geared to the supply of inputs for capital formation and production in the oil and gas industry both within the region and in other areas. Thus, the existence of these strong linkages between the petroleum industry and other sectors set the stage for large interindustry or Leontief multiplier effects. The resulting increases in income also led to Keynesian multiplier impacts arising from additional final demand expenditures, especially those in the form of local consumption.

These effects were further enhanced by two other linkages. First, it is well established that interregional migration is driven to a large degree by regional differentials in employment and income opportunities (see Greenwood, 1975, for a dated but still very useful survey of the determinants of interregional migration). Consequently, the increases in these opportunities in the oil and gas producing regions associated with the Leontief and Keynesian multiplier effects resulted in a substantial rise in net immigration. For example, between 1972 and 1981 annual net migration to Texas rose from just under 150 thousand to about 420 thousand and in Alberta it went from thirteen thousand to over sixty thousand.[8] This induced migration, in turn, produced a population multiplier effect by further increasing consumer, investment and government demands for goods and services in these regions.

The second linkage, referred to as the accelerator mechanism, involves the relationship between investment and changes in population and income in the region. The effect is to transform any initial demographic and economic expansion into rapid growth in overall capital formation, and this provides a further stimulus to the regional economy. It is useful to note that this mechanism, along with the capital intensive nature of the oil and gas sector, worked to make investment the dominant engine of growth in these economies over the 1973-1981 period. This is perhaps best illustrated by the case of Alberta, where real investment as a percentage of real Gross Domestic Product rose from an average of twenty-three percent in the decade preceding 1973 to almost forty percent in 1981. As explained later, this certainly added to the inherent variability of the petroleum based regional economies and subsequently led to large errors in the forecasts underpinning land use and infrastructure planning.

There is also an important transmission mechanism involving interregional trade. Specifically, the increase in energy prices meant a dramatic improvement in the terms of trade for the oil and gas surplus regions. That is, the rise in the value of their exports relative to the price of their imports generated a significant increase in wealth and purchasing power within these regions. Moreover, unlike the case of international trade, there is no opportunity for offsetting exchange rate adjustments since interregional trade involves a common currency. In any case, unless the additional wealth and purchasing power is stored in the form of a fiscal surplus by the regional government or drained out of the region by federal fiscal policy, the result for these surplus regions is typically a combination of higher prices (and wages) and higher employment, production and per capita income. This expansion also involves the multiplier and accelerator mechanisms outlined above.

Another linkage involves the role of energy prices in the location of industry. The general argument here is that the dramatic increases in oil prices over this period may have created a stronger tendency for energy intensive industries to locate near the energy source or to locate so as to further reduce transportation costs (since rising oil prices will presumably increase transportation costs). While there were no doubt some instances of such locational shifts which favored the oil and gas surplus regions, this mechanism is not generally believed to represent a significant part of the explanation of the rapid growth in these regions during the 1970s (Schmenner, 1984).

The other transmission mechanisms involve somewhat more round about processes. First, there is the energy rent distribution mechanism. That is, higher oil and gas prices meant larger energy rents and a significant proportion of these were collected by the governments of the producing regions through severance taxes or royalties, bonuses, land rentals and so on. The rapid growth in the fiscal surpluses of these governments not only allowed them to greatly expand infrastructure and the provision of public goods over this period but, also, to do this without increasing taxes and draining off private demand. Hence, this provided a further impetus for growth in these regions. Second, it has been argued by some authors (for example, Winer and Gauthier, 1982) that the associated increase in net fiscal benefits (measured as the difference between the value of public amenities provided for residents of the region and the taxes they must pay to support them) induced more migration to the oil and gas surplus regions than would otherwise have been the case. At this point, it will suffice to note that the empirical evidence concerning the existence and importance of fiscally induced migration is mixed.

Taken together, these mechanisms transformed rising oil and gas prices into very rapid growth for Texas, Oklahoma and Alberta. Much of this growth was of the extensive rather than the intensive variety, and, as such, it had important implications for land use planning at the regional and urban level. Nevertheless, it did have some noticeable impacts on intensive growth.   For example, between 1973 and 1981, per capita income in all three regions relative to the national averages increased by approximately ten percentage points over the historic or long run average levels.[9] This is particularly noteworthy given the rigidity of long run regional income differentials in both countries.

Sectoral Impacts: While these shifts in aggregate variables are important, they disguise many of the even more dramatic changes at the micro or sectoral level that are of special concern to land use planners. As shown by the location quotients displayed in Table 6.1, one of these was the increased specialization in mining and construction activities. The growth in the relative size of the construction sector is particularly significant and it reflects a shift noted earlier; namely, the movement to an increasingly investment driven economy. Other noticeable changes include reductions in the relative size (that is, relative to their magnitude in the national economy) of one or more of the following sectors: Transportation Communication and Utilities; Wholesale and Retail Trade; Finance Insurance and Real Estate; Community Business and Personal Services; and, Government.

Even this level of disaggregation hides the full extent of the structural twisting that occurred in these regions during the period of rising energy prices. A more detailed analysis reveals a pattern consistent with the predictions of the 'booming sector' models (Corden and Neary, 1982; Corden, 1983; Campbell, 1984; Neary and Wijnbergen, 1985). These models were developed to explain the effects of the North Sea oil boom on the Netherlands economy, especially the adverse effects (referred to as Dutch Disease) in the form of worsening competitive positions of many of the region's non-resource sectors. As outlined in a regional context by Norrie and Percy (1983, 1982) and Mansell (1987), a rise in oil prices generates the following sequence of events in an oil and gas surplus region:

(i)   the investment multiplier and terms of trade effects lead to an expansion of aggregate demand in the region. After a temporary decline, the relative size of the oil and gas sector increases significantly. There is also rapid growth in the industries (such as construction and some manufacturing, service and transportation industries) that are most closely linked to the oil and gas sector.

(ii)   given the temporary shortages of specialized labor, wage and salary levels in the wage setting sectors (especially mining and construction) rise sharply. This then sets the stage for wage and cost increases in other sectors as they compete for labor and other input requirements. The net in-migration induced by the rising income and employment opportunities reduces the upward pressure on wages but also serves to enhance the growth in aggregate demand and, especially, the demand for infrastructure.

(iii) with tight local supply conditions, imports to the region increase sharply, as do the prices of commodities, such as housing and local services, that are non-tradeable across regional boundaries. In a sense, the energy rents associated with rising oil and gas prices become 'capitalized' in the form of high prices for these non-tradeables and for regional inputs (labor, capital and land).

(iv) at the same time, industries in the region which face competition from suppliers in other regions face downward pressure since they cannot pass the higher costs along in the form of higher prices. Thus, for example, non-energy related manufacturing activity in the region declines.

In general then, the end result is that while most sectors expand, the economies of the oil and gas surplus regions become less diversified away from the energy sector or more specialized in energy production and related activities. Further, they become less stable as the result of the dominance of investment-related activities, the existence of large rents in the prices of locally produced non-tradeables (such as housing and commercial real estate) and the greater propensity for speculative types of behavior.

The Post-1981 Period

This period saw a sharp reversal in the economic fortunes of the oil and gas surplus regions. In 1982 the world oil price dipped for the first time in many years, and this undermined the widely-held expectations of continued energy price increases. In addition, the high interest rates which initiated the general recession in both countries hit these investment driven economies particularly hard and, in the case of Alberta, the National Energy Program produced a massive drainage of income from the provincial economy and initiated an exodus of energy investment. Then, in 1986 oil prices collapsed to levels of about one-third of what they were in 1981 and have yet to recover to levels greater than fifty percent of those in 1981. Natural gas prices have followed a similar path.

Macro Impacts: There are some differences in the timing and severity of the downturns in Texas, Oklahoma and Alberta. In particular, because of the National Energy Program, Alberta's post-1981 downturn was sharper and occurred earlier than that in Texas or Oklahoma. On the other hand, Alberta's downturn after the collapse of oil prices in 1986 was less severe than that in the two states (Mansell and Percy, 1989). Nevertheless, the general patterns are similar. Relative to the situation nationally, real output and income declined, unemployment rose, per capita income fell and population growth slowed markedly. (See Figure 6.2 for trends in relative unemployment rates.) This shift in relative economic performance is perhaps best illustrated by the swing in net migration (it will be recalled that net migration is sensitive to changes in the income and employment opportunities in a region relative to those in other regions). In Texas, net migration fell from about +420 thousand in 1981 to roughly -40 thousand in 1987; in Alberta it went from about +60 thousand in 1981 to more than -30 thousand by 1984; and in Oklahoma the out-migration between 1983 to 1984 was so large that it more than offset natural increase and produced an actual decline in population. Even in spite of the substantial drops in population growth brought about by these reversals in migration patterns, relative per cap-

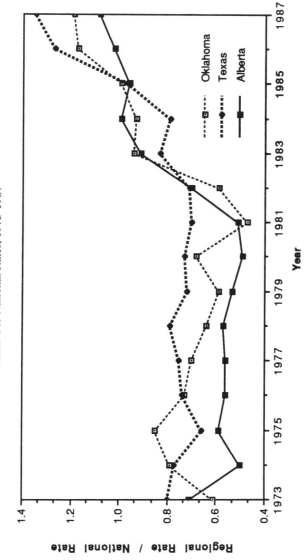

Figure 6.2

Unemployment Rates for Texas, Oklahoma and Alberta
Relative to National Rates, 1973-1987

Source: Based on data from U.S. Department of Commerce, *Employment and
Earnings, States and Areas,* and Alberta Bureau of Statistics, *Alberta*
Statistical Review.

ita incomes   fell by more than five percentage points from the 1981 levels in all three regions.

As demonstrated by this experience, most of the mechanisms outlined previously also work in reverse. That is, a decline in energy related investment brought about by changing expectations about future oil and gas prices, high interest rates or energy policy, sets in motion negative Leontief and Keynesian-type multipliers. Added to this is the decrease in the growth of demand for infrastructure resulting from the shift in migration patterns and the decline in regional government expenditure or increase in non-energy taxes in response to shrinking severance or royalty tax revenues. Finally, the accelerator, in combination with these multiplier effects, works to amplify the downward adjustment. Using Alberta as an example, real investment in 1986 was only 61 percent of its 1981 level and, whereas real investment accounted for 39 percent of real GDP in 1981, in 1986 it represented only 22 percent.[10]

Other elements of the explanation of the economic 'bust' in these regions include the decline in their terms of trade, especially after 1985, and the revival of the economies of the industrial heartlands in the two nations. The latter was, at least in part, due to lower energy prices and general economic recovery and it included a shift in migration patterns in their favor and away from the oil and gas surplus regions. Further, as noted earlier, many of the features of these surplus regions (such as their market responsiveness, labor and population mobility and the relative paucity of wage and price rigidities) served to enhance the speed and the extent of the macro adjustments to the oil and gas sector downturn. While this high degree of adjustability augurs well for economic efficiency over the long run it is not without significant social and economic costs and dislocations. Moreover, as explained later, it adds another dimension to land use planning in these regions.

Sectoral Impacts: One of the most noticeable effects of the post-1981 downturn in the three regions has been the shrinkage of the construction sector. The location quotients for this sector have declined significantly (see Table 6.1) and this reflects the   collapse of investment discussed above.[11] There are also signs of a reversal of the earlier sectoral shifts associated with rising energy prices but it is too early to assess their significance. About all that can be said is that, based on the predictions of the booming sector models, one would expect a reversal of Dutch disease or, put differently, the emergence of market induced diversification. However, if only because prices and costs generally have less downward than upward flexibility, this process is likely considerably slower than the de-diversification associated with rising energy prices.

A consequence of falling oil prices predicted by these models that has been more clearly evident in the main gas and oil surplus regions is the collapse of asset values. Just as high energy prices resulted in some of the associated rents being cap-italized in the prices of non-tradeables (for example, land, hous-ing, and commercial real estate), the rents evaporated with fal-ling energy prices and the values of many non-tradeables declined sharply, as did the prices of inputs for the previously booming sectors. This downward adjustment was enhanced by two other changes: the shrinking macro economy in the regions and the excess infrastructure capacity which emerged as the economic and demographic growth in the regions fell below the projections used in planning.

Some of the costs of this adjustment process are highly visible since they show up in the form of vacant buildings, uncompleted industrial parks or half developed residential sub-divisions. Others are less apparent but no less important. For example, the decline in the prices of non-tradeables reduced the value of the assets (mortgages, business loans, etc) held by regionally based financial institutions to the point where many became insolvent. The long term effects are difficult to calcu-late but, because of the enhanced perceptions of risk to lending in these regions, they will likely mean reduced availability of credit and/or less favorable credit terms in the future (Dow, 1987). Similarly, there are the substantial costs incurred by many thousands of individuals in these regions through reduc-tions in their business or home equity or through foreclosure as the equity became negative. However, there is also a positive feature   of these asset revaluations. Specifically, they allow many activities and investments that had been economically viable only under boom-type conditions to become viable in the less favorable regional economic environment produced by falling or low oil prices.

Given the magnitude of the social and economic costs associated with these macro and sectoral shifts and adjustments, it is not surprising that the interest in policies to stabilize the economies of the oil and gas surplus regions has been rekindled. The main focus in this regard is typically on policies aimed at diversifying the economic base away from petroleum. However, it remains to be seen whether this is a realistic or achievable goal. First, as noted earlier, the oil and gas sector has very much shaped the character and structure of the economies and these features are not easily changed. Not only does such change require long periods of sustained effort but, also, it involves counteracting the powerful macro and sectoral impacts associated with shifting energy prices. Second, there is the fundamental conflict between, on the one hand, specialization in the areas of comparative advantage and achieving the high per capita incomes arising therefrom and, on the other, diversifying away from these areas of advantage and sacrificing some growth in the average standard of living. Finally, in most of these regions the fiscal capacity to bring about change is closely tied to the level of oil and gas prices. Thus, when energy prices are high and the fiscal capacity is available it is difficult to achieve diversification if only because of the market induced specialization or Dutch Disease; and, when prices are low or falling, the decline in fiscal capacity makes it difficult to finance diversification initiatives and, more often than not, requires the regional governments to cut expenditures or raise taxes, both of which serve to further deflate the economy.

Although there are other, and, in many respects, better approaches to stabilizing these regional economies,[12] it is likely that their sensitivity to energy price shifts and the endemic variability in their economic and demographic growth rates will remain distinguishing features. The implications of this for land use planning are explored in the following section.

Implications for Planning

Most of the research concerning the relationship between energy prices and land use planning has taken a demand side or energy use viewpoint. Thus, a fair amount is now known about the implications of these prices for urban and transportation structures, the location of industry, types of housing and so on (Melvin and Scheffman, 1983; Downs and Bradbury, 1984). Indeed, energy costs, utilization and conservation have been key factors in land use planning for a considerable length of time (for example, see Brookhaven National Laboratory, 1978). However, little attention has been paid to the implications arising from the supply side or production of energy and this must be of special concern to planners in the oil and gas surplus regions. As demonstrated in the foregoing sections, the character, structure and growth of the economies of these regions are heavily influenced by the petroleum sector and swings in oil and gas prices and in most cases these supply side ramifications outweigh those associated with the demand-side. The objective in this section is to outline the implications of these characteristics for land use planning.

It should be noted at the outset that the following discussion concerns land use planning generally, within both a regional and urban context, rather than specific types of land use planning. As such it is relevant to many of the planning objectives (such as preserving agricultural land and critical environmental areas, regulating land development on the urban fringe and areas affected by major public facilities, and controlling urbanization, the distribution of urban areas and the development of public infrastructure) but without special reference to any one. Also, many of the implications are as relevant to regional and urban planning in these regions as they are to land use planning.

Planning Under Uncertainty

While there are many different approaches to land use planning (for example, see Chapin and Kaiser, 1979), they all contain one key ingredient; namely, projections of the rate and structure of economic and demographic change in the region. With these in hand the objective is then to accommodate, shape or restrict this expected change so as to maximize some community or regional welfare function. In most cases the traditional methods and models used are capable of generating demographic and economic forecasts which are sufficiently accurate to allow for effective planning. However, the situation in the oil and gas surplus regions is quite different. As explained, demographic and economic change in these regions is heavily influenced by oil and gas prices, as well as by interest rate policies (because of the high capital intensity) and national energy policies. Thus, at a minimum, accurate forecasts of oil and gas prices are required in order to obtain reasonably accurate economic and demographic forecasts and herein lies a fundamental problem for land use planners in these regions.

Especially in recent years, oil and natural gas prices have proven to be extremely difficult to accurately forecast, and this is in spite of the development of many sophisticated models designed for this purpose. Indeed, the behavior of much of this industry during the 1970s, the behavior of the banks which financed the expansion based on extrapolations of rapidly rising prices, and the fact that neither group foresaw the oil price collapse in 1986, would suggest that these prices could not be predicted by even those most directly involved and affected. Although much has no doubt been learned about the dynamics of oil and gas markets and prices from this experience, there remain rather formidable problems in forecasting many of the determinants of these prices with any degree of precision (the determinants include: the future growth rates of the industrialized economies; the trend in energy conservation and the extent to which this trend will be reversed if energy prices remain low; the degree of stability of the OPEC cartel; and, future rates and costs of new non-OPEC discoveries). This, in turn, translates into considerable uncertainty about future economic and demographic growth rates for the oil and gas surplus regions. The challenge for land use planners in these areas is to accommodate this uncertainty.

As noted by Frankena and Scheffman (1980), there is a variety of well developed analytical techniques that are relevant to land use planning but which have yet to find generalized use in this context. A number of these explicitly deal with the problem of planning or decision making under risk and uncertainty and the objective here is to briefly outline how they might be applied to land use planning in the energy surplus regions where reliable medium or long term baseline projections are unavailable.

One approach is to work with a range of economic and demographic forecasts based on a variety of oil and gas price scenarios. Provided that probabilities of occurrence can be attached to these scenarios, it is possible to construct decision trees which show expected outcomes, and the variance of the expected outcomes, for the various combinations of plans and states of nature (Brigham and Pappas, 1976, is a useful reference for this technique). The states of nature in this case would represent the range of possibilities regarding future oil and gas prices and the structure and growth of the region's economy associated with each set of prices. Assuming risk aversion, the objective is to select the plan which produces the most favorable expected outcome with the lowest variance.

Cost Benefit Analysis (CBA) represents a somewhat more comprehensive approach (see Pearce, 1983, for an overview). In addition to providing an array of techniques for incorporating the many non-market variables that the land use planner must typically deal with (such as aesthetics, noise, pollution, congestion and so on), CBA embodies methods to take account of the risks associated with a variable and highly uncertain future economic environment. For example, expected values (computed as the sum of the products of probabilities and outcomes) can be used for the future costs and benefits associated with a particular plan, a risk premium can be added to the discount rate used, or the terminal point used in the analysis can be varied to reflect the amount of risk. Two other concepts developed in the CBA literature which are relevant in this context are 'certainty equivalents' (the amount which must be assured to make the decision maker or planner indifferent between   this certain sum and the expected value associated with a project, policy or plan for which the outcome is uncertain) and 'preservation benefits' (the appropriate value to be attached to an irreversible change, such as that when agricultural land is converted to urban use or when an inner city residential area is converted to commercial use).

It is entirely possible that there is insufficient information to even establish the probabilities associated with the various energy price, economic and demographic scenarios. In this situation, a potentially useful approach is to adopt a game theoretic framework. Game theory has a long history (see Shubik, 1981, for a survey) and was developed for decision making under uncertainty. It is also frequently incorporated in CBA (Pearce, 1983). The applications of game theory in a regional and urban context are summarized by Isard (1976) and they generally involve a two step procedure. The first step is to construct a 'payoff' matrix which shows the outcome for every combination of 'states of nature' and 'planning strategy.' In the present context, the former would represent the various possibilities concerning the economic and demographic environment, ranging from that under a low energy price scenario to that under a high price scenario. The strategies represent the alternative land use decisions that could be incorporated in the plan. Although it may be possible in some cases to calculate a cardinal measure of the net benefit (or cost) associated with each strategy under each of the 'states of nature,' in most situations it would be an ordinal measure simply to distinguish among, say, highly undesirable, moderately undesirable, neutral, moderately desirable and highly desirable outcomes. For example, the 'payoff' for a plan involving the extension of an urban fringe might receive a value of +50 for the case of rapid demographic growth (or high oil prices) and a value of -50 for the low growth (or low oil price) case.

The second step involves the selection of the 'optimal' strategy, given the uncertainty about the future economic and demographic environment, through the use of a decision criterion. As outlined by Isard, there are a number of different criteria that can be used. These include mini-max, equal probability and mini-max regret. In general the objective is to ensure against highly undesirable outcomes irrespective of the 'state of nature' that actually materializes. With this approach probabilities can also be attached to the various 'states' or 'scenarios' if they are available and the solution can involve mixed strategies. For example, the optimum might be represented as a portfolio of land use with specific percentages of land allocated to each of the various uses.

In summary, these approaches or other methods for decision making and planning under uncertainty would, at a minimum, provide a useful way of framing the land use planning problem in areas where economic growth and structural change is closely tied to unpredictable shifts in oil and gas prices. There would also appear to be considerable potential for them to form an integral part of the quantitative aspects of land use planning under these and other types of uncertainty. Thus, further explorations along the lines outlined in this section would be useful.

The Variability Problem

As perhaps best illustrated by their experiences in recent years, many of the oil and gas surplus regions are characterized by a high degree of economic and demographic variability. For example, Figure 6.1 reveals annual changes in the populations of Texas, Oklahoma and Alberta ranging from -0.5 percent to almost +5.0 percent. In fact, based on variations in gross product, personal income and employment over the period 1961-1985, Alberta has the most variable regional economy in Canada. The value for the regional economic instability index based on employment is 183 for Alberta compared to 34 for Canada; in the case of Oklahoma the index value is 128 compared to 63 for the U.S. and many parts of Texas exhibit levels of variability comparable to those for Oklahoma and Alberta (Mansell and Percy, 1989).

Many of the reasons for this high degree of variability of the oil and gas surplus regional economies were outlined earlier and they include: their capital intensive nature and their heavy reliance on investment as the engine of growth; their exposure to volatile and externally determined prices and policies; their highly mobile population and labor force; the relative paucity of market rigidities; the tendency for energy rents to be capitalized in the prices of inputs and non-tradeables (land, housing, etc); and the instability of regional government revenues. The end result tends to be large swings in many of the parameters of critical importance to the land use planner. Examples include: the substantial variations in net migration and, hence, in population growth rates and population structures (since migration tends to be highly selective especially with respect to age); and, large shifts in the rate and structure of economic growth.

Much can be gained simply through the recognition and appreciation of this variability. For example, consider a case of rapid growth due to high energy prices such as that experienced in these regions during the 1970s. As explained earlier, there are a number of predictable consequences. One is a dramatic increase in real estate values, especially in the central business districts of the cities whose fortunes are most directly tied to those of the petroleum sector. This, in turn, has an adverse effect on the health and viability of inner city communities, especially once the strong speculative element is factored in (this element is enhanced given the tendency for energy rents to become capitalized in asset values and the above average responsiveness of markets in these regions). In addition, there is a twisting of the sectoral structure and, most likely, a shift in the structure of housing demand (for example, the rapid in-migration and increases in housing prices would generally result in a disproportionate increase in the demand for multiple family units).

In these cases there is likely to be strong pressures for land use planners within the region to respond to or accommodate these market-induced structural and macro shifts. However, if this situation is recognized as part of an inherent boom-bust cycle, rather than a movement to a higher long run growth path, there will be less pressure to respond to these shifts and a greater incentive for planners to focus on land use patterns consistent with longer run goals and objectives.

A similar argument can be made in the case of a sharp drop in oil and gas prices such as that experienced in 1986. Based on the observed responses to the large upward and downward shifts in these prices over the 1970s and 1980s, it is now clear that the price elasticities of both energy supply and energy demand are considerably larger than previously thought. The net result is that decreases in oil and gas prices will set in motion forces (reduced domestic supply and increased demand) that will strengthen these prices over the medium and longer term. Similarly, the responses to high prices (increased domestic supplies and reduced demand) will ensure that real oil and gas prices will not grow at rapid rates over a long period. Rather, the most realistic scenarios are those exhibiting long cyclical swings in petroleum prices. Thus, much can be gained simply through the avoidance of land use policies and planning based on projections of very rapid or very slow long term growth in the oil and gas surplus regions (that is, projections which fail to recognize the inherent cyclical element in energy prices).

Land use planners are always faced with a conflict between two fundamental elements. On the one hand, their plans must accommodate market forces and contain sufficient flexibility to allow for the inevitable shifts in those forces; on the other, in order to effectively shape land use patterns so they are consistent with broad community and social objectives, their plans must usually control or alter these market forces. However, as demonstrated by the foregoing example, these elements and the conflict between them are enhanced in oil and gas surplus regions and this creates a further challenge for land use planners.

At the one end of the spectrum, greater attention must be given to the need for flexibility. One facet of this would be more of an emphasis on incrementalism. For example, new subdivisions might be of a smaller scale and sequenced so that they would be satisfactorily developed and occupied even if the economic and demographic growth which spawned them proved to be of short duration. Another aspect would be greater designed-in flexibility regarding such things as lot sizes, industrial parks and the land requirements for transportation and other infrastructure. In general, the objective would be the avoidance, to the greatest extent possible, of the types of circumstances commonly found in the oil and gas surplus regions in the post-1981 period. Included here are situations such as partly completed high income subdivisions because of the shift to low or moderately priced housing as the economy deteriorated, large amounts of vacant office space in the cores of the major urban centers, or fringe land zoned out of agricultural use and dedicated to uncompleted or partly used industrial parks. Aside from the economic losses and waste, such situations of over-supply clearly exacerbate the problem of instability. The substantial downward shifts in prices and rents required to restore some sense of equilibrium bring with them large financial losses, perceptions of high risk and a reluctance by investors to finance new development even long after economic recovery in the region.

At the other end of the spectrum is the need for land use planning to "lean against the winds of boom and bust," and it must be balanced against the need for flexibility and responsiveness to market forces. In general, this approach involves a greater emphasis on the land use patterns consistent with long run growth and planning objectives and less emphasis on responding to the types of macro and sectoral shifts discussed in earlier sections. It is important to emphasize that the adoption of such an anti-cyclical planning response in itself will be of little consequence unless other planners and decision makers in the region embrace a similar anti-cyclical stance (for example, through the stabilization of the revenues of regional governments and a more aggressive use of anti-cyclical fiscal policy by those governments, through sector specific stabilization schemes and through policies aimed at diversifying the industrial structure and expanding the range of products and markets for existing industries[13]). However, with proper coordination it can have a significant stabilizing effect. Deliberate attempts can be made to shift some public infrastructure expenditures from the periods of rapid growth to the periods of slow growth. Also, greater diversity can be designed into land use patterns. For example, attempts can be made to reduce the homogeneity (in terms of the direct dependence on the oil and gas sector) of industrial parks, residential areas and central business districts. With a greater diversity in the economic bases of these units, they would be somewhat more stable even if the regional economy as a whole remained just as sensitive to swings in energy prices. Put differently, the objective would be to more evenly spread the effects of both the boom and the bust. Finally, consideration might be given to the wider use of special enterprise zones as a way to stimulate diversifying activities and reduce some of the Dutch Disease or de-industrialization effects associated with an energy boom.

To this point the focus has been on random variability (fluctuations associated with seemingly unpredictable events such as the dramatic increases in oil prices in 1973 and the collapse of these prices in 1986) and cyclical variability (that is, the repetitive swings commonly found in the markets for primary products). However, the concern about secular instability represents yet another element of the variability problem that must be taken into account by land use planners in the oil and gas surplus regions. The traditional view has been that since oil and gas are depletable resources, the economies of these regions must eventually decline as energy production falls. Consequently, this possible outcome, and the importance of developing plans consistent with diversification to avoid it, have been of concern to planners in these regions. However, it is now recognized that a secular or long run decline of this industry in the U.S. and Canada is far from inevitable over the foreseeable future even though it is true that the reserves are finite. There are several reasons for this change. First, it has long been recognized that after the initial developmental phase there is a decline in finding rates for new reserves. However, rather than a continued exponential decline in these rates, there is now evidence that, even in the mature producing areas of Texas and Oklahoma, they have levelled off and are likely to remain fairly constant for a considerable period of time (Fisher, 1987). Second, the experience of the 1970s has demonstrated that prices are a key determinant of the supply of oil and gas. That is, it is not the physically fixed reserve base (which is of unknown size) that is relevant so much as it is the size of the economically recoverable reserve base and this depends on the prices of oil and gas. In other words, since oil and gas prices cannot, over the long run, rise above the levels which would make alternative or backstop energy sources (oil from tar sands, synthetic gas from coal, etc) economic, the oil and gas base can never be completely exhausted. Thus, the growth or decline of this sector in both countries over the foreseeable future will very much depend on what happens to energy prices.

Unfortunately, this does not resolve the planner's problem since these prices will continue to be primarily determined by factors which are largely beyond the control of the governments of these two nations and which, for the most part, cannot be predicted. About all that can be said is that logical scenarios can be constructed for generally rising (real) energy prices over the next decade and for flat or declining real prices. Given this situation, the previously-discussed framework of 'decision making under uncertainty' may be particularly appropriate in the development of longer run land use plans in these regions.

As with planning in general, land use planning is more of an art than a science. Hence, it is not possible to convert the implications outlined above into a set of easily applied rules and principles. Rather, in most cases they simply represent an additional set of qualitative factors and nuances which the planner in these regions must incorporate in the search for an optimal land use pattern.

Summary

With the dramatic increases in energy prices during the 1970s, considerable attention has been focused on the implications for national economies and, in the context of land use planning, on the implications for housing, urban and industrial structures arising from higher heating and motive costs. While these are important, they overlook the many regional ramifications associated with the production of energy. In both the U.S. and Canada, there are numerous regional economies whose fortunes are directly tied to those of the oil and gas sector and where the dominant effects of energy price shifts are determined on the energy production rather than the energy use side of the equation. This, in turn, results in additional considerations in land use planning within these regions. The objectives in this paper were to examine the manner in which both rising and falling energy prices affect the character, structure and performance of the economies of the oil and gas surplus regions and to discuss the implications for planning within these regions.

Using Texas, Oklahoma and Alberta as representative cases, it was shown that the oil and gas sector tends to produce a regional economy with certain identifiable characteristics. These include: a high degree of capital intensity and a large investment component of aggregate demand; an industrial structure dominated by backward and forward linkages to the petroleum sector; a very mobile population and labor force; regional governments that rely heavily on petroleum as a source of revenue; an above-average exposure to fluctuations in international commodity markets and in national policies; and, regional markets with a high degree of price and wage flexibility.

These characteristics and various mechanisms were used to explain the linkage between energy prices, on the one hand, and on the other, the performance and structure of these petroleum-based regional economies. For the period of rising oil prices (1973-81) it was argued that their strong economic and population growth can be explained by a combination of effects involving Leontief and Keynesian multipliers, investment accelerators, regional terms of trade, interregional migration and the energy rent collection/distribution mechanisms. Also, the booming-sector model was used to explain the structural consequences of rising energy prices. This included the increased specialization in mining (oil and gas) and construction activities and de-industrialization (or Dutch Disease). Similarly, these mechanisms were used to explain the downturns and structural shifts in these economies in the post-1981 period.

Finally, the implications for land use planning in these regions were discussed. Here, attention was focused on the forecasting and variability problems. It was noted that since it is unlikely that oil and gas prices can be accurately forecasted, one of the key ingredients (that is, accurate economic and demographic forecasts for the region) of traditional planning approaches is absent. To deal with this problem a general framework based on 'decision making under uncertainty' was suggested. The second problem discussed was that of instability or variability arising from random or cyclical swings in energy prices and policies. A variety of changes in the orientation of land use planning in this boom-bust environment were suggested, including attempts to design-in greater flexibility and to pursue more of a 'leaning against the wind' planning stance.

It is not possible to convert these connections between energy prices and the character, structure and growth of the oil and gas surplus regions, or the implications of these connections for land use planning, into a set of easily-applied rules and principles. Rather, at this point they simply represent an additional set of qualitative factors and nuances which the planner in these regions must incorporate in the search for an 'optimal' land use pattern. However, there appears to be considerable potential to go beyond this. As noted, there are numerous analytical techniques designed to deal with the types of problems (for example, planning and decision making under uncertainty and variability) that greatly complicate the land use planners tasks in these regions. Techniques such as cost benefit analysis, game theory, risk analysis and a variety of methods used to evaluate financial portfolios and regional economic instability are particularly noteworthy in this regard. Further research is required to determine if and how these approaches can be systematically incorporated in or added to the conventional land use planning methodology.

NOTES

1. In the case of electricity, prices are typically regulated, and they do not exhibit the volatility observed for oil and gas. Also, any economic rents associated with the production of electricity are generally distributed via regulated pricing rather than, as in the case of oil and gas, through royalties and taxes collected and then redistributed by governments. Moreover, compared to petroleum and natural gas, the contributions to regional exports and the development of backward and forward linkages in the region are typically less extensive. Although the coal industry does share some important characteristics of the oil and gas industry (for example, in some cases it makes substantial contributions to the region's balance of trade), it does not face the same degree of price volatility or exposure to the vagaries of the international marketplace. In addition, it is much less capital intensive, the economic rents associated with production are considerably more modest, and it is generally afforded less strategic importance.

2. Employment data are from U.S. Department of Commerce, *Employment and Earnings, States and Areas* (various issues) and from Alberta Bureau of Statistics, *Alberta Statistical Review* (various issues).

3. For example, in 1941 prior to the development of the petroleum industry in Alberta the respective populations of Alberta and Saskatchewan were 818,000 and 896,000, whereas by 1971 they were 1,628,000 and 926,000. Similarly, total personal income in Alberta in 1941 was only slightly larger than that in Saskatchewan but by 1971 it was more than double and almost all of this difference can be explained by the emergence of the oil and gas industry in Alberta (Mansell, 1987.)

4. Data for Texas from Bob Bullock, Texas Comptroller of Public Accounts, *Fiscal Notes,* Issue 87:3 (March 1987) and data for Alberta from Alberta Treasury, *Financial Summary and Budgetary Review, 1980-81.*

5. Based on data from Alberta Bureau of Statistics, *Alberta Economic Accounts, 1986* (Table 13) and *Alberta*

Statistical Review, Third Quarter 1987 (Table 19). Comparable data are not available for Texas and Oklahoma. However, since the technology used in each of the sectors does not vary significantly across regions it is reasonable to expect the same magnitude of differences in capital intensity between the petroleum sector and other sectors in these states.

6. For example in the case where the growth in total income is reduced by, say, a decline in oil prices, the resulting decrease in net in-migration (or increase in net out-migration) slows population growth and thereby reduces the fall in per capita income.

7. Calculated from data in U.S. Department of Commerce, Bureau of the Census, *Current Population Reports* (various issues); U.S. Department of Commerce, *Employment and Earnings, States and Areas* (various issues) and Alberta Bureau of Statistics, *Alberta Statistical Review* (various issues).

8. Estimates from Bob Bullock, Texas Comptroller of Public Accounts, *Fiscal Notes,* Issue 87:5 (May 1987) and Alberta Bureau of Statistics, ASIST Matrix Number 6128. It is also useful to note that the increased net in-migration to the oil and gas surplus regions was not just related to the economic expansion in these regions that resulted from rising energy prices. Also important was the decline of some of the heavily industrialized regions in the two countries, especially those tied to automobile manufacture and other activities that were negatively affected by high oil prices.

9. Based on data from U.S. Department of Commerce, Bureau of Economic Analysis, and Alberta Bureau of Statistics, *Alberta Economic Accounts.*

10. Data from Alberta Bureau of Statistics, *Alberta Economic Accounts, 1986* (March 1988).

11. By way of an example it is interesting to note that between 1981 and 1986 total employment in Alberta's construction sector fell from 122 thousand to 67 thousand. Alberta Bureau of Statistics, *Alberta Statistical Review,* Third Quarter, 1987 (Table 19).

12. These approaches include: the more active use of interregional fiscal transfers and sector specific stabilization policies by the federal government to smooth out regional cyclical and random fluctuations; more aggressive use of anticyclical fiscal policy by regional governments; policies to encourage the development of instability insurance schemes for volatile sectors; and, policies aimed at diversifying the markets for existing basic industries and expanding the range of products and degree of upgrading by these industries (as opposed to policies to alter the industrial structure of the economy). See Mansell and Percy (1989) for details.

13. Revenue stabilization involves broadening the tax base, the accumulation of larger fiscal surpluses during periods of rapid growth and, perhaps, the use of a capital fund (such as the Alberta Heritage Savings Trust Fund) to convert unstable resource revenues into a stable flow of interest and dividends. Sector-specific stabilization involves such things as taxation and resource royalty regimes that are responsive to changes in resource prices or schemes which allow firms in highly variable sectors such as agriculture and energy to purchase 'insurance' against income shortfalls brought about by depressed prices. For further details see Mansell and Percy, 1989.

REFERENCES

Brigham, E.F. and J.L. Pappas, 1976, *Managerial Economics,* Hinsdale, Illinois: Dryden.

Brookhaven National Laboratory, 1978, *The Planner's Energy Workbook: A Users Manual For Land Use and Energy Utilization,* New York: Brookhaven.

Campbell, H., 1984, *Exhaustible Resources and Economic Growth: The Case of Uranium Mining in Canada,* Economic Council of Canada, Discussion Paper 270, Ottawa: Supply and Services, Canada.

Chambers, E. and D. Gordon, 1966, "Primary Products and Economic Growth: An Empirical Measurement," *Journal of Political Economy* 74: 315-332.

Chapin, F. Stuart, Jr. and Edward J. Kaiser, 1979, *Urban Land Use Planning* (Third Edition), Chicago: University of Illinois Press.

Corden, W.M., 1983, "The Economic Effects of a Booming Sector," *International Social Science Journal* 35: 441-454.

Corden, W.M. and J.P. Neary, 1982, "Booming Sector and Deindustrialization in a Small Open Economy," *Economic Journal* 92: 825-848.

Dow, Sheila C., 1987, "The Treatment of Money in Regional Economies," *Journal of Regional Science* 27: 13-24.

Downs, Anthony and Katherine L. Bradbury (eds), 1984, *Energy Costs, Urban Development, and Housing,* Washington, D.C.: Brookings Institution.

Fisher, William L., 1987, "Can the U.S. Oil and Gas Resource Base Support Sustained Production?" *Science,* American Association for Advancement of Science (June 26, 1987).

Frankena, M.W. and D.T. Scheffman, 1980, *Economic Analysis of Provincial Land Use Policies in Ontario,* Toronto: University of Toronto Press.

Greenwood, M.J., 1975, "Research on Internal Migration in the United States: A Survey," *Journal of Economic Literature* 13: 397-433.

Hanson, Eric J., 1958, *Dynamic Decade: The Evolution and Effects of the Oil Industry in Alberta,* Toronto: McClelland and Stewart.

Hill, John K., 1986, "Energy's Contribution to the Growth of Employment in Texas, 1972-1982," *Economic Review,* Dallas: Federal Reserve Bank of Dallas.

Hunt, Gary L., 1987, "The Impact of Oil Price Fluctuations on the Economies of Energy Producing States," *Review of Regional Studies* 17/3: 60-76.

Isard, W., 1976, *Introduction to Regional Science,* New Jersey: Prentice Hall.

Landsberg, Hans H. and Joseph M. Dukert, 1981, *High Energy Costs,* Baltimore: Johns Hopkins University Press.

Lean, William, 1969, *Economics of Land Use Planning: Urban and Regional,* London: Estates Gazette.

Mansell, Robert L., 1987, "Energy Policy Prices and Rents: Implications for Regional Growth and Development," in

W.J. Coffey and M. Polese (eds), *Still Living Together: Recent Trends and Future Directions in Canadian Regional Development,* Montreal: Institute for Research on Public Policy.

Mansell, Robert L., 1981, "Texas and Alberta: A Comparison of Regional Economies," *Texas Business Review* 55: 241-246.

Mansell, Robert L. and M. Percy, 1989, *Strength in Adversity: A Study of the Alberta Economy,* Toronto: C.D. Howe Research Institute (forthcoming).

Mansell, Robert L. and L. Anderson, 1984, "Energy Prices and Economic Growth," *Review of Regional Economics and Business* (University of Oklahoma) 9/2: 9-18.

Melvin, J.R. and D.T. Scheffman, 1983, *An Economic Analysis of the Impact of Oil Prices on Urban Structure,* Toronto: University of Toronto Press.

Miernyk, William, 1982, "The Differential Effects of Rising Prices on Regional Incomes and Employment," in Hans Landsberg (ed), *High Energy Costs,* Baltimore: Johns Hopkins University Press.

Miernyk, William H., Frank Giarratani and Charles F. Socher, 1978, *Regional Impacts of Rising Energy Prices,* Cambridge, MA: Ballinger.

Neary, J. Peter and Sweder Van Wijnbergen (eds), 1985, *Natural Resources and the Macroeconomy,* Cambridge, MA: MIT Press.

Norrie, K.H., 1984, "A Regional Economic Overview of the West Since 1945," in A.W. Rasporich (ed), *The Making of the Modern West: Western Canada Since 1945,* Calgary: University of Calgary Press.

Norrie, K.H. and M.B. Percy, 1983, *Economic Rents, Province Building and Interregional Adjustment: A Two Region General Equilibrium Analysis,* Economic Council of Canada, Discussion Paper No. 230, Ottawa: Supply and Services, Canada.

Norrie, K.H. and M.B. Percy, 1982, *Energy Price Increases, Economic Rent and Industrial Structure in a Small Regional Economy,* Economic Council of Canada, Discussion Paper No. 220, Ottawa: Supply and Services, Canada.

Pearce, D.W., 1983, *Cost-Benefit Analysis,* London: Macmillan.

Perloff, H.S., E.S. Dunn, E.E. Lamphard and R.F. Muth, 1960, *Regions, Resources and Economic Growth,* Baltimore: Johns Hopkins Press.

Perroux, F., 1955, "Note on the Concept of Growth Poles," in D.L. McKee, R.D. Dean and W.H. Leahy (eds), *Regional Economics: Theory and Practice,* New York: Free Press.

Perry, George L., 1975, "The United States," in Edward R. Fried and Charles L. Schultze (eds), *Higher Oil Prices and the World Economy,* Washington, DC: Brookings Institution.

Perryman, Ray M., 1988, "The Impact of Oil Price Fluctuations on the Economies of Energy Producing States: A Comment," *Review of Regional Studies* 17: 77-78.

Richards, John, 1985, "The Staple Debates," in D. Cameron (ed), *Explorations in Canadian Economic History: Essays in Honour of Irene M. Spry,* Ottawa: University of Ottawa.

Shmenner, Roger W., 1984, "Energy and the Location of Industry," in A. Downs and K.L. Bradbury (eds), *Energy Costs, Urban Development and Housing,* Washington, DC: Brookings Institution.

Stabler, J.C., 1968, "Exports and Evolution: The Process of Regional Change," *Land Economics* 44: 11-23.

Watkins, M.H., 1963, "A Staple Theory of Economic Growth," *Canadian Journal of Economics and Political Science* 29: 141-158.

Winer, S.L. and D. Gauthier, 1982, *Internal Migration and Fiscal Structure,* Economic Council of Canada, Ottawa: Supply and Services, Canada.

Shubik, M., 1981, "Game Theory Models and Methods in Political Economy," in K.J. Arrow and M.D. Intriligator (eds), *Handbook of Mathematical Economics, Volume 1,* New York: North Holland.

Energy Flows in a Spatial Context:
A Comparison between Canada and the U.S.

Stephen Lonergan

The higher energy prices of the 1970s stimulated a concern on the part of professional planners, architects, engineers and academics about the spatial context of energy production and consumption activities. Why does energy consumption per capita vary markedly between countries; is urban or rural living more energy intensive; what is the most energy efficient building structure; and why does energy consumption vary not only between industrial sectors, but within the same sector? These are but a few examples of the questions raised regarding energy-spatial relations. Higher prices also resulted in a move to more energy efficient modes of production, as governments in North America and Europe encouraged energy conservation in industry through "off oil" programs, and in the household sector through programs like the Canadian Home Insulation Program which provided grants to homeowners. The concern with energy efficiency is, or should be, of continued importance to society; it is becoming increasingly evident that many of our environmental problems are the result of the production and combustion of fossil fuels.

It has been hypothesized that the spatial configuration of our activities is very much dependent on energy production and consumption considerations. Once the energy crisis arrived, there was an immediate search for alternative sources of supply, resulting in considerable investments in "mega-projects", such as tar sands in Canada, shale oil in the U.S., and synthetic fuels in New Zealand. These projects were often located in frontier areas and with little consideration of the land use effects that might accompany their development (Lakshmanan and Johansson, 1985). Resource development projects in Canada included offshore oil development in the Atlantic and the Beaufort Sea; tar sands and heavy oil projects in Alberta and Saskatchewan; and hydroelectric projects in Quebec. While there has been a considerable decline in activity in the Beaufort, activities in the other regions have continued, in part due to recent initiatives from the federal government. The remote locations of these developments is relevant, however, because they are energy intensive operations and they attract a considerable population, particularly during the construction phase. Development of these resources will ultimately yield a transfer of capital from present areas of high energy consumption (Zucchetto, 1980). This will, in turn, result in isolated pockets of very energy intensive activity in remote areas of the country.

Most of the work on energy in a spatial context relates to demand side issues. Some believed that higher energy prices and reductions in supply would lead towards population concentration (Ostro and Naroff, 1980; Wardwell, 1980). It was also argued that the dispersed settlement pattern resulting from population deconcentration in North America over the past few decades was energy inefficient and environmentally destructive; and that higher prices would encourage consumers to purchase smaller, more energy efficient dwellings, and to seek residences nearer to work to minimize travel costs. The resulting savings on space heating and cooling and on commuting costs would result in a more concentrated land use pattern. The mayor of one northeastern U.S. city went so far as to claim the energy crisis was a panacea for our urban ills (New York Times, 1978).

This expected concentration is strongly refuted by many researchers, based on two propositions. First, the savings in energy consumption (and costs) associated with moving to the city (or simply to more high density living) fall short of the costs of such a move, both psychic and real (Small, 1980). Choices involving technological change and less disruption in lifestyle rather than locational change would be much more likely. Retrofitting homes with additional insulation and weatherstripping or purchasing smaller, more fuel efficient cars are obvious examples. Second, a very concentrated land use pattern may well *not* be the most energy efficient type of living, particularly when all energy costs are considered. The most energy efficient type of land use pattern might be small, polynucleated cities (Odum, 1973; Romanos, 1978; Van Til, 1979).

There are other energy related factors that may also affect the location of industry and population in North America. Recently, the Province of Quebec offered firms guaranteed low cost electricity for twenty years if they would locate in the province (and, in particular, certain poorer regions of the province). In this case, energy acts as an incentive to development and also, because of its low cost, as a stimulus for energy inefficiency.

Since the supply and price of energy is spatially variable, it is difficult to generalize about energy and land use across regions. Nevertheless, since energy is an important input to production, it appears that either: industry may seek regions that guarantee lower priced energy in the future; or, within a given industrial sector, firms that are more energy efficient may be at a competitive advantage in times of higher energy prices, less energy supply or, more likely, in the face of regulations to improve energy efficiency as a means of achieving pollution emission requirements.

These issues have significant implications for regions as well. Since industry accounts for over forty percent of commercial energy consumption in North America, regions that house energy inefficient industries may also be at a disadvantage, as firms move elsewhere, or as market share for these firms declines. The recent free trade agreement between Canada and the U.S. brings this concern to the international level. The major energy component of the agreement is the establishment of a North American Energy Market, basically allowing the U.S. equal access to Canada's energy resources, even in times of shortage. But what about the energy efficiency of Canadian versus U.S. industries? Will industries in one country or another be at a competitive disadvantage relative to energy in the future? How do regions (both urban and rural) in the U.S. and Canada compare as to their energy intensity? The main objective of this paper is to compare the energy intensity of industries and regions in the U.S. and Canada, to determine if there are significant differences in the spatial pattern of energy consumption. Although these two countries are the highest consumers of energy per capita and per dollar of output in the world (Canada is slightly higher), it is likely that this masks large regional differences within the countries as well as across their border. The discussion below presents data on energy consumption in industry over time, simply as an initial excursion into identifying differences in regional energy flows. It does not account for many of the spatial variations that undoubtedly cause these differences, such as climate, age of infrastructure or, except in passing, price differentials. Data are then aggregated by metropolitan area (the most recent year available for this information in Canada is 1981) to promote a comparison of regional energy intensities. The remainder of the paper is structured as follows: it begins with a brief discussion of the theory of energy flows and regional competition. This is followed by a comparison of industrial energy consumption in the U.S. and Canada. The third section presents energy intensity data for metropolitan areas in the two countries. The final section discusses the implications of these findings for free trade and for regional competitiveness in general.

Energy Flows and Spatial Competition

An interesting theoretical argument exists for concerning ourselves with energy when considering competitive advantages between regions. Odum (1983; 1971) contends that the basic design principle of self-organizing systems can be termed the "maximum power principle". Based on work done by the biologist Alfred Lotka (1922), Odum hypothesized that systems which maximize power and use this power most effectively will survive in competition with other systems. This applies to social as well as biological systems. The notion that energy plays an important role in system survival, however, predates even Lotka. Boltzmann (1886) noted that survival can be presented as a struggle for available energy.

The implications of the maximum power principle for urban and regional systems has not been well developed (see Lonergan, 1985; 1983). Zucchetto (1975) used the City of Miami as a case study and developed a simulation model of urban growth based on energy flows. He concluded that the decline in the importance of the city relative to other regions in the state (prior to 1972) was due to decreasing net energy flows in the city. The inability of the city to capture energy (as tourism moved to other regions in the state) and, in turn, maximize power, led to its decline.

Another of Odum's students (Brown, 1981) examined energy flows through the urban hierarchy in Florida by similar methods, but there is little discussion of the relationship between these flows and the maximum power principle. Providing an explicit definition for terms like maximum power production in the context of social systems has posed a serious obstacle to further refinements of the theory.

An important aspect of the maximum power principle for regional systems, however, has conspicuously been ignored by Odum and his students. Developed countries have very high throughput of energy already and, as prices rise, supplies decrease or limits on consumption are imposed, it will be those regions that *use* energy most efficiently that will win out in competition with other regions. The future of postindustrial society is one of continued high throughput of energy with minimum degradation. Pollution and wastes, forms of social entropy which have been directly related to high levels of energy consumption in the past, must be minimized. This application of what is now termed the minimax criterion (Kirkaldy, 1965) to social systems has been proposed by Kirkaldy and Black (1972) and Kirkaldy and Lonergan (1984).

The need to assess social and economic activity in terms of energy flows and concepts of social entropy has been suggested by Georgescu-Roegen (1971) and Miernyk (1982) as well. Spatial competition is a natural extension of these concepts, and the hypothesis that certain energy efficient regions may be at an advantage in the future seems consistent with the above theories. One important note, however. Implicit in these theories is the concept of embodied energy; that all flows of goods and services in an economy can be converted to energy units. Calculating embodied energy flows across regions is a major undertaking and far beyond the scope of this paper. Instead, direct energy consumption statistics are used to suggest how a theory of energy flows would treat spatial and land use issues.

The energy theories expressed above and their application to regional development issues is largely based on work conducted by Lotka, Odum and Kirkaldy pertaining to natural or physical systems with extensions to social systems. This is simply one of perspective (and a minor one to be sure) on the development of regions. Debate on how regional development occurs has had a long history; modernization theory, dependency theory, and heartland-hinterland paradigms are but a few of the theories that have been discussed. Nevertheless, viewing regional development from an energy perspective is appealing in its analogy to natural systems. It provides another perspective on regional growth and change, and is worthy of consideration even though the theory itself as applied to social systems remains undeveloped.

Industrial Energy Consumption in the U.S. and Canada[1]

The pattern of energy consumption in the industrial sectors of developed countries remained remarkably stable from 1950 to 1973, comprising roughly forty-one percent of total energy consumption in the largest OECD countries, and exhibiting an annual rate of growth of approximately five percent (IEA, 1983). Rapid increases in the real price of energy to industries subsequent to 1974 (Figure 7.1), however, triggered substantial decreases in the energy intensities of industry and a decline in the factor share of specific energy intensive industries relative to the output of the manufacturing sector as a whole. The recent rapid decline in energy consumption per unit of

Figure 7.1

Energy Consumption per Unit of Output and Real Energy Prices
for the Seven Largest OECD Countries
1960-1980

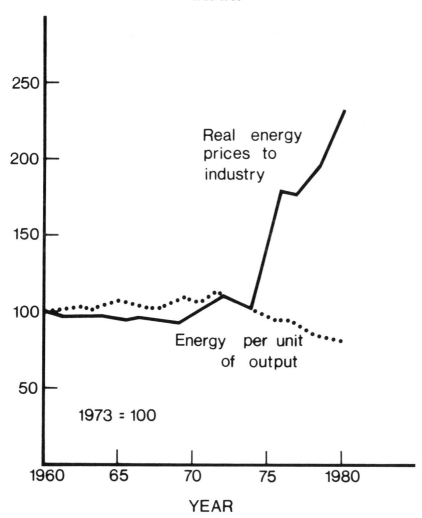

national   output, which began in 1969, is undoubtedly due in part to conservation efforts within industry, but may also reflect changes in industrial composition, decreasing capital/labor ratios or simply the decline in output of certain energy intensive industries.

The two OECD countries consuming the greatest amounts of energy per capita are Canada and the United States. Canada is also the highest consumer of energy per dollar of gross national product and, while the energy intensities of all OECD countries have declined since 1973 (measured as energy consumed per constant U.S. dollar of GNP), Canada has shown the least decline, followed by France (which consumes only sixty percent of the energy per dollar of output that Canada does) and the U.S. (IEA, 1983). International comparisons of energy/GNP ratios are of little use in examining the pattern of energy consumption and its role in economic development and spatial competition between countries. Comparing energy intensities between sectors or across regions, however, can be of particular utility in identifying international differences that may become more pronounced as real prices of energy increase. This section examines changes in energy consumption in the manufacturing sector in the U.S. and Canada, concentrating on eleven of the largest energy consuming industries, during the period 1967 to 1980. Although it would be convenient to associate most of the changes described below with the 1973-74 Arab oil embargo and the subsequent quadrupling of oil prices by OPEC, energy consumption patterns in manufacturing began well before 1973 (Dorf, 1978). The eleven industries studied comprise 46.4 percent of the energy consumption in the manufacturing sector in the United States and almost 69 percent in Canada. Considerable potential exists for energy conservation in a number of these sectors (Brummel, 1984) and comparisons are useful both to note international differences as well as to identify sectors which would contribute significantly to energy conservation and self-sufficiency goals that are the cornerstone of both countries' energy policies.

A detailed examination of energy consumption, cost of fuels and value of shipments was undertaken for the following industries: petroleum refining; steel mills and blast furnaces; industrial organic chemicals; paper and pulp mills; cement; primary aluminum; motor vehicles; motor vehicle parts; glass manufacturing; synthetic organics; and alkalis and chlorine (Table 7.1). Data are based on the Annual Survey of Manufacturers conducted by the U.S. Bureau of the Census, and the Detailed Energy Demand and Supply and Census of Manufacturers publications by Statistics Canada. The data cover energy feedstocks (i.e. energy products consumed in the manufacturing sector) and include coke and coal, natural gas, gasoline, diesel fuel, kerosene, heavy fuel oil, light fuel oil and electricity, reported in physical units and standardized to kilowatt hour equivalents (KHEs).

A number of deficiencies in the data should be noted at this juncture. The data omit captive energy, which results in an understatement of the total requirements for energy. This problem is particularly relevant for petroleum refining and steel mills and blast furnaces, where captive sources often account for more energy than is purchased (Dorf, 1978). In the pulp and paper industry, bark and waste products also may account for a large proportion of total energy consumed. It is assumed, accordingly, that captive fuel in a given sector provides a similar percentage of total energy requirements regardless of country of origin. Measures of the energy efficiency of a given sector between countries, therefore, would not be affected.

A second problem relates to the classification system used for the manufacturing sector in the U.S. and Canada. The Standard Industrial Classification systems are unique to each country and some of the sectors are not entirely consistent between countries. Attempts have been made through the description of sectors provided by the respective governments to ensure consistency, a task that is simplified by summing the disaggregated listings of manufacturing sectors that are reported in the above documentation (U.S. Bureau of the Census, 1974; Statistics Canada, 1980). The confidentiality requirement inherent in all published data does appear in certain circumstances when using disaggregated data, but the selection of the largest manufacturing sectors (in terms of

Table 7.1
Changes in Industrial Energy Efficiency, U.S. and Canada, 1967-80

Energy Consumption (KHE's) per dollar (1976 U.S.)

Manufacturer	1967 U.S.	1967 Canada	1971 U.S.	1971 Canada	1974 U.S.	1974 Canada	1976 U.S.	1976 Canada	1980 U.S.	1980 Canada
Petroleum Refining	11.8	1.8	13.6	2.5	6.9	1.9	5.6	1.7	2.5	1.8
Blast Furnaces and Steel Mills	13.5	16.1	13.2	13.5	9.3	8.1	11.8	7.1	11.1	8.5
Industrial Organic Chemicals	-	26.2	-	26.6	16.1	17.8	15.9	18.5	15.1	15.9
Pulp and Paper Mills	18.5	21.3	21.2	23.9	14.6	15.8	17.9	15.7	13.5	13.8
Cement	65.7	54.5	61.1	43.6	55.0	49.4	53.6	42.6	41.2	40.4
Primary Aluminum	32.8	14.3	36.8	16.2	32.5	18.4	39.1	17.7	22.9	13.8
Alkalies and Chlorine	50.9	2?.?	52.6	28.4	35.9	30.0	28.2	20.7	19.7	21.6
Synthetic Organics	13.7	9.2	9.4	9.1	8.3	6.5	7.8	6.4	7.3	4.8
Glass Manufacturing	15.5	13.6	15.4	12.8	14.9	10.8	14.1	11.0	12.0	10.5
Motor Vehicle Parts	1.5	2.9	1.6	2.0	1.4	1.7	1.7	1.4	1.3	1.9
Motor Vehicles	.8	.7	.6	.7	.6	.6	.8	.6	.6	.6

energy consumption, but also in terms of value of shipments) minimizes this difficulty.

The data presented below on energy consumption, value of shipments and energy costs in the manufacturing sector of the U.S. and Canadian economies represents only the eleven industries listed above, for the years 1967, 1971, 1974, 1976 and 1980. This is followed, however, by a comparison between all major industrial groups in the two countries for a single year, 1981. The efficiency of energy use is calculated by dividing the total energy consumed in KHE by the total value of shipments, adjusted to 1976 U.S. dollars. Figure 7.2 depicts the growth in total energy consumption for the eleven industries, normalized to a value of 100 for 1967 consumption. Consumption in Canada grew at a faster rate than in the U.S., due to a more rapid growth in output and a somewhat lower cost of purchased energy. The disparity in the cost of energy to industry between the U.S. and Canada increased in 1980, as a time lag existed between energy price deregulation efforts in the two countries, but this difference has decreased over the past few years.

The efficiency of energy use in the manufacturing sector is greater in the United States than in Canada throughout the period, with the exception of 1976, when the value of shipments in the U.S. declined substantially from 1974. This result is not entirely unexpected, since Canadian firms paid slightly less for industrial energy during this period. Income elasticities of energy demand over the period are +0.36 for Canada and +0.17 for the U.S. This is particularly significant, since the eleven industries studied account for two thirds of all energy consumed in the manufacturing sector in Canada, but less than a half in the U.S. In addition, the overall energy efficiency in the manufacturing sector in the U.S. is less than a half of the average efficiency of the industries studied (that is, the other industries use far *less* energy per dollar of output), while the domination of the large energy consuming industries is much more apparent in Canada, resulting in a much higher level of consumption of energy per dollar of output overall in Canada. Obviously, industrial mix *is* an important factor in energy/GNP levels across countries, and the findings reported here should not

Figure 7.2

Total Energy Consumption for Eleven Industries Studied
U.S. and Canada, 1967-1980 (1967 = 100)

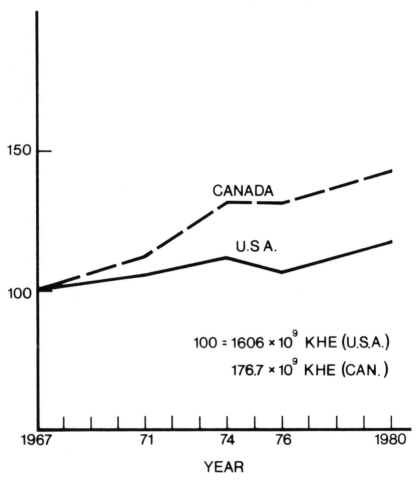

YEAR

be viewed as an indictment of a country's national energy or industrial policy, but rather as an indication, in part, of the effect of industrial composition on national energy consumption. As will be shown later, the varying industrial mix across regions has a significant effect on the energy intensity of those regions as well.

Changes in the consumption of energy per dollar of output since the early 1970s can be attributed to short term price induced conservation and possibly some technological substitution. Increases in the real cost of purchased energy between 1971 and 1974 resulted in a decrease in energy consumption per dollar of output in both the U.S. and Canada. The trend continued in the 1974 to 1976 period, with the exception of a lower total value of shipments in the U.S. resulting in a temporary stabilization of the energy/output ratio. During the period 1976 to 1980, however, as the price of energy to industry increased (not as rapidly in Canada as in the U.S.) and the value of shipments increased in both countries, the energy/output ratio in Canada for the eleven manufacturing industries actually rose slightly, implying that the eleven industries in Canada were less efficient in energy use than in the U.S., a trend that was consistent between 1967 and 1974.

In addition to these general changes in the energy/output ratio, interfuel substitution significantly affected the fuel mix of total purchased energy consumption in manufacturing during the 1967 to 1980 period. Fuel oil increased from 9.2 to 15.0 percent of total manufacturing energy consumption in the U.S., while in Canada it actually decreased from 27.9 to 26.1 percent (Table 7.2). Similarly, electricity consumption has historically been much greater in the Canadian manufacturing sector, comprising 23.8 percent of total energy consumed in 1967 and 25.9 percent in 1980. Natural gas, on the other hand, accounted for 49.0 percent of total energy consumption in the manufacturing sector in 1980 in the U.S. compared to only 32.4 percent in Canada.

The reasons for the substantial variation in fuel mix in any given period are likely due to the spatial variation in the price of particular types of energy between the U.S. and Canada.

Table 7.2
Percent of Total Energy Consumption
Attributable to Various Fuels, Manufacturing Sector
U.S. and Canada, 1967, 1976 and 1980

| | Percent of Total Consumption | | | | | |
| | 1967 | | 1976 | | 1980 | |
Energy Type	U.S.	Canada	U.S.	Canada	U.S.	Canada
Electricity	12.3	23.8	17.4	24.6	18.2	25.9
Natural Gas	46.5	23.3	49.2	35.9	49.0	32.4
Fuel Oil	9.2	27.9	14.3	28.4	15.0	26.1

Disaggregating by type of energy yields the information listed in Table 7.3. Electricity prices are substantially lower in Canada than in the U.S. and greater consumption of electricity in all sectors might be expected. The price of fuel oil was also thirty percent less in Canada than in the U.S., while the opposite situation was true for natural gas. Accordingly, higher rates of electrical and fuel oil consumption in the manufacturing sector could be expected in Canada, with the U.S. exhibiting higher rates of natural gas consumption. This was, in fact, the case, as shown in Table 7.2.

Table 7.3
Purchased Energy Average Dollar Cost (1976 U.S. $)
for the Manufacturing Sector
U.S. and Canada

| | Cost ($/KHE x 10^3) | | | |
| | 1976 | | 1980 | |
Energy Type	U.S.	Canada	U.S.	Canada
Electricity	20.00	9.40	23.80	10.40
Natural Gas	3.50	4.10	4.16	4.57
Fuel Oil*	8.00	5.30	9.50	7.28

*Light fuel oil, heavy fuel oil, kerosene and diesel fuel.

Industrial energy efficiency values for the eleven industries from 1967 to 1980 are listed in Table 7.1. Although Canada exhibits higher levels of energy use per dollar of output in manufacturing throughout the time period, with the exception of 1976, this is not the case for each industry. Of the four industries that consume more than seventy percent of the total energy of the sectors listed, Canada has an efficiency advantage in three. These are steel mills and blast furnaces, primary aluminum and cement. In the fourth major energy consuming sector, pulp and paper, recent efficiency improvements in U.S. mills have lowered the energy/output ratio marginally below that in Canada.

Figures 7.3 and 7.4 present energy and labor intensity data for all major industry groups in Canada and the U.S. Note that these groups are not equivalent to the industries listed in Table 7.1, and estimates of their energy intensities should not be compared. Five groups stand out in terms of their energy intensity: primary metals, paper and allied industries, non-metallic minerals, chemicals and petroleum and coal products. The levels of energy use per dollar of output for these groups is quite different between the two countries, as is the relative ranking of the groups. The only group with a similar level of energy intensity is primary metals, despite the fact that steel mills are less energy intensive in Canada than in the U.S., as noted previously. In three cases, Canadian industrial groups are far more energy intensive than their U.S. counterparts, while for petroleum and coal products, the opposite is true. Variations between the remainder of the groups are minor, and of less concern given the domination by the "big five."

These figures prompt two speculations. First, the substantial difference in energy intensities between similar industrial groups in Canada and the U.S. may reflect a relative advantage of one country over another with the advent of free trade. This argument is tempered somewhat by the fact that within each group there are substantial variations in energy intensity. Second, regions that are highly dependent on one or more of the first five groups will be at a competitive disadvantage in a future of higher energy prices and reduced supply, particularly

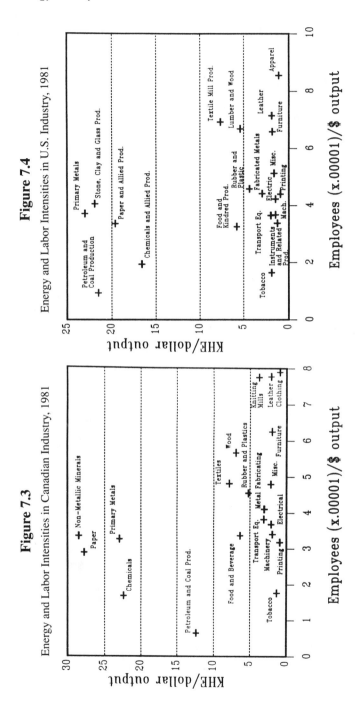

Figure 7.4

Energy and Labor Intensities in U.S. Industry, 1981

Figure 7.3

Energy and Labor Intensities in Canadian Industry, 1981

if these regions also harbor firms that are energy inefficient relative to similar firms in the other country. Competition from abroad could pose a significant problem for growth in these regions.

Spatial Differences in Energy Intensity

Industrial energy consumption remains the most important item in a region's energy budget. Just as differences in energy intensities are noticeable across industries, regions exhibit their own energy intensities. Figures 7.5 and 7.6 illustrate the energy and labor intensities of regions in the U.S. and Canada, based solely on their energy consumption and total output in manufacturing. For the United States, twenty Standard Metropolitan Statistical Areas (SMSAs) were selected and for Canada, the twenty-two Census Metropolitan Areas (CMAs) were used. For each metropolitan area, data on energy consumption, by type of energy, employment and value of output was obtained, standardized in KHEs and 1976 U.S. dollars, and aggregated to yield energy and labor intensities. As might be expected, those regions with a high concentration of energy intensive industries also exhibited high spatial energy intensities. In the U.S., three metropolitan areas, New Orleans, Houston and Pittsburgh, stand out; all have a high concentration of at least one of the "big five" energy intensive industrial groups. These three exhibit energy intensities over twice that of all the other SMSAs studied except for Tulsa and Birmingham. Houston also has the distinction of being the least labor intensive of the twenty-five SMSAs. In general, Canada has fewer metropolitan areas that could be described as very energy intensive. Thunder Bay, Ontario, is the only CMA with a KHE/dollar ratio greater than ten, whereas five such regions exist in the U.S. This might be explained by the fact that Canadian metropolitan areas do not exhibit as high a concentration of energy intensive industries as do those of the U.S., or that, with almost ten times the population and industrial output, one might expect the U.S. to have more energy intensive cities.

U.S. metropolitan areas tend to be of similar labor intensity relative to Canadian CMAs. Most U.S. regions are

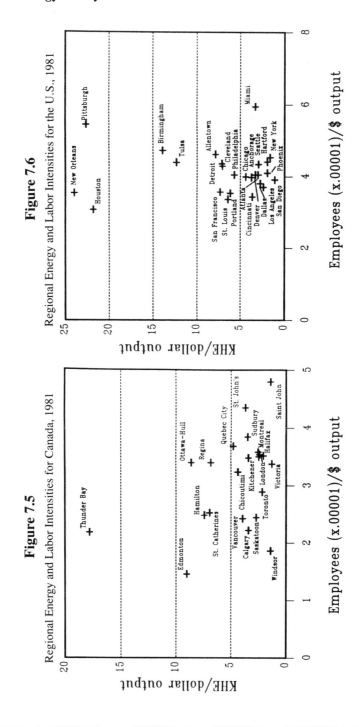

Figure 7.6

Regional Energy and Labor Intensities for the U.S., 1981

Figure 7.5

Regional Energy and Labor Intensities for Canada, 1981

clustered around a value of .00004 employees per dollar of output, while the Canadian regions are distributed quite evenly between .000018 and .00005. But what does this imply for the future of these regions? There are two possibilities, as noted above. With the advent of free trade, industries in the U.S. and Canada compete directly with one another for North American market share. To be more energy efficient will imply an advantage as energy prices rise or as supplies become limited (by market forces or artificially). Firms that are less energy efficient will lose business, and the regions that house these firms will consequently suffer.

Within a country there will be disruptions as well, as higher energy prices and limitations on supply affect regions differently (Wilbanks, 1981). Regions that are more energy intensive will be more affected during these periods, with a resulting loss in jobs as firms rationalize, or fewer wage concessions as energy becomes a more costly input to production. Although science by analogy is dubious at best, there is a certain logical consistency with the minimax theory: regions which maximize their throughput of energy will do well in times of energy surplus and low prices, but during times of shortages or higher prices, those regions which are most energy efficient will benefit.

Discussion and Conclusion

The spatial context of energy supply and demand in North America is one that is very much dominated by the energy intensive, highly industrialized metropolitan areas. Examining the energy intensities of particular industries and of metropolitan areas provides an interesting perspective on problems of interregional competition, free trade and general systems behavior. But to concentrate solely on these regions would be to ignore other aspects of energy and land use that may be equally important. As the U.S. and Canada encourage domestic fossil fuel production, non-metropolitan areas will experience considerable growth, and pockets of energy intensive activity will occur. Development of the tar sands and heavy oil projects in Alberta and Saskatchewan; shale oil in Colorado; offshore oil in Hibernia (off Newfoundland) and in the Beaufort Sea will very likely have a dramatic effect on the spatial distribution of energy supply activities (when, and if these projects begin; tar sands and the Hibernia offshore oil project have just received large federal subsidies).

The attempt in this paper has been to compare the energy intensities of industries and regions in the U.S. and Canada to determine if there are noticeable differences in the spatial pattern of energy consumption. It has been shown that some regions in each country are very energy intensive; the implication being that in times of supply disruption or higher prices, these regions may be at a competitive disadvantage. But these are not the only regions with high levels of energy consumption per capita. Anomalies exist with respect to resource extraction areas as well as remote communities. In the face of tremendous environmental consequences resulting from our continued use of fossil fuels, more research on the spatial context of energy production and consumption activities is needed. If we are approaching limits on our consumption of fuels, the spatial implications of our energy activities need to be well understood.

NOTE

1. Portions of the section on industrial energy consumption in the U.S. and Canada were written with the help of James Zucchetto and Takao Nishimura.

REFERENCES

Boltzmann, L., 1886, "Der Zweite Hauptsatz der Mechanischen Warmtheorie," *Almanach der K. Acad. Wiss. Mechanische,* Wien 36.

Brown, M.T., 1981, "Energy Basis for Hierarchies in Urban and Regional Systems," in W.J. Mitsch, R.W. Bosserman and J.M. Klopatek (eds), *Energy and Ecological Modeling,* New York: Elsevier Scientific.

Brummel. A., 1984, "Global Scenarios for Energy Planning," paper presented at the 2nd International Congress of Arts and Sciences, Rotterdam.

Dorf, R.C., 1978, *Energy, Resources and Policy,* Boston, MA: Addison-Wesley.

Georgescu-Roegen, N., 1971, *The Entropy Law and the Economic Process,* Cambridge, MA: Harvard University Press.

IEA (International Energy Agency), 1983, *World Energy Outlook,* Paris: IEA Publications.

Kirkaldy, J.S., 1965, "Thermodynamics of Terrestrial Evolution," *Biophysical Journal* 5: 965-979.

Kirkaldy, J.S. and D.M. Black, 1972, "Social Reporting and Education Planning," Toronto: Ontario Ministry of Education.

Lakshmanan, T.R. and B. Johansson (eds), 1985, *Assessing the Regional Consequences of Large Scale Energy Projects,* Amsterdam: North-Holland.

Lonergan, S.C., 1985, "Regional Development as an Entropic Process: A Canadian Example," in F.J. Calzonetti and B.D. Solomon (eds), *Geographical Dimensions of Energy,* Amsterdam: Reidel.

_____, 1983, "Regional Growth and Environmental Disruption: A Thermodynamic Approach," *Man, Environment, Space and Time* 3: 143-160.

Lotka, A.J., 1922, "Contributions to the Energetics of Evolution," *Proceedings of the National Academy of Sciences,* 18.

Miernyk, W.H., 1982, *The Illusions of Conventional Economics,* Morgantown, WV: West Virginia University Press.

New York Times, March 17, 1978, Comments made by Mayor K. Gibson of Newark, New Jersey.

Odum, H.T., 1983, *Systems Ecology,* New York: Wiley Interscience.

Odum, H.T., 1973, "Energy, Ecology and Economics," *Ambio* 2: 220-227.

Odum, H.T., 1971, *Environment, Power and Society,* New York: Wiley Interscience.

Ostro, B.D. and J.L. Naroff, 1980, "Decentralization and the Demand for Gasoline," *Land Economics* 56: 169-180.

Romanos, M.C., 1978, "Energy-price Effects on Metropolitan Spatial Structure and Form," *Environment and Planning A* 10: 93-104.

Small, K., 1980, "Energy Scarcity and Urban Development Patterns," *International Regional Science Review* 5: 97-117.

Statistics Canada, 1980, *Standard Industrial Classification,* Ottawa: Supply and Services, Canada.

U.S. Bureau of the Census, 1974, *Census of Manufacturing, 1972,* Washington, DC: U.S. Government Printing Office.

Van Til, J., 1979, "Spatial Form and Structure in a Possible Future," *Journal of the American Planning Association* 45: 318-329.

Wardwell, J.M., 1980, "Energy Constraints on Population Dispersal," paper presented at the Annual Meeting of the Population Association of America, Denver, Colorado.

Wilbanks, T., 1981, "Energy Self-sufficiency versus Interdependency: Implications for Regional Income Distribution," *Regional Development Dialogue* 2: 78-94.

Zucchetto, J., 1980, "Energy and Human Settlement Patterns," presented at the North American Meetings of the Regional Science Association, Milwaukee, Wisconsin.

_____, 1975, "Energy-economic Theory and Mathematical Models for Combining the Systems of Man and Nature, Case Study: The Urban Region of Miami, Florida," *International Journal of Ecological Modeling* 1: 248-268.

A Sustainable Tomorrow
Means Transitions Today

Andrew F. Euston

Sustainable tomorrows mean transitions today. Americans have a pivotal role to play in this process. We have many extraordinary tools and attributes to work with. With them we may seek to reshape our ever-compounding resource dependencies. We need especially to reconceive options and to reshape our urban choices about land and about energy. This paper discusses our prospects for making such transitions.

It is widely agreed that production of carbon dioxide emissions must be greatly curbed. The First World is not preparing to stop this, much less to slow down. The Third World will burn more and more until it has wholly acceptable technical alternatives. Today, both worlds are committed to being urban. Clearly the fixed patterns of nature and the prevailing habits of urbanized civilization are poised in dire conflict. It is not nature which has to bend. Our common test ahead is to bring forward social and technical solutions to this conflict so as to neutralize and contain it.

The transitions we choose to shape now could well preoccupy the next century. If action is chosen in time, some important economic, environmental, social and conceptual transitions are possible around this pivotal topic of land/energy. On the economic and environmental dimensions, a livable planet and a providential global village might emerge intact. On the social and conceptual dimensions, two key routes for transition are in place in the U.S. Both concern communications, these being the fuller development of the human potential and the wider use of modern information systems.

The global sustainability of human well-being is everybody's business now. Sustainability is, in effect, the overarching framework in which all societal choices about the future may be best understood. If and when it should prove undeniable that humanity's present collective course is inane, the First World will see that it has the most to lose. Hopefully, this understanding of global sustainability may come about before the options are closed.

Part I observes how civilization's struggles have led to over-exploitation of land and a virtual dependency upon carbon based burning. Part II explores the new potential for taking corrective action. Part III posits several conceptual frameworks that embrace the larger societal transitions that are required of us.

What follows is an excursion in a search for our transition to sustainability, and for perceptions about mobilizing shifts in how we behave as a race towards the earth and its systems of balance.

Part I: Transitioning From What?

Urbanization: Impetus for
Global Decline and Recovery

Contemporary urbanization is acutely dependent upon energy and land derived resource consumption. This condition is new enough here in the U.S., which was less than ten percent urban at the time of its founding, and is over seventy-five per-cent so today. Now, as urbanization becomes the rule for most populations, a most critical added factor has entered in: urban sustainability.

If cities have the potential for supporting decency and well-being for society, by any reckoning these virtues can be questioned today. Paris, Toronto, Nairobi, Osaka and San Francisco may still suggest urbane delight, but Bhopal, Chernobyl and Love Canal convey a darkening side of urban reality. Although the latter are extreme cases, every urban settlement has its negative impact upon earth's ecological systems of support for life. Cities have become a primary impetus for global decline, and they have a job ahead to change this.

Historically, cities have been one of humanity's great glories. Much has depended upon critical assets of climate, setting, layout, design, verve or culture. Now the humaneness of all communities is at risk ecologically, owing to society's flawed technological choices - choices about what we make, what we consume and what we build.

These ecological risks can become certainties unless wiser choices are made. Urban communities must begin systematically to defend themselves from the unintended consequences. American communities are capable of responding, if the options are made clear. At present these are not clear at all, and the effort to sort them out is way behind the need. Specifically:

- cities must seek to reverse global ecological decline, if they are to sustain human well-being;

- cities must identify their wisest options in all aspects of their affairs around technology;

- actions taken collectively by cities are crucial to future global sustainability; and

- public attitudes in cities are most probably the critical factor in the arrest of global decline, and their ecological threats to human well-being.

Modern cities have available a variety of land related measures that could help curb or offset fossil fuel burning. These range from the urban forest movement, "greenline" parks, waste recycling, urban district heating and cooling networks, thermal storage, waste treatment marshes and a wide range of alternative electric power sources not based on burning (wind, geothermal, solar, hydro, tidal). In fact, the range of viable options that cities have for reversing global decline is truly vast. What we lack is the vision that is necessary to bring them into being.

Will Land/Energy Transitions
Happen on Their Own?

America can convert to a wide array of renewables, to be sure: wood wastes, methanol from wood, ethanol from corn, methane from garbage. It can adapt to non-combustibles: solar, geothermal, wind, hydro, etc. Our towns and cities can invest in some efficient community energy infrastructure systems that create "islands" of buildings that are tied into district heating and cooling thermal networks. It can do so now on an orderly and graduated transitional basis, but it is unlikely to seize the precious opportunity so long as:

- oil stays cheap;

- business requires a three to five year return on investment;

- the U.S. is the only major nation attempting such reforms;

- major competitors keep their nuclear option and we do not;

- there are no subsidies or incentives through taxation or pricing;

- there is no aggressive alternative energy technical research and development; or

- there is no alerted sense of priority backed by the conscious concern of a public mandate.

Energy competitive community development investments are of many kinds, encompassing many investment routes, including those of construction, conservation, production, movement, land use, landscape and broader integrative urban/rural social and economic systems. When energy costs again become heavily burdensome, for instance should its increase again outpace growth in the economy, then we may expect to turn belatedly to a very wide range of previously available recourses.

Over the next decade or two what can be anticipated is a range of energy related developments emerging:

- oil prices eventually will increase;

- natural gas pricing will rise, along with oil;

- as fuel costs rise, conservation will again become attractive and then absolutely necessary;

- with increased global warming, gas of all varieties will be the burning fuels of choice, although use of fossil fuel natural gas will always represent an added burden of atmospheric carbon;

- to foster economic competitiveness and keep local dollars at home, there will be pressure to promote the renewables, methane production and far wider use of waste heat (from power plant stacks, industry, sewage effluent and many other sources).

Given Chernobyl's devastating European impacts, when matched with the vast capital investments now dedicated to operational nuclear plants in numerous countries, the debates on the right to a nuclear option should out-distance those on the laws of the sea. We have here the ultimate "NIMBY" scenario, for the world's literate have learned through Chernobyl and earlier disasters that when it comes to nuclear fallout, one's "backyard" now circles the globe. On the other hand it may cost dearly to lose the nuclear option.

One might argue there is still time, based upon available non-renewable fuel resources, if these were truly safe. Unfortunately this is not the case. In the short term, humanity can buy time only if it increases conservation. During the 1980s, as measured against work force productivity, conservation levels have stayed substantially the same. In the longer term, we are compelled to seek a new route.

Earth As Civilization's
Resource Stomping Ground

One primary concern for human well-being is the oxygen productivity of the soils and the seas. Many cities suffer toxic air inversions, as we know. Now we are learning that globally we may be bringing upon our own suffocation. The oceans were in balance until recent decades. Now with atmospheric ozone depletion the oceans' oxygen producing organisms are at risk. Land based industrialization and chemical pollution practices have been known as threats to aquatic life generally. We have heard about land locked waters such as the Dead Sea and the Great Salt Lake, where fish other than adapted shrimp do not live. The number of ocean connected dying seas is on the increase, not to mention the legions of acid rain affected dead lakes and ponds.

Ocean borne organisms provide about one third of the world's fresh oxygen. The Amazonian jungles alone provide almost a third. They are fast being burned and chopped away. As for soil, humanity has a history of depleting it. That history is part of the current reality which is to be confronted.

It was very different when people were beginning to cultivate domesticated grains along the Nile. Glaciers were still to their north. Back then much of arid North Africa was forested as were the Fertile Crescent, Turkey, Southern Italy and Spain. In the Middle East can be found large numbers of defunct ancient wells dug hundreds of feet deep which meet with perfect accuracy the companion tunnels which were hand dug for miles from their downgrade irrigation outflows. In India on the Ganges can be found gigantic former impoundments, somewhat like mill ponds in principle, but devised to tap the fast and seasonally flooding waters, where former cities of great size flourished.

In Mexico and Peru large scale irrigation was widely employed. In Mexico City, just a century or so before Cortez, the Aztecs built a vast island network of fertile, floating gardens on what was then a large lake. Like neighboring Lake Pazzucaro, its gradually diminishing shore lines are marked by settlements and temple sites that are high and dry. In fact, the lake where Cortez found Montezuma's island citadels has been evaporated almost from sight in just a few centuries.

Along dry Peruvian hillsides streams were horizontally diverted for many miles to irrigate precious fields. As tectonic forces intermittently tilted some of these terraces inland, entirely new channels were built for the growing to continue but, given the geometry, on ever diminishing irrigation plains until they had to be abandoned.

It has been during the past five thousand years, the epoch of civilization itself, when human society and the planet's ecosystems have come into severe conflict. Up until now one might say this has been for society an anarchy in which each clan, nation, empire, theology, and ideology has been positioning itself. It is now imperative to find ways to transcend this civilized positioning. Collectively, human social evolution has to turn such a corner or decline.

Civilization has lost ground with its soils. There is ample reason even for Americans to be concerned. It costs less to grow on prime land, and much of that is being urbanized. Our prevailing farming methods invite accelerated erosion of the soil. Most of our farmland is demineralized and denatured. Water is in diminishing supply as well depths increase and urban uses outbid agricultural. We will be more concerned about arable, watered soil soon enough. California has more demand for than supply of water. The Bureau of Land Management has determined that no new water supply is to be expected west of the Mississippi. When in five years or so the choice should come up, urban and industrial uses will replace agricultural uses in several Western states. As farming returns eastward shorter growing seasons and higher prices will ensue.

Ultimately for industrial based U.S. agriculture a major constraint will become its elevated energy consumption costs. In terms of energy, as with many other aspects of agriculture, much depends upon the place of the more labor intensive modes of growing. Is a permanent agrarian underclass to emerge, or some   new high-tech homesteader variant or something in between resembling traditional peasantry?

These are real options, especially if structural unemployment and in-migration are here to stay. Meanwhile energy optimal scenarios for farm/forest production have not as yet become an integral part of our own calculus. These are perceived as lesser contingencies. Eventually they will have to be confronted. Despite recent declines in oil prices, the confrontation could be soon.

In the face of this problematic history, exploding world population has been committing itself for decades to the predominant source of global degradation: industrial civilization. Even if we wanted, we could not turn back that clock. One pattern is that urbanization also increases, and another appears to be the gradual reduction of reproduction rates with industrialization. We do not know when or how population growth will taper off globally. We do see that industrialization has risen in lands with great population explosions and with it the externalities of greenhouse effects, acid rain and global degradation.

Part II: Transitioning Along What Routes?

Civilization has got to devise its own ecological transitions. The word transition here is meant to imply a kind of ethos, a mode of personal participation in something larger than most of what goes on for us. It is a kind of activity meant to be around for a very long time, something to evolve as it goes along. It entails education, communication, the arts, sciences and special competencies of all sorts.

In the sections following, both inner and outer routes for transitioning are introduced. Underlying this is a point of view, one which holds that here in the U.S. people must first be helped to appreciate the seemingly distant, mostly imperceptible, global ecological threats now at play. What is involved in them can be evasive. It does not hit most people; not yet. Hence ecological decline is not perceived as the "crisis" of the moment. Most influential of all, energy remains relatively inexpensive here. Once alerted, informed and engaged by whatever means, people may begin to cast away their prevailing disconnectedness from humanity's increasingly compromised future.

Land/Energy Transitions
Along an Ecopotential Route

Humanity shares a need to find transitions towards sustainable ways of life. We already possess miraculous tools for restoring balance, if such becomes our choice. Some such tools are touched upon below, relating to land/energy. We urgently need to identify the attainable choices which honor the planet's ecological potential for sustaining life. This may not prove easy, but it should prove more honest and upholding than idly perpetuating further damage to our planetary legacy. A few premises about such possibilities for overcoming them are in order now.

Premise 1: "civilization" now means all of us, most currently extant human beings. Shifts needed within it mean that shifts are needed within us.

Premise 2: civilization is now determining the well-being of life at every bend in the globe and how it is going to go for all humanity from here on.

Premise 3: it is the current reality that civilization is in the process of deciding:

• what creatures go extinct;

• how long growing seasons shall be;

• how healthy food is to be;

• if there is food to feed the world;

• how much skin cancer people get;

- how many genetic booby traps will be planted;

- where soil remains tillable, water potable, waters fishable;

- how much phytoplankton is at sea; and

- how much oxygen there is to breathe.

Premise 4: civilization could use a vision of the transitions needed to shift current reality and make over the way things are heading.

Premise 5: those for whom the future well-being of life matters need to become clear that such transitions are for civilization to act on right now.

Premise 6: individuals, groups, even nations can seek their own visions of what they would prefer to see and then pursue these.

Premise 7: if such concerns are valid, most people who care to act on them are free to help generate aspects of the transitions they choose to envision coming about.

If the systems approach helped in focusing the Manhattan Project or NASA's achievements, it is unlikely to serve in mobilizing people to care and to respond about ecology. It is unsuited as a way to solve the problem at hand of sustaining life by mobilizing greater world understanding of what is going on ecologically. What might be a scenario for coming to grips with such an awesome challenge?

As Transitions Begin:
Urban Energy Competitiveness

This section presents some underlying assumptions about the urban energy choices that lay ahead, if a transition to life sustaining society is to have its beginnings today. First it defines three terms. "Ecopotential" is a word coined here to signify the positive life sustaining options we mortals may employ without our robbing natural-systems-Peter to pay human-systems-Paul. "Energy competitiveness" signifies the notion of communities having a direct role in creating their own transitions towards economic competitiveness in the global marketplace. Since energy comprises ten percent of U.S. expenditures (compared to five percent in Japan) it behooves each community to optimize its own energy efficiency and production standing.

The term "sustainable" is involved here repeatedly. Dictionary definitions of "sustainability" cite terms such as endure, carry a burden, bear up. Ecologist Richard Forman calls it "meeting the needs of the present without jeopardizing the needs of the future". He speaks about achieving stability without trying to design a ridgidly constant world and about the importance of sustaining essential variables over generations. Geographer Kingsley Haynes views sustainability as a matter of incremental adjustments and equilibrium shifts, each having a time dimension and a beneficiary dimension (i.e. whether the next generation is to be left to pay for the mortgages and the bonds).

Our society is an urban one. Typically today cities are in constant change. What might be the place of urban sustainability? Unless there is a boom or a catastrophe we do not take much notice of the change. This helps to explain why people tend to be oblivious of their living environment's profound yet unperceived changes in direction.

Urbanization means resources in abundance to put in place and with which to replace. Our conventional building methods bind us to cheap, abundant energy. Unless our technology choices deem it to be otherwise, the luxury of cheap, unquestioned energy supplies is foreseeably nearing an end. Meanwhile, the imperatives of infrastructure maintenance, deteriorated building stock, poorly insulated construction and routine refurbishing continue. Transitions are implicit here in how the choices get made and who gets to make them.

One focus for transitioning to sustainable urbanization is embodied energy. We need to keep more stuff in place. A brick in place embodies the energy behind its assembly, its firing, its transport, its storage, its placement, its foreseeable maintenance.   Transitions are due here. One would be to extend significantly the time frame of relative permanence we anticipate as we design and build in order to minimize lost motion, lost energy. In a culture of planned obsolescence such as ours this adjustment will be a radical one.

Another shift would be in the kinds of products used and in their detailed design. One could see a shift to bamboo from plastics and metals for many purposes: reinforcing bars in light construction, for example. This is being done successfully already. Another would be an emphasis on local resources that reduce transport. Another is interchangeability in the designs of structures so as to minimize demolition in the future.

Generic lists of plausible substitutes for materials and products that reduce net energy costs could be assembled and kept current rather readily. Similarly there could be available checklists of specific local energy investments to be encouraged, ones that serve a local economy by reducing its losses of investment capital to fuel purchases outside the local economy. The transitions for energy competitiveness ahead are plentiful:

- **Urban forests**: which have been shown to lower the ambient temperature of a city's hot weather "heat islands" by 15 °F, if local tree canopies are sufficiently mature. Since the summer's hottest day air conditioning demands set the peak load level for typical electric power facility designing, a way exists for communities to invest in their own energy competitiveness.

- **Sewer marshes**: places that contain grasses and riverine plants capable of taking out of raw sewage its toxic metals and other compounds without need for external energy resources.

- **Heat pumps**: equipment for extraction of heat and cooling to be found in great quantity within suitable underground water aquifers, deep wells, industrial waste heat, electronically intensive office buildings and municipal sewage. The latter is to be put to use soon for the district heating of downtown Lincoln, Nebraska, for example.

- **Methane from trash:** which is increasingly being tapped from America's plethora of "Mount Trashmores."

- **Recycling:** which has a reuse potential varying from fifteen to perhaps thirty percent, and waste-to-energy burning, which offers additional efficiency gains over transporting and land fill burying. Trash burning pollution of some wastes have their own constraints which are still in process of resolution technically and in the courts.

- **District heating and cooling:** which can double the energy efficiency of a power plant by using its waste heat.

- **Public transportation:** which offers potential fuel conservation over private vehicle patterns, is the focus of the Advanced Transit Association. ATRA is very hopeful about TAXI-2000, a transit system patented by the University of Minnesota that promises subway volumes at five or ten percent of infrastructure cost.

As for routes by which to mobilize such transitions:

- **Net energy cost:** another concept to use for urban energy competitiveness is that of "net energy cost," that is, comparisons to show the energy effects of one course of action versus another as we build and produce. An example offered by U.S. DOE's Lawrence Berkeley Laboratory is of a five million dollar assembly facility for highly efficient windows which is anticipated to produce sufficient sash in two decades to obviate a parallel equivalent need for the building of a several hundred million dollar power plant.

- **Goal programming:** this is a mathematical technique devised for the Iowa Energy Office which is useful in allocating scarce resources among competing activities and in reconciling conflicting objectives. It uses a worksheet format, adds a heavy input of quantification to the process so as to portray options more crisply, and is intended to build consensus decision making around specific items.

- **Strategic energy planning:** this is a variant on the familiar corporate planning mode of problem assessment. A publication, *The Hidden Link,* is available from Public Technology Inc. of Washington, D.C. on this approach.

- **Metabolic units:** this is a term currently applied in the work of appropriate technologist Pliny Fisk, director of the Center for Maximum Potential Building Efficiency. Working with Israeli arid area agronomists on a farming demonstration for the State of Texas, Fisk emphasizes the use of residual products from all activities and resources on the farm site, such as energy, foods, fluids, manure, husks and other materials. "Metabolic units" are a way of describing things that are designed to be interdependent within a system. Rather than perpetuating ours as a "throw away" society, this direction calls for seeking out efficiencies through linkages.

- **Urban constellations:** this gives a strategic potential to urbanization in relationship to its resource base of adjoining rural areas. The concept of Phillip Lewis, director of the Environmental Awareness Center of the University of Wisconsin, these constellations are the actual "necklaces" of urbanization which are linked in connected corridor loops of varying shapes. It will be on this large urban regional scale which we soon shall have to organize our resources. Such a concept as this offers a simple, imageable and defined basis upon which to act. In effect, urban constellations constitute the largest manageable ecological units for society to work with.

- **The Sustainable City:** this is the title used by a small group of local energy directors now at work in a common effort to define the best use of their cities' efforts to achieve energy competitiveness and energy security in the uncertain years immediately ahead. The cities (San Jose and San Francisco, California, Portland, Oregon, and Tacoma, Washington), are unique in this effort and are enjoining cooperation from several other communities in other geographic quarters. Their findings will constitute transitions needed in all U.S. communities.

These then are a variety of tools and themes for mobilizing the transitions ahead in land and energy consciousness. The option for using them is not in some distant crisis but now.

As Transitions Begin:
The Land/Energy Interconnection

There are interconnections to be examined between the land resource and energy production, if the transition toward optimization for both is to come about. Renewable fuels have fewer polluting side effects than coal or oil, yet these also contribute to carbon dioxide levels. Non-polluting alternatives exist: solar, geothermal, water power sourced and, in the view of the French, nuclear power. Society has a truly prodigious sorting out to do with all of these.

In the real estate business they speak of three fundamentals, "location, location and location". Not quite so in energy, but this can be important. Traditional and new fuel sources are closely related to their physical origin in or on land: wood, peat and biomass (ranging from sugar cane, riverine plants, beet residuals to wood shavings and urban yard wastes).

Nuclear fuel is in a class by itself, given the astronomical land related and other costs being incurred for its storage sites, clean ups and quarantines. Chernobyl's explosions have had devastating after effects on the food sales of Poland and Germany. Lapp herds have been dispatched in large numbers due to ingestion from fallout concentrated in moss.

Coal has wide ranging relationships to land. Coal freight's costs affect coal's competitiveness. Today, ready access to low sulphur coal influences whether some utilities choose coal at all. In the longer term, use of coal as a fuel is bound to be heavily influenced by tightening ecological restrictions. Coal extraction is another issue in terms of land, for surface mining has shown a marginal likelihood of restoring disturbed land back into productive use. Surface and tunnelled mines cause acid runoff, killing streams and often parts of rivers. Coal burning exhaust yields high levels of sulphur and carbon dioxide, if not treated, being comparable in influence to vehicle exhaust as the principal causes of acid rain.

Acid rain is of enormous consequence for the land. Germany's Black Forest is decimated. The days of the New England maple's fall colors are numbered. Acid tolerant forests will have to be planted all over the urbanized world. The causes of our fishless lakes, dying forests and ailing farm lands so widespread in the northeastern quadrant of North America are traced directly to upwind coal burning point sources, primarily coal burning power plants.

In Scandinavia, highly effective use is made of precipitators, catalysts, fluid mists and such, not only to clean up coal burning exhaust but also to reclaim its useful by-products. Significantly, once burned, coal's fly ash can produce a form of concrete equivalent in performance to, and at an energy use level only a few percentage points of, what is true of Portland cement.

In addition, solar energy has its land relationships. For rooftop collectors to become of major value in cities this will call for larger, dedicated land areas. Conceivably in some communities, flat roof structures will become required to support collectors. Sun technology should be coming into its own by the end of the century as competitive with other heat sources. This would be especially true were more communities served by district heating and cooling (DHC) thermal piping systems. Scandinavia has increasing numbers of such communitywide networks. Seoul is now building a vast interconnected citywide system.

Most urban architectural space needs are for "low quality" energy, that is, below steam temperature, which can be best served by solar resources. This relates to DHC thermal networks as well as the individual building. Still another facet of combined solar and district heating is the future promise of thermal seasonal storage. This implies summer heat stored in sizeable water tanks, insulated reservoirs and underground chambers, including appropriate aquifers from which heat is later extracted when needed. Winter ice storage has a similar potential. The related infrastructure, electric heat pump power and operational costs must first become supportable for these alternatives to begin to spread.

In future years, when the solar collection/thermal network option comes into its own, collector fields will have to compete for space. In built-up areas the efficiencies of large fields will be harder to locate where most needed. The higher the density of energy consuming urbanization, the longer the thermal piping networks are likely to be for solar heat sourcing. The wise community will plan ahead for this need.

For widest use of district heating and cooling to take hold, oil prices above $24 per barrel would be needed. Their fuel efficiencies and air quality benefits may in time become a standard determinant of urban land use planning designed to aggregate building massing into higher density urban "heat islands."

For buildings, the use of passive solar design, including daylighting refraction, has become increasingly widespread. Even urban row house retrofitting for passive solar has proven cost effective at today's lower fuel prices. To encourage solar architecture, a variety of solar access laws have been introduced which govern land uses affecting a property's sun rights.

As a footnote on solar collectors, earlier residential systems offered a low financial return on investment, given their high installation costs, imperfect designs, complexities of sustained operation and, above all, current lower cost of fuel. However, new hybrid glass tube systems combining photovoltaics with fluid thermal circulation mediums may be competitive. Such a system may offer an average home sufficient capacity for hot water from the thermal component and power enough to run a refrigerator. These two appliances are the major energy consumers in most households.

We have ample domestic natural gas transmission pipe infrastructure, so that gas has few geographic constraints. Shipping via liquid natural gas tank cars and tankers is risky.

Most port access is in urban locations such as Brooklyn and the Delaware River. This implies that, for example, the U.S. would not be likely to purchase gas from the abundant U.S.S.R. reserves.

Biomass methane is still another matter. Brazil now exports its oil and limits its vehicles to using locally produced biomass derivatives. Widespread, a large scale and long term biomass gasahol option, however, will compete with global food/fiber needs. Also, these cleaner sources, like natural gas itself, still add to global carbon dioxide build-up.

Investment in other future renewable power sources may also depend upon geographic proximity. The electrical grid principle, if liberally applied to the wheeling of renewably resourced, clean power production, would make electric energy sourcing an important post-petroleum recourse. Wind energy sites could be widely distributed, but prime locations tend to be in mountain, plains and coastal ridge areas away from population centers. Most of our country's vast geothermal potential is in the West and Northwest, and proportionately inaccessible to urban concentrations for its thermal potential. Tidal power potential is greatest well north of the forty-eight states.

As for land relatedness and land impact, the newer technologies may bring their own visual and ecological consequences, those such as wind driven, tidal and wave systems or kinetic water impoundments, subsurface aquifer heat pumping and riverine hydro. Uses of each will need to be weighed with an eye to the future.

As this discussion indicates, future fuel sourcing will have its own increasing consequences for land use. A great many alternative energy technologies already have promise, and more are to come.

Land/Energy Transition:
the Forest Conservation Route

During 1988, Conservation International, Inc. secured a large Bolivian rainforest region in return for its retiring of certain bank discounted national debts. Increasingly, such land reservation initiatives are underway to protect forest preserves and ecological habitats. In the U.S., private utilities have become parties to forest protection arrangements so as to offset specific environmental incursions here.

The concept of national land reservations in this country is not new, having begun with the placement of our Indian reservations and, around the turn of the century, with our major national parks and forests. What is new is the wide diversity of purposes now tied to these. Increasingly, groups such as Conservation International, Inc. (protection of large biomes), World Vision, Inc. (food relief), World Resources, Inc., Trust for Public Land, Inc. (ecological land banking) and others integrate local economic opportunity within conservation frameworks to foster local acceptance.

Early in the 1970s, UNESCO introduced MAB (the Man in the Biosphere Program) in over a hundred countries. Its "ideal biosphere reserve" concept combines maximum ecosystem diversity with local research, training and demonstrations in satellite areas around a conservation "core zone." MAB's progress is in the face of an exponential population and land development growth of recent decades. One MAB Project, the International network of Biosphere Reserves, now has over two hundred designated reserves. About fifty of these are in the U.S., mainly existing designated parks. MAB epitomizes the tremendous positive value of the information route. It is both a conservation breakthrough and an information breakthrough. Sophisticated interdisciplinary methodology is coming into use as one result not only for biome conservation inventory, analysis and alerting purposes but for human welfare as well.

Part III: Transitioning to Sustainable Enterprise

By no means has a full exposition of our habitat's ecological decline been attempted here. In structuring the February, 1989 national conference on "Energy Competitiveness and the Environment" for the Federal Departments of Energy and of Housing and Urban Development, the author has had numerous direct encounters with scientific and public interest groups concerned with this nation's environmental quality options. Much was said to be grave ahead that for brevity's sake has been bypassed above. One recent attempt to put it all together is *State of the World 1989 - a Worldwatch Institute Report on Progress Toward a Sustainable Society*. Yet that industrious group has not thus far addressed the spectrum of alternative investment transitions needed to respond to the ecological crisis of urban civilization. We do not yet know what the sustainable enterprise marketplace is to contain.

Remarkably, given our predominantly entrepreneurial culture, the profile of such a marketplace has not been given attention. It is fair to say that, relative to the ecological urgencies at play, until recently this culture has failed to act comprehensively on this system wide set of problems. Given the order of magnitude economic and societal shifts implicit in these urgencies, American denial and avoidance are both grave and understandable.

Yet, sustainability offers civilization a new paradigm, a framework for its choice making. Lots of people today talk about "paradigms" and paradigm "shifts". Such shifts are when big new ideas congeal into one big new perspective that redefines for everyone the rules of the game for some significant playing field. For society as a whole, for instance, such shifts came first with a collectivized structuring of agriculture, urban settlements and bureaucracy (scribes, soldiers, priests, lawyers, administrators), next the great spiritual religions and then with the mind-focused arrivals of reason, industrialization, and now electronic prosthesis (extension) of the brain.

The principle of *ecologically sustainable enterprise* is the logical next global paradigm within which the acceptability of future physical and human resource investment choices can best be undertaken and best be understood throughout human society. Ecologically based sustainability as a primary criterion is appropriate and necessary to our own economy's choices.

An Ecologically Sustainable Enterprise Marketplace

We Americans started out as practitioners of frontier enterprise. Whether it has been about industry, science, social progress or outer space, we have been choosing new frontiers since before the beginning of this century. Time has come to opt for one more frontier: one that balances our prosperity with the future well-being of those to come. We can do it by creating a marketplace for sustainable enterprise.

This paper has argued that an abundance of remedial technologies and remedial methodologies are attainable. We only need to take maximum advantage of our society's great capacity for creative invention and experiment, capacities which are an article of our faith. We constantly make things up and do it well. If we choose to seek a new marketplace for sustainable enterprises, however, we must first find some viable bridges to it. There is a variety of promising bridges available for transitioning towards ecologically sustainable enterprise. These may take such forms as bridging *precoursers,* bridging *resources* and bridging *forums.*

The nature of a bridging precourser would be a route which has partly paved the way. This might include the alternative energy and energy conservation practices of the 1970s, innovations funded out of oil overcharge corrections in the 1980s, recent waves of alternative agriculture developments or a range of urban and rural development themes still underway such as historic preservation, urban transportation joint development and waterfront recapture projects, high occupancy vehicle lanes for commuters, planned unit residential development for the suburbs, urban fringe agricultural land preservation   easements, and many more such valuable precedents.

One of the most potent bridging resources we have, along with communications itself, is the field of Urban Environmental Design. This field embraces local government design administration, the several environmental design professions (architecture, planning, etc), a multitude of special competencies (such as law, market analysis, political science), community development focused non-profit organizations and citizen activists.

This enormous body of talent and skills exists in the majority of our communities as an outgrowth of the environmental ethic and the surge of urban development over the past two or three decades. The diversity of values which this "field" can balance makes it a unique bridge for transitioning to a new ecologically sustainable enterprise marketplace paradigm.

The diversity typical of the urban environmental design resources to be found in a majority of our communities is best characterized, in microcosm, by the historic preservation movement. Within it are the ingredients of culture, the built environment, public sector design administration, private investment, professional skills, legal and financial tools (such as demolition ordinances and revolving funds) and the communications media. We have proven throughout every state and region that these resources can be blended into a powerful force for private enterprise and public interests combined. We have learned, too, that it helps to have some physical fabric to focus upon as a way to bring people's energies to bear upon an issue.

Bridging forums follow an assortment of situations, typical of others here in America, where sustainable enterprise has a future. Each suggests a potential context for fostering the sustainable marketplace:

- Richmond, Indiana: a small rustbelt city in a rural region with a fine stock of old architecture, a small college, a hands-on planning process and people willing to explore their potential as an economic hub for rural sustainability.

- Austin, Texas: the City Gate industrial and commercial park being packaged at the edge of town for ventures using urban and rural residual materials.

- San Jose, California: a major city with an aggressive energy, municipal waste, water and open space quality agenda, a model for emulation.

- Lawrence, Massachusetts: where a major communications college is to relocate in the environs of the state's second largest linguistic minority population, positing the potential for creating a major marketing bridge to Central and South America.

Transitioning Towards Sustaining Life

World census profiles for the ten largest cities as of 1985 averaged fourteen million. Of these at least half are in impoverished nations. India estimates 160 million homeless, heading for 300 million by the year 2000, the equivalent of half its present population. America already has significant homelessness which is not expected to decline but to increase. Recent findings of the Worldwatch Institute indicate that, for hundreds of millions, the causes of homelessness are ecological in nature: from soil decline to development's displacement, climatic change and war.

Ours is a lifetime of transitions, and our children's shall be even more so. It is a challenge to hold in mind the idea of the world becoming a much better place and at the same time the reality of the egregious suffering and calamity now actually taking place all over the world. These two are painful opposites, but the latter does not rule out the former. Rather, it demands a response.

Select Bibliography on Energy and Land Use Planning

Alonso, W., 1978, "Metropolis Without Growth," *The Public Interest* 53: 68-86.

Anas, A. and L. Moses, 1978, "Transportation and Land Use in the Mature Metropolis," in C.L. Levin (ed), *The Mature Metropolis,* Lexington, MA: Heath.

Appalachian Regional Commission, 1973, *The Development of Environmental Guidelines for Land Use Policy, Applicable to Flood Prone and Mine Subsidence Prone Areas in Pennsylvania,* Report ARC-73-185-2563, Washington, DC: Appalachian Regional Commission.

Armen, G., 1982, "Energy and Land Use Patterns in the City," *Canadian Institute of Planners Conference Proceedings 1982:* 139-142.

Banister, D., 1981, *Transport Policy and Energy: Perspectives, Options and Scope for Conservation in the Passenger Transport Sector,* University College London, Town Planning Discussion Paper 36.

Beaumont, J.R. and P. Keys, 1982, *Future Cities: Spatial Analysis of Energy Issues,* New York: Research Studies Press/Wiley.

Beaumont, J., M. Clarke, and A.G. Wilson, 1981, "Changing Energy Parameters and the Evolution of Urban Spatial Structure," *Regional Science and Urban Economics* 11: 287-315.

Berry, B.J.L., 1975, "The Geography of the United States in the Year 2000," in J. Friedman and W. Alonso (eds), *Regional Policy: Readings in Theory and Applications,* Cambridge, MA: M.I.T. Press.

Blowers, A. and D. Pepper, 1987, *Nuclear Power in Crisis: Politics and Planning for the Nuclear State,* London: Croom Helm.

Brooks, David B., 1974, "Mineral Resources, Economic Growth, and World Population," *Science* 185, No. 4145, July 5: 13-19.

Burns, M.E. (ed), 1988, *Low Level Radioactive Waste Regulation: Science, Politics and Fear,* Chelsea, MI: Lewis Publishers.

Bradbury, K.L., A. Downs, and K.A. Small, 1982, *Urban Decline and the Future of American Cities,* Washington, DC: Brookings Institution.

Brundtland, Gro Harlem (chair), 1987, *Our Common Future: World Commission on Environment and Development,* New York: Oxford University Press.

Burby, R.J. and A.F. Bell, 1978, *Energy and the Community,* Cambridge, MA: Ballinger.

Burchell, R.W. and D. Listokin, 1982, *Energy and Land Use,* New Brunswick, NJ: Center for Urban Policy Research, Rutgers University.

Burgwald, B., W. Cole, and C. Wagner, 1981, *Investigating the Relationship Between Land Use Planning, Transportation, and Energy Consumption,* Washington, DC: National Technical Information Service.

Burton, D.J., 1979, "Energy and Urban Form," in G.A. Tobin (ed), *The Changing Structure of the City,* Beverly Hills, CA: Sage.

Byrne, J. and D. Rich, 1988, *Planning for Changing Energy Conditions* (Energy Policy Studies 4), New Brunswick, NJ: Transaction Books.

_____, 1985, *Energy and Cities,* (Energy Policy Studies 2), New Brunswick, NJ: Transaction Books.

Byrne, J., C. Martinez, and D. Rich, 1985, "The Post-industrial Imperative: Energy, Cities and the Featureless Plain," in Byrne and Rich.

Byrne, R.M. "The Impact of Energy Costs and Supply Prospects on Land Development Practices," *Urban Land* 38, 8 (September): 6-12.

Calzonetti, F.J., 1980, *Energy and its Effect on Regional Metropolitan Growth in the United States,* Edward Arnold.

Calzonetti F.J. and B.D. Solomon (eds), 1985, *Geographical Dimensions of Energy,* Amsterdam: Reidel.

Carrol, T.O., R. Nathans, P.F. Palmedo, and R. Stern, 1976, *The Planner's Energy Workbook: A User's Manual for Land Use and Energy Utilization Relationships,* Upton, NY: Policy Analysis Division, Center for Analyzing Energy Systems, Brookhaven National Laboratory.

Carter, L.J., 1987, *Nuclear Imperatives and Public Trust: Dealing with Radioactive Waste,* Washington, DC: Resources for the Future.

Center for Renewable Resources, 1984, *Renewable Energy in Cities,* New York: Van Nostrand Reinhold.

Champion, G., 1989, "Counterurbanization in Britain," *Geographical Journal* 155: 52-59.

Christensen, B.A., and C. Jensen-Butler, 1982, "Energy and Urban Structure: Heat Planning in Denmark," *Progress in Planning* 18: 57-132.

Cope, D.R., 1984, "Radioactive Waste Management and Land Use Planning," in Cope, Hills, and James.

_____, 1982, "Deep Mining of Coal and Land-use Planning: Technical Change and Technical Competence," *Minerals and the Environment,* 4: 105-110.

Cope, D.R., P.Hills, and P.James, 1984, *Energy Policy and Land-Use Planning,* Oxford: Pergamon.

Corbett, J and T. Hayden, 1981, "Local Action for a Solar Future," *Solar Law Reporter* 2: 953-969.

Coyle, D. et al, 1988, *Deadly Defense: Military Radioactive Landfills,* New York: Radioactive Waste Campaign.

Crandall, D., 1982, "Maximizing Energy Conservation through Site Planning and Design," in Burchell and Listokin.

Crowell, W., A. Shapiro, and W. McShane, 1981, *Transportation During the Next Energy Crisis: The Special Problems of Small Urban Areas,* Washington, DC: U.S. Department of Transportation.

Cubukil, A. et al, 1981, *The Energy Implications of Suburban Intensification,* Toronto: Ontario Ministry of Energy.

Curtis, F.A. and B.G. Braitman, 1982, "The Potential for Energy Conservation through Land Use Planning: The Ontario Experience," in F.A. Curtis (ed), *Energex '82, Conference Proceedings,* Solar Energy Society of Canada, Winnipeg.

Curtis, F.A. and J. Hunnef, 1982, "The Roles of the Land Use Planner in Energy Conservation," in F.A. Curtis (ed), *Energex '82, Conference Proceedings,* Solar Energy Society of Canada, Winnipeg.

Dantzig, G. and T.L. Saaty, 1973, *Compact City: A Plan for a Liveable Urban Environment,* San Francisco, CA: Freeman.

DeChiara, J. and L. Koppelman, 1984, *Time-Saver Standards for Site Planning,* New York: McGraw Hill.

Dendrinos, D.S., 1979, "Energy Costs, The Transport Network and Urban Form," *Environment and Planning A* 11: 655-664.

Donovan, Hamester, and Rattien, Inc., 1976, *Energy, The Environment, and Land Use: Literature Review,* Washington, DC: Donovan, Hamester, and Rattien, Inc.

Downs, A. and K.L. Bradbury, 1984, *Energy Costs, Urban Development and Housing,* Washington, DC: Brookings Institution.

Duensing, E., 1980, *Solar Access: The Right to Light and its Effect on Land Use Planning and the Law,* Monticello, IL: Vance Bibliographies.

Economic Commission for Europe, 1978, "The Impact of Energy Considerations on the Planning and Development of Human Settlements," *Ekistics* 45: 193-200.

Edmonton Metropolitan Regional Planning Commission, 1982, *Energy Conserving Land Use Planning,* Edmonton, Alberta: The Commission.

Erley, D. and M. Jaffe, 1979, *Site Planning for Solar Access: A Guidebook for Residential Developers and Site Planners,* Washington, DC: U.S. Department of Housing and Urban Development, Office of Policy Development and Research, in cooperation with U.S. Department of Energy.

Erley, D., D. Mosena, and E. Gil, 1979, *Energy Efficient Land Use,* Chicago, IL: American Planning Association.

Euston, A.F., 1985, *Community Development, Urban Design and Energy or "Rome Wasn't Retrofitted in a Day,"* unpublished mimeo.

Frankena, M.W. and D.T. Scheffman, 1980, *Economic Analysis of Provincial Land Use Policies in Ontario,* Toronto: University of Toronto Press.

Goldemberg, Jose, et al (eds), 1988, *Energy for a Sustainable World,* New York: Wiley.

Glasson, J., 1984, "Local Impacts of Power Station Developments," in Cope, Hills and James.

Gordon, R.L., 1988, "Coal in U.S. Land Policy," in Byrne and Rich.

Gough, M and J.O. Lewis, 1984, "Renewable Energy Resources and Planning in Ireland," in Cope, Hills and James.

Greene, D.L., 1980, "Urban Subcenters: Recent Trends in Urban Spatial Structure," *Growth and Change* 11: 29-40.

Haines, V.A., 1986, "Energy and Urban Form - A Human Ecological Critique," *Urban Affairs Quarterly,* 21: 337-353.

Harmon, R.B., 1981, *Architectural Aspects of Energy - Efficient Land Use: A Selected Bibliography,* Monticello, IL: Vance Bibliographies.

Harwood, C.C, 1977, *Using Land to Save Energy,* Cambridge MA: Ballinger.

Hawkes, Dean (ed), 1987, *Energy and Urban Built Form,* (Papers presented at the International Seminar on Urban Built Form and Energy Analysis), Cambridge U.K., Boston MA: Butterworths.

Hills, P., 1984, "Planning for Coal," in Cope, Hills and James.

Hoch, I., 1976, "City Size Effects, Trends and Policies," *Science* 193: 856-863.

Huffman, J. and Fleming, D., 1975, "Allocative and Energetic Implications of Land Use Planning," *Environmental Law* 5: 477-513.

Jackson, G.A. and Masnick, G.S., 1983, "Take Another Look at Regional U.S. Growth," *Harvard Business Review,* (March-April): 76- 87.

Janssen, A.H.M., 1984, "Nuclear Power and Land Use Planning in the Netherlands," in Cope, Hills and James.

Johnston, S.J., 1982, *Energy Sensitive Land Use Planning: Adapting Traditional Municipal Land Use Policy Tools to Achieve Energy Conservation in American Residential Communities,* New York: Columbia University Press.

Kasarda, J.D., 1980, "The Implications of Contemporary Distribution Trends for National Urban Policy," *Social Science Quarterly* 61: 201 and 373-400.

Kasperson, R.E. (ed), 1983, *Equity Issues in Radioactive Waste Management,* Cambridge, MA: Oelgeschlager, Gunn and Hain.

Keyes, D.L., 1981, "The Influence of Energy on Future Patterns of Urban Development," in Solomon, *The Prospective City,* Cambridge, MA: M.I.T. Press.

_____, 1978, "Energy and Land Use: An Instrument of U.S. Conservation Policy," *Energy Policy* 4: 225-236.

Keyes, D.L. and G.E. Peterson, 1980, *Urban Development Patterns,* Washington, DC: Urban Institute.

_____, 1977, *Metropolitan Development and Energy Consumption,* Washington, DC: U.S. Government Printing Office.

Knowles, Ralph L., 1974, *Energy and Form: An Ecological Approach to Urban Growth,* Cambridge, MA: M.I.T. Press.

Kowalski, J.S., 1983, *Energy Costs and the Changing Spatial Structure of Cities,* National Technical Information Service.

Kraus, M., 1987, "Energy Forecasting: The Epistemological Context," *Futures* 19: 254-275.

Lamm, J.O., 1986, *Energy in Physical Planning: A Method for Developing the Municipality Master Plan with regard to Energy Criteria* (Document D14: 1986), Stockholm: Swedish Council for Building Research.

Landsberg, H.H., 1979, *Energy: The Next Twenty Years,* Cambridge, MA: Ballinger.

Lang, R. and A. Armour, 1982, *Planning Land to Conserve Energy: 40 Case Studies from Canada and the United States,* Ottawa: Environment Canada, Lands Directorate, Land Use in Canada Series 25,

Lave, C.A., 1978, "Transportation and Energy: Some Current Myths," *Policy Analysis* 4: 297-315.

League of Women Voters, 1985, *The Nuclear Waste Primer* (S. Wiltshire and I. Weber) New York: Nick Lyons Books.

Lee, H., 1982, *Energy at the State and Local Level,* John F. Kennedy School, Harvard University.

Levinson, H.S. and Strate, H.E., 1981, "Land Use and Energy Intensity," *Transportation Research Record,* no. 812.

Lichtenberg, A., 1980, "Lifestyles, Energy and Urban Design in Sweden and the U.S.," in D. Morley, S. Proudfoot, and T. Burns (eds), *Making Cities Work,* Boulder, CO: Westview Press.

Lonergan, S., 1987, "Energy Flows and the City of Hamilton," in M.J.Dear, J.J.Drake, and L.G.Reeds, *Steel City: Hamilton and Region,* Toronto: University of Toronto Press.

Long, J.F., 1981, *Population Deconcentration in the United States: Special Demographic Analysis,* Washington, DC: U.S. Bureau of the Census.

_____, 1980, *The Impact of the Energy Shortage on Population Deconcentration in the United States,* Paper presented at the Annual Meeting of the Population Association of America.

Lounsberry, J., L. Sommers, and E. Fernald (eds), 1981, *Land Use: A Spatial Approach,* IA: Kendall-Hunt Publishers.

Lovins, A., 1977, *Soft Energy Paths,* Harmondsworth, UK: Penguin.

Lundqvist, L., L-G Mattson, and E.A. Erilson, 1989, *Spatial Energy Analysis: Models for Strategic Decisions in an Urban and Regional Context,* Aldershot, UK: Gower.

Macdonald, R., G. Desfor, et al, 1980, "The Energy Problem and Urban Innovation," in Morley, Proudfoot and Burns, *Making Cities Work,* Boulder, CO: Westview Press.

Mackay, G.A., 1984, "North Sea Oil; The British Experience," in Cope, Hills and James.

Manohar, S., 1985, "Urban Land Use Planning and Energy Conservation," *Sunworld* 9.1: 22-25.

_____, 1984, "Urban Planning for Energy Conservation," *Sunworld* 8: 118-122.

McCutchen, M and J. Hamm, 1983, "Land Use Regulations to Promote Ridesharing," *Transportation Quarterly* 37: 479-491.

Meier, R.L., 1974, *The Design of Resource Conserving Cities,* Cambridge, MA: M.I.T. Press.

Melvin, J.R. and D.T Scheffman, 1988, "The Effects of Oil Price Changes on Urban Structure: Some Theoretical and Simulation Results," in Byrne and Rich.

_____, 1983, *An Economic Analysis of the Impact of Oil Prices on Urban Structure,* Toronto: University of Toronto Press.

Meyer, J. and J. Gomez-Ibanez, 1981, *Auto Transit in Cities,* Cambridge, MA: M.I.T. Press.

Miernyk, W.H., 1984, "Energy and Regional Development," in Downs and Bradbury.

_____, 1981, "Energy Development and State Economic Development," *Journal of Energy and Development* 7.2: 163-171

_____, 1977, "Rising Energy Prices and Regional Economic Development," *Growth and Change* 8,3 (July):2-7.

_____, 1976, "Regional Economic Consequences of High Energy Prices in the United States," *Journal of Energy and Development* 1: 213-239.

Miernyk, W.H., F. Giarratini, and C.F. Sober, 1978, *Regional Impacts of Rising Energy Prices,* Cambridge, MA: Ballinger.

Miller, A,S,. 1979, "Legal Obstacles to Decentralized Solar Energy Techniques," *Solar Law Reporter* 1: 595-612 and 761-783.

Mills, E.S, 1980, "Population Redistribution and the Use of Land and Energy Resources," in Berry and Silverman, *Population Redistribution and Public Policy,* Washington, DC: National Academy of Sciences.

Mogridge, M.J.H., 1985, "Transportation, Land Use, and Energy Interaction," *Urban Studies* 22: 481-492.

Morley, D., S. Proudfoot, and T. Burns, 1980, *Making Cities Work,* Boulder, CO: Westview Press.

Morris, D., 1982, *Self-Reliant Cities: Energy and the Transformation of Urban America,* San Francisco, CA: Sierra Club Books.

Morrison, P.A. and A. Abrahamse, 1982, *Is Population Decentralization Lengthening Commuting Distances?*, Santa Monica, CA: Rand Corporation.

Muth, Richard F., 1984, "Energy Prices and Urban Decentralization," in Downs and Bradbury.

Nadel, S., 1979, *Soft Energy Paths and Urban Areas*, Middletown, CT: Wesleyan University.

Nadler, P.S., 1975, "New Chance for Cities: High Cost Energy will Tip the Scales in Favor of Cities over Suburbs and Exurbs," *Real Estate Review*, 4: 24-28.

Nathans, R., 1980, "Energy and Land Use: An Integrated Approach," in Morley, Proudfoot and Burns.

Neels, K., 1981, *Families, Houses and the Demand for Energy*, Santa Monica, CA: Rand Corporation.

Newman, P.W.G. and J.R. Kenworthy, 1989, "Gasoline Consumption and Cities: A Comparison of U.S. Cities with a Global Survey," *Journal of the American Planning Association* 55: 24-37.

Newton, P.W. and J. Parin, 1983, "The Social Impact of Industrial and Resource Development on Local Communities: A Survey of Residents' Views," *Australian Journal of Social Issues* 18: 245-258.

Nivola, Pietro S., 1986, *The Politics of Energy Conservation*, Washington, DC: Brookings Institution.

Odell, Peter R., 1980, "Energy and Regional development: a European Perspective," *Built Environment* 11: 9-21.

Oldfield, M., 1981, *Reducing Energy Consumption Through Urban Form Change*, Ottawa: Energy Probe.

O'Neill, Kevin, 1986, "Solar Access Zoning," *Journal of Planning Literature* 1: 260-268.

Ontario Ministry of Energy, 1983, *Energy Handbooks for Executive Summary*, Toronto: Ontario Government Publications.

_____, 1980, *Energy Efficient Community Planning: Bibliography*, Toronto: Ontario Government Publication (revised edition).

Ontario Ministry of Municipal Affairs and Housing, 1984, *Land Use Planning for Energy Conservation*, Toronto: Ontario Government Publications.

_____, 1982, *Energy Conservation Through Official Plans: A Guideline,* Toronto: Ontario Government Publications.

_____, 1982, *Handbook for Energy Efficient Residential Subdivision Planning,* Toronto: The Ministry.

Openshaw, S., 1982, "The Siting of Nuclear Power Stations and Public Safety in the UK," *Regional Studies* 16: 183-198.

Organization for Economic Cooperation and Development, 1978, *Environment and Energy Use in Urban Areas,* Paris: O.E.C.D.

O'Riordan, T., 1984, "Energy Projects and the Planning Process: A Canadian Perspective," in Cope, Hills and James.

Osofsky, H.R., 1983, "Solar Building Envelopes: A Zoning Approach for Protecting Residential Solar Access," *Urban Lawyer* 15: 637-652.

Owens, S., 1986, "Strategic Planning and Energy Conservation," *Town Planning Review* 57: 69-86.

_____, 1985, "Energy, Participation and Planning: The Case of Electricity Generation in Great Britain," in Calzonetti and Solomon.

_____, 1986, *Energy, Planning and Urban Form,* London: Pion.

_____, 1985, "Potential Energy Planning Conflicts in the UK," *Energy Policy* 13: 546-555.

_____, 1984, "Energy and Spatial Structure: A Rural Example," *Environment and Planning A* 16: 1319-1337.

Parker, J.H., 1982, "An Energy and Ecological Analysis of Alternative Residential Landscapes," *Journal of Environmental Systems* 11: 271-288.

Pasqualetti, M.J. and Dellinger, M., 1989, "Hazardous Materials from Site Specific Energy Development," *Journal of Energy and Development* (in press).

Pasqualetti, M.J. and B.A. Miller, 1984, "Land Requirements for the Solar and Coal Options," *Geographical Journal* 152: 192-212.

Perryman, R.M., 1988, "The Impact of Oil Price Fluctuations on the Economics of Energy Producing States: A Comment," *Review of Regional Studies* 17: 77-78.

Raine, J.W., 1980, "Energy and its Local Implications," *Town Planning Review* 51: 399-408.

Real Estate Research Corporation, 1974, *The Costs of Sprawl: Environmental and Economic Costs of Alternative Residential Development Patterns at the Urban Fringe,* Washington, DC: U.S. Government Printing Office.

Rickaby, P.A., 1987, "Six Settlement Patterns Compared," *Environment and Planning B,* 14: 193-223.

Ridgeway, J., 1980, *Energy Efficient Community Planning: A Guide to Saving Energy and Producing Power at the Local Level,* Emmaus, PA: JG Press.

Roberts, P.W., 1988, "Energy Policy and Planning in the U.K. - The Case of Coal and Regional Development," in Byrne and Rich.

Roberts, P. and T. Shaw, 1984, "Planning for Gas in the United Kingdom," in Cope, Hills and James.

Robinson, I.M., 1985, "Energy and Urban Form: Relationships Between Energy Conservation, Transportation and Spatial Structures," in Byrne and Rich.

_____, 1983, "How Will High Energy Costs Affect Social Forms and Patterns: Relationships Between Energy-Conservation, Transportation, and Spatial Structure," in *Proceedings of the Symposium on Energy: Challenges and Opportunities for the Middle Atlantic United States,* Baltimore: Johns Hopkins University, Energy Research Institute.

_____, 1981, *Canadian Urban Growth Trends: The Need for a National Settlement Policy,* Vancouver: University of British Columbia Press.

Romanos, M.C., 1978, "Energy Price Effects on Metropolitan Spatial Structure and Form," *Environment and Planning A,* 10: 93-104.

Ross, M.H. and R.H. Williams, 1981, *Our Energy: Regaining Control,* New York: McGraw-Hill.

Sargious, M.A., D. Szplett, and N. Jonarthanan, 1981, "Potential Price Induced Fuel Conservation and Changes in the Canadian Urban Transport System," *Journal of Energy and Development* 7: 61-71.

Savitz, M. and G.S. Leighton, 1977, "Energy Management through Land Use Planning: An Overview of Federal

Research   Development and Demonstration," *Environmental Comment,* July 1977: 10-13.

Schmenner, R.W., 1984, "Energy and the Location of Industry," in Downs and Bradbury.

Sewell, W.R.D. and H.D. Foster, 1980, *Analysis of the United States Experience in Modifying Land Use to Conserve Energy,* Ottawa: Environment Canada.

_____, 1980, *Energy Conservation Through Land Use Planning: A Synthesis of Discussions at a Symposium held in Montreal 26-28 March 1980,* Ottawa: Environment Canada, Lands Directorate, Working Paper 6.

Sharpe, R., 1982, "Energy Efficiency and Equity of Various Land Use Patterns," *Urban Ecology* 7: 1-18.

Shelley, F., B. Solomon, M.J. Pasqualetti, and G.T. Murauskas, 1988, "Locational Conflict and the Siting of Nuclear Waste Disposal Repositories," *Environment and Planning C* 6: 323-333.

Shrader-Frechette, K.S., 1988, "Values and Hydrogeological Method: How Not to Site the World's Largest Nuclear Dump," in Byrne and Rich.

Slayton, W.L., 1976, "Tomorrow's City will look like a Collection of Small Towns," *Planning* 42, 7 (August): 14-16.

Small, K.A., 1980, "Energy Scarcity and Urban Development Patterns," *International Regional Science Review* 5: 97-117.

Solomon, B. and F. Shelley, 1988, "Siting Patterns of Nuclear Waste Repositories," *Journal of Geography* 87: 59-71.

Smith, P.L., A.E. Gatze, and S.T. McCreary, 1980, *Land Use and Environmental Impacts of Decentralized Solar Energy Use,* Springfield, VA: National Technical Information Service.

Solar Energy Research Institute, 1982, *Solar Envelope Zoning: Application to the City Planning Process,* Springfield, VA: National Technical Information Service.

Spirn, A.W., 1984, *The Granite Garden: Urban Nature and Urban Design,* New York: Basic Books.

Steadman, P., 1980, *Configuration of Land Uses, Transport Networks and their Relation to Energy Use,* Center for

Configurational Studies, Open University, Milton Keynes, U.K.

Sternlieb, G. and Hughes, J.W., 1979, "Back to the Central City: Myths and Realities," *Traffic Quarterly* 33: 617-636.

Street, A.L., 1982, "Energy Considerations in Local Planning," *Town Planning Review* 53: 423-438.

Tabb, P., 1984, *Solar Energy Planning: A Guide to Residential Settlement,* New York: McGraw Hill.

Talarcheck, G.M., 1984, "Energy and Urban Spatial Structure: A Review of Forecasting Research," *Urban Geography* 5: 71-86.

Thrall, G.L., 1982, "The Effect of Increasing Transportation Costs upon Urban Spatial Structure: An Analysis using the Geographical Consumption Theory of Land Rent," *Urban Geography* 3: 121-141.

Throgmorton, J.A., 1987, "Community Energy Planning: Winds of Change from the San Gorgonio Pass," *Journal of the American Planning Association* 53: 358-367.

Tombs, F., 1983, "Coal and our Future Environment," in *Energy and Our Future Environment* (Conference Proceedings), London: Institute of Energy.

Tomlinson, P., 1982, "The Economic Impact of Opencast Coal Mining," *Town Planning Review* 53: 5-28.

Tonn, B.E., 1986, "500 Year Planning: A Speculative Provocation," *Journal of the American Planning Association* 52: 185-193.

Underwood McLellan, 1984, *An Introduction to Energy Conservation in Residential Development,* Ottawa: Canada Mortgage and Housing Corporation.

United Nations, 1980, *Energy Considerations in Urban and Regional Planning,* U.N. Economic and Social Council.

Unseld, C.T., D.E. Morrison, D.L. Sills, and C.P. Wolf (eds), 1979, *Sociopolitical Effects of Energy Use and Policy,* Washington, DC: National Academy of Sciences.

Urban Land Institute, 1983, *Land Use Planning and Development,* Springfield, VA: National Technical Information Service.

U.S. Congress, 1980, *Compact Cities: Energy Saving Strategies for the Eighties,* Report by the Subcommittee on the City,

288 Energy Policy Studies

Committee on Banking, Finance and Urban Affairs, House of Representatives, 96th Congress, Second Session, July 1980, Washington, DC: U.S. Government Printing Office.

_____, 1979, *Renewable Energy and the City,* Joint Hearings before the Subcommittee on the City, Committee on Banking, Finance, and Urban Affairs and the Subcommittee on Oversight and Investigations of the Committee on Interstate and Foreign Commerce, House of Representatives, 96th Congress, First Session, October 1979, Washington, DC: U.S. Government Printing Office.

U.S. General Accounting Office, 1981, *Greater Efficiency can be achieved through Land Use Management,* Washington, DC: G.A.O.

U.S. Office of Technology Assessment, 1984, *Environmental Protection in the Federal Coal Leasing Program,* Washington, DC: O.T.A.

Van Til, J., 1986, "Comment on Energy and Urban Form," *Urban Affairs Quarterly* 21: 355-357.

_____, 1982, *Living with Energy Shortfall,* Boulder, CO: Westview.

_____, 1980, "A New Type of City for an Energy Short World," *Futurist* 14: 64-70.

_____, 1979, "Spatial Form and Structure in a Possible Future: Some Implications of Energy Shortfall for Urban Planning," *Journal of the American Institute of Planners* 45: 318-328.

Wardwell, J.M. and C.J. Gilchrist, 1980, "The Distribution of Population and Energy in Nonmetropolitan Areas: Confluence and Divergence," *Social Science Quarterly* 61: 567-580.

Weijo, R., G. Didge, and W. Rudelius, 1983, "Stimulating Energy Conservation by Homeowners: A Planning Model for Local Governments," *Public Administration Review* 43: 433-443.

Wene, C.O. and B. Ryden, 1988, "A Comprehensive Energy Model in the Municipal Energy Planning Process," *European Journal of Operational Research* 33: 212-222.

Werth, Joel T. (ed), 1979, *Energy in the Cities Symposium* (sponsored by the Office of Policy Development, U.S.

Department of Housing and Urban Development), Chicago IL: American Planning Association.

White, A.G., 1986, *Energy and Spatial Form: A Selected Bibliography,* Monticello, IL: Vance Bibliographies A 1713.

Wilkinson, Kenneth P. et al, 1982, "Local Social Disruption and Western Energy Development: A Critical Review," *Pacific Sociological Review* 25: 275-296.

Windheim, L.S. and R.R. Wooder, 1976, "Cities as Energy Systems," *Building Systems Design* 73, 2 (February/March).

Windsor, D., 1979, "A Critique of the Costs of Sprawl," *Journal of the American Institute of Planners* 45: 279-292.

Zelinsky, W. and D.F. Sly, 1981, *U.S. Population Distribution and Personal Energy Use,* Washington, DC: National Academy of Sciences.

Zucchetto, James, 1982, *Energy and the Future of Human Settlement Patterns: Theory, Models and Empirical Considerations,* Philadelphia, PA: University of Philadelphia, Working Paper 60.

_____, 1975, "Energy-Economic Theory and Mathematical Models for Combining the Systems of Man and Nature - Case Study: The Urban Region of Miami, Florida," *International Journal on Ecological Modeling* 1: 241.

_____, 1975, *Energy Basis for Miami, Florida, and Other Urban Systems,* Ph.D. Dissertation, University of Florida.

Contributors

Lester R. Brown is President and Senior Researcher with Worldwatch Institute and Project Director of the Institute's annual *State of the World* reports. Formerly Administrator of the International Development Service of the U.S. Department of Agricultural Development Service, he is author of several books including *World Without Borders* (New York: Random House, 1972), *By Bread Alone* (New York: Praeger, 1974), *The Twenty-Ninth Day* (New York: Norton, 1978), and *Building a Sustainable Society* (New York: Norton, 1981).

Diane M. Cameron is an environmental scientist at the Natural Resources Defense Council in Washington, D.C. She was formerly the nuclear waste project manager for the League of Women Voters Education Fund, Washington, D.C. She also heads a study on recycling and solid waste management options for the League of Women Voters of Prince Edward's County, Maryland. She has published articles in the fields of energy policy and water pollution.

J. Barry Cullingworth is Unidel Professor of Urban Affairs and Public Policy and a senior research associate in the Center for Energy and Urban Policy Research at the University of Delaware. He has published over thirty books on housing, planning and public policy including three volumes of the U.K. Official History of Environmental Planning (London: Her Majesty's Stationery Office, 1975-1981), *Urban and Regional Planning in Canada* (New Brunswick, NJ: Transaction Books, 1987) and *Town and Country Planning in Britain* (Unwin Hyman, 10th edition, 1988). His current research is focused on land use planning.

Andrew F. Euston is a member of the American Institute of Architects. He is the Senior Urban Design and Energy Program Officer for the U.S. Department of Housing and Urban Development. Currently he is leading "the conceptual development of the sustainable enterprise theme of economic development through energy competitive and environmentally balanced investment."

Jodi L. Jacobson is a researcher with Worldwatch Institute and co-author of *State of the World 1987*. She is a graduate of the University of Wisconsin-Madison, where she studied economics and environmental sciences.

Stephen Lonergan was formerly an associate professor in the Department of Geography, McMaster University and associate director of the McMaster Institute for Energy Studies. He is now in the Department of Geography at Victoria University. He received his B.Sc. from Duke University and his Ph.D. in regional science from the University of Pennsylvania. His research interests are in the areas of energy analysis, environmental and social impact assessment related to climate change, and environmental, energy and economic growth issues in Asia.

Robert Mansell is professor of economics at the University of Calgary. His main research areas are energy and regional economics, and he has written numerous articles and monographs dealing with regional modeling, the regional impacts of energy policy and prices, the evaluation of large scale projects and regional economic disparities. Dr. Mansell has also undertaken many consultant reports for government and industry dealing with regional, energy and economic development issues.

Susan Owens is a lecturer in the Department of Geography and a Fellow of Newnham College at the University of Cambridge, U.K. She has published many articles in the energy/environment field, and is the author of Energy, *Planning and Urban Form* (Pion, 1986).

Martin J. Pasqualetti (Ph.D. University of California, Riverside) is an associate professor of geography at Arizona State University. His research and publications have addressed the conflicts between energy development and land use. He has emphasized the development of site specific energy resources in the western states, and has recently been concentrating on the geosocial costs of decommissioning nuclear power plants. He is co-founder and past president of the Energy Specialty Group of the Association of American Geographers.

Barry D. Solomon is a policy analyst with the global change program at the U.S. Environmental Protection Agency. He previously worked at the U.S. Department of Energy and has held academic appointments at Indiana University and West Virginia University. Dr. Solomon is the author of over thirty research articles on energy policy, the co-editor of *Geographical Dimensions of Energy* (Boston: Riedel/Kluwer Academic Publishers, 1985), and co-author of a forthcoming book on the politics of nuclear waste.